SIMPSON

IMPRINT IN HUMANITIES

The humanities endowment
by Sharon Hanley Simpson and
Barclay Simpson honors
MURIEL CARTER HANLEY
whose intellect and sensitivity
have enriched the many lives
that she has touched.

The publisher gratefully acknowledges the generous support of the Simpson Humanities Endowment Fund of the University of California Press Foundation, which was established by a major gift from Barclay and Sharon Simpson.

The publisher and author gratefully acknowledge the generous contributions to this book provided by Westminster College and Moki Mac River Expeditions.

THE GRAND CANYON READER

THE GRAND CANYON READER

EDITED BY LANCE NEWMAN

UNIVERSITY OF CALIFORNIA PRESS BERKELEY LOS ANGELES LONDON

Frontispiece: *Panorama from Point Sublime,* by William Henry Holmes.
Reproduced by permission of the David Rumsey Map Collection,
www.davidrumsey.com.

University of California Press, one of the most distinguished university
presses in the United States, enriches lives around the world by
advancing scholarship in the humanities, social sciences, and natural
sciences. Its activities are supported by the UC Press Foundation and
by philanthropic contributions from individuals and institutions. For
more information, visit www.ucpress.edu.

University of California Press
Berkeley and Los Angeles, California

University of California Press, Ltd.
London, England

Library of Congress Cataloging-in-Publication Data

The Grand Canyon reader / edited by Lance Newman.
    p.   cm.
    Includes bibliographical references.
    ISBN 978-0-520-27078-7 (cloth : alk. paper) — ISBN 978-0-520-27079-4
(pbk. : alk. paper)
    1. Grand Canyon (Ariz.)—Description and travel.   2. Colorado River
(Colo.-Mexico)—Description and travel.   3. Natural history—Arizona—
Grand Canyon.   4. Natural history—Colorado River (Colo.-Mexico)
5. Grand Canyon (Ariz.)—Literary collections.   6. Colorado River
(Colo.-Mexico)—Literary collections.   I. Newman, Lance.
    F788.G7555   2011
    979.1'32—dc22   2011009200

Manufactured in the United States of America

20   19   18   17   16   15   14   13   12   11
10   9   8   7   6   5   4   3   2   1

This book is printed on Cascades Enviro 100, a 100% post consumer
waste, recycled, de-inked fiber. FSC recycled certified and processed
chlorine free. It is acid free, Ecologo certified, and manufactured by
BioGas energy.

To the river guides of Grand Canyon

The book is open, and I can read as I run.

JOHN WESLEY POWELL

CONTENTS

THE PEOPLE

ACKNOWLEDGMENTS

The author would like to thank Richard Quartaroli of the Cline Library at Northern Arizona University, Roy Webb of the Marriott Library at the University of Utah, Paul Hirt of the Department of History at Arizona State University, Betty Upchurch of the Research Library at Grand Canyon National Park, and Brad Dimock of Fretwater Press for invaluable assistance in identifying and locating materials. Thanks also to Kim Robinson, Jacqueline Volin, and Bonita Hurd of the University of California Press, who did remarkably careful and thoughtful work at all stages of the editing process. Finally, this book would not have been possible without the generous support of the Quist family, Hal and Barbara Newman, David and Vicki Mackay, Fred Phillips, Dwight Worden, Latimer Smith, and Matt Herrman.

INTRODUCTION

Stories of the Great Unknown

John Wesley Powell, leader of the first recorded river expedition though Grand Canyon, looked downstream from a beach near the mouth of the Little Colorado River on August 13, 1869. For more than two and a half months, he and his crew had been working their way down the Colorado from their starting point in Green River, Wyoming, carrying their heavy boats and equipment around most of the rapids. They were exhausted, battered, and hungry. They hoped to reach the mouth of the Virgin River where it enters the lower Colorado, but maps of the region showed only terra incognita, a blank space that they would need to cross to get to safety. Wondering what might wait around the bend where the canyon turned sharply to the west, Powell wrote in his journal, "We are now ready to start on our way down the Great Unknown."

Today, when we first look out from the rim, Grand Canyon can still seem not only unknown but even unknowable. As we struggle to comprehend the view, we often start by trying to compute the canyon's size. It is as much as six thousand feet deep and eighteen miles wide. The Colorado River flows 277 miles from Lees Ferry to Pierce Ferry at an average rate of 17,850 cubic feet per second. There are more than 75 named rapids, with a total combined drop of more than two thousand feet. The rocks in the canyon's walls range from about 270 million years old to about 1.8 billion years old, or about two-fifths the age of the planet. Numbers like these offer a rudimentary sense of scale, but in the end they are just numbers. So next we try to comprehend the canyon by comparing it to more familiar things. The area between the rims is twice the size of Massachusetts. Four Empire State Buildings stacked one atop the other would not reach the rim. All of the billions of human beings alive today could be packed into the inner gorge, and they would not be visible from the rim. In the end, though, even startling images like these fail to take the measure of the canyon.

There is one tool that makes this unintelligible space into a meaningful place: the story. Stories fill the Great Unknown with human action, thought, and desire. Stories transform this immense emptiness into the place that visitors come to see: Grand Canyon. In the tradition of the Hopi tribe, the canyon is Ongtupka, the place of salt, where human beings emerged into this, the fourth world. In previous worlds, the people had strayed from the ways of peace, so the creator gave them a beautiful but challenging new home where the sheer difficulty of survival would help hold their community together. For John Wesley Powell, the canyon was the open Book of Nature, and he dedicated his life to reading its record of earth's geologic history. Powell saw himself as an explorer and scientist working in the service of human progress. His account of his exploration of the canyon inspires readers with a story of the triumph of reason and science over fear and ignorance. For Ann Zwinger, the story of a hike to an ancestral Puebloan grave site offers an opportunity to think about modern society's relationship with nature. Contemplating the fate of a woman buried near the mouth of Bright Angel Creek almost a thousand years ago, Zwinger wonders whether we, too, will find the limits of our ability to thrive in such a challenging and fragile land.

I have selected the essays, journals, and poems in *The Grand Canyon Reader* from more than forty-two thousand writings about Grand Canyon published in the last five hundred years. The twenty-seven selections tell compelling and thought-provoking stories about people inhabiting, exploring, surviving, and attempting to understand this incomparably wild landscape. Some of the readings are classics not only of Grand Canyon literature but also of American literature as a whole. Others are obscure and even unpublished texts that deserve to be better known. Lively, rough-hewn tales written by unschooled river runners stand side by side with finely crafted literary works by such beloved authors as John McPhee, Linda Hogan, and Terry Tempest Williams. I have made a special effort to place the voices of women and Native Americans alongside the more familiar works of European and Euro-American men. In short, the readings in this book represent the widest possible range of human feelings about Grand Canyon.

Unlike most books of its kind, *The Grand Canyon Reader* is organized in reverse chronological order. It meets readers on the common ground of the present moment, and then it makes three separate journeys backward in time. The first two sections focus on the major landscapes that visitors encounter when they drive, hike, or float through the park: the rim and the river. The readings in these sections move from the most contemporary views to the more unfamiliar perspectives of older generations, including those of the first authors to write about Grand Canyon as a natural wonder that every American should visit. The third section places both contemporary and traditional Native American stories alongside journal entries and reports written by the conquistadors and explorers who "discovered" the canyon and the people who had always called it home.

These three journeys combine to tell another story, a story of the circular evolution of human attitudes toward the canyon. Contemporary writers like Craig Childs and Barry Lopez see the canyon as an open-air classroom, a special place that offers unparalleled opportunities for the study of nature and ourselves. From their perspective, the canyon can teach us how to live thoughtfully in our world; if we approach it with open eyes, this wild landscape can help us overcome the human-centered, time-bound attitudes that are, in part, responsible for our modern society's destructiveness. This contemporary way of thinking contrasts sharply with the work of earlier generations of writers, most of whom saw the canyon as a resource for personal enrichment. The riches they sought might be material, intellectual, or spiritual, but the basic story was often the same: go to the canyon and come away with treasures, like precious metals, divine favor, scientific reputation, game trophies, aesthetic experiences, or exciting adventures. At the end of five centuries of such conquests, the work of the living writers included here harks back to the traditional stories of the canyon's native peoples, who learned from their homeland that not only survival but also well-being require selfless respect for the complexity and delicacy of the natural world.

Because *The Grand Canyon Reader* includes such a wide range of stories across such a long span of history, it gives readers a chance to choose for themselves the meanings that will shape their encounters with the Great Unknown. Almost all readers will be changed by their experiences of the canyon. For despite their differences, almost all stories about Grand Canyon, across time and cultures, share one idea: it is a place apart, a unique place so strange that it forces us to think anew about ourselves and our world.

My own encounter with Grand Canyon began on a February morning many years ago, when I woke up and stepped out of my car in a parking lot at South Rim Village. Six inches of dry snow had fallen overnight, and I could hear a raven preening its breast feathers in the total silence of the ponderosa forest. With a quiet mind, and still warm from my sleeping bag, I walked to the rim and looked into the canyon for the first time. The sun lit the upper walls and snow-covered slopes, though the inner gorge was still shrouded in deep shadow. I stood there, waiting for the canyon to speak to me. The vast panorama of rock, as still and silent as a blank screen, said nothing. The cold began to find its way through my jacket, and I turned to find the cafeteria.

After breakfast, I walked to the nearest trailhead. By the time I had hiked downward for an hour or two, the sun had warmed the air and melted the snow, so I stripped to shorts and a T-shirt. I rinsed off in a creek, then laid down on a sun-warmed rock. The walls rose three thousand feet to snow-dusted pines. The sky was brilliant blue and cloudless. The only sound was the murmur of the creek in its bed. It was a beautiful spot for a rest. But at that moment, it meant nothing more. I got up, hiked out, and drove home.

If I came away having heard nothing that day, it was because I had not learned how to listen. A few years later, my neighbor Abel Nelson offered to take me along as a volunteer assistant crewmember, a "swamper," on a raft trip down the Colorado River. I took his offer, since I had nothing better to do. I thought that I had signed up for little more than a whitewater adventure. Once we left Lees Ferry, the rapids were as thrilling as I had hoped, but what really got my attention were the stories he told day after day as we floated through the canyon. The riffle below Soap Creek is where Frank Brown, who was too thrifty to buy life jackets, drowned in 1889. On the Unkar Delta, an Ancestral Puebloan village carved out a living for a century before suddenly abandoning the canyon for good. Two-thirds of the way down Hance Rapid, the much-loved guide Whale spent a long day with his boat stuck on the big rock on the left. Abel sang Steve Goodman's "Grand Canyon Song" in an alcove near the Marble Canyon dam site, read aloud from Powell's journal after dinner, and, over a shot of whiskey after our clients had bedded down for the night, he told tales of hijinks and mayhem. At the end of our trip, I called in to quit my job in town and stayed in the canyon for the rest of the summer.

Soon it was my turn to tell stories, so I began to read about the canyon. Walking out from Phantom Ranch later that summer, I visited my resting spot at Indian Gardens for the second time. I now understood that this broad, well-watered flat on the Tonto Platform was the ancestral farmland of the Havasupai people, who grew corn, beans, and squash here during the spring and fall. Their source of irrigation water, Garden Creek, flows from a spring formed where limestone meets impermeable shale laid down in the Tapeats Sea half a billion years ago. The Kolb brothers hiked up and down Bright Angel Trail for decades, just so they could use the water here to develop the photographs they took of early visitors to the South Rim and then sell them to their subjects. Soon after the park was established, the Havasupai were forced to stop farming here. A campground took the place of their fields, and Indian Gardens became the most visited spot below the rim. What I had once seen as an anonymous stop on a trail that could be anywhere, I now knew as a particular place with a name and with stories that gave it rich and sometimes difficult layers of meaning.

Since then, during twenty summers on the river, I have collected stories of my own that give Grand Canyon particular meanings for me. Every time I run Horn Creek Rapid, I cringe, recalling the time I misjudged my run, hit a rock hard, and one of my clients suffered a massive hematoma near her left eye. When I pass the mouth of 75-Mile Canyon, I remember the time I woke to the sound of a rattlesnake buzzing on my chest. I somersaulted out of my sleeping bag, sending the snake flying into a stand of brittlebush. Passing Cave Springs, I always recall a storm that struck as Matt Herrman and I passed by while looking for camp late one afternoon. It rained so hard that I could not see the nose of my boat. Just as we floated blindly through the next riffle, at Silver Grotto, a section of wall broke loose and covered the lower end of the beach with rubble. Everyone who spends much time in the canyon has a similar mental map of places made meaningful by stories like these. But such experiences fade into unimportance when I recall hundreds of days spent floating on quiet stretches of the river; explaining geology to curious clients; hiking with them to places like Upper Stone Creek and Whispering Springs; listening to the songs of yellow-breasted chats, Lucy's warblers, and canyon wrens; and watching sacred datura flowers open as the moon rises.

Other places in the canyon have taken on an especially personal significance for me. Floating through Conquistador Aisle on a hot July day, I fell in love with my wife. A few years later, we got married at Fire Point, up the road from her mother's house in the House Rock Valley. I met Jon Olivera when we were working as volunteers on our first Grand Canyon trip. Riding through Hermit Rapid was the biggest rush we'd ever experienced, and we swore we would come back in our own boats. I once had a huge argument with Dave Brown about where to tie up our boats on the rocks at Tuna Creek; we were a bit agitated because our friend Bert had just swum Crystal Rapid while trapped beneath an overturned raft. Last summer, Dave and I took our young daughters on their first river trip. In short, my family is grounded in Grand Canyon and so is my closest circle of friends.

There are hundreds of other circles of family and friends who, like mine, have come to know each other in this place full of stories. Many of these communities span generations. One day years ago, I watched O'Connor Dale's young daughters, Emily and Ann-Marie, hike to Upper Elves Chasm on one of their first river trips. Both are now guides, raising their own children in and around the canyon. Another time, I found an ostrich egg in a crack near the mouth of Havasu. I still believe that Paul Thevenin's son, Fred, who was in his teens at the time, brought the egg in from Kanab and hid it to baffle someone like me. Of course, he will never admit it. Fred owns a rafting company now, he is serving a term as president of Grand Canyon River Guides, and his children will be working on the river before long. Another time, not long ago, Amil Quayle and I led a group of clients up Clear Creek, where we were looking for a break from a hot August afternoon. Coming around a bend in the narrow gorge, we met Amil's son Bruce and his grandson Eric, who were making their way back downstream with a string of their own clients in tow. Instantly, the ancient cliffs of Vishnu Schist became the walls of a living room as the three Quayles, three generations of guides, whose careers together spanned more than fifty years, took a few minutes to swap hugs and catch up on family gossip in a patch of shade.

Grand Canyon's many circles of family and friends are held together not only by the stories we share but also by a mutual commitment to care for the place where we work and live. The national park welcomes more than four million visitors every year. Like many of them, when we first looked over the rim, and when we first read scientific accounts of the canyon's formation by implacable natural processes over eons, we saw ourselves from new perspectives. We suddenly felt small and unimportant, lost in reaches of time and space far deeper than we had ever before imagined. But for many of us, that feeling of insignificance changed with the understanding that, for many people over hundreds of years, the Great Unknown has been home. When we heard their stories, we came to understand our time in Grand Canyon and our lives together in the passing present as opportunities not only to enjoy the outdoors and learn about nature but also to work for the preservation of the beautiful and sustaining home given to us by time. One way we do that work is by sharing stories like those in *The Grand Canyon Reader*.

THE RIM

GRAND CANYON

Amil Quayle

After working as a guide during the early years of commercial river-running in Grand Canyon, Amil Quayle ran a cattle ranch while he earned a doctorate in English from the University of Nebraska at Lincoln, and then he returned to his childhood home, a small house his father had built near the Henry's Fork of the Snake River in St. Anthony, Idaho. His two sons, Bruce and Manx, and two of his grandchildren, Eric and Kyndle, are now Grand Canyon river guides. Quayle's two award-winning books of poetry, *Pebble Creek* (1993) and *Grand Canyon and Other Selected Poems* (2009), draw on his family's long intimacy with the rugged landscapes and rural cultures of the American West. Most of his poems give readers a finely detailed and sometimes sorrowful view of the changes that have overtaken the West's human and natural communities during the last century. In this, the title poem of his second book, he digs even deeper into time, finding a metaphor for the shape and texture of his life experience in the geology of the Grand Canyon.

. . .

I speak now of that Grand Canyon
which lies within each of us. There
are pre-Cambrian rocks at the center,
the core, and talus from yesterday's fall;

marble and granite grown hard from the
pressure and heat of heartbreak and
passion; crumbling sandstone, layer on
layer of sediment, sentiment piled on
over a lifetime's experience. The sun
bursts on us each morning then dies
and we are in darkness, but moon shadows
tease our walls. We listen to the pulsating
rhythm of time's river lapping at our
shores. The sandy places slide, diffuse,
move closer to the sea. A billion years
of erosion is magnified, demagnified into
sixty or seventy years as we measure time.
Perhaps in a million years your shinbone
will be a fossil in another Grand Canyon,
cold in a bed of rock next to mine.

FEAR OF GOD

Craig Childs

Acclaimed environmental writer Craig Childs earned his knowledge of nature the hard way. After growing up in Colorado and Arizona, he spent ten years living out of his pack and hiking the most remote backcountry of the Four Corners. When he returned occasionally to town, Childs worked as a river guide, gas station attendant, and beer bottler. He slept in his pickup truck and wrote on legal pads in Laundromats and cafes, telling stories of the incredible things he had seen. One of the strongest voices in a new generation of environmental writers, Childs describes nature at its most elemental and most extreme. His work is rich with sensory images in a way that reflects his long years living outdoors on the plateaus and in the canyons of his home, the desert Southwest. In this chapter from his 2000 book, *The Secret Knowledge of Water*, he chases a flash flood off the North Rim into a remote side canyon, where he experiences firsthand the power of running water that carved Grand Canyon.

. . .

In the morning came the banging pots and pans of distant thunder. I rolled from my bag into the thin blue dawn, shuffled across the sand, and stood there naked, peeing on a broom snakeweed. All parts of the planet lay below. This was the top, four thousand feet off the floor of the Grand Canyon, between Fern Glen Canyon and Kanab Canyon. To the west an unsettled broth of storms emerged from Nevada. I ran my fingers over my head, stretched my arms into the air. It was early for this kind of weather. I would usually not see storms of this size until at least noon, when the atmosphere had a chance to embroil itself in rising late-summer thermals. The ocean must have been shedding a healthy layer of moisture in this direction. Now that I was looking, rubbing my eyes and walking to the rimrock, I saw that the storm was about the size of one of the New England states. It dragged lightning over the ground the way someone distractedly pets a cat. From here it looked like toothpicks touching ground, holding up the storm.

I had been waiting, patient, walking these canyons for weeks while sorting through flood debris, counting flood stones of different sizes, using delicate tools to measure the angles of carved bedrock. Mostly, though, I lurked in shadows, waiting for the unexpected arrival of a flood, looking up now and then to see a small cloud heading north. The late-summer storms I had been counting on had spun in every direction, ravaging Olo Canyon while I was at Shanub Point, tearing the insides out of Deer Creek while I hunted for drinking water at the rim of Tuckup Canyon. At night I sat with my knees to my chest, watching the faint blue flashes, hearing a dim rumble, ostracized by another storm heading to another place, missing me entirely.

There would not be much time before this storm arrived. I realized this and sorted through my gear. The storm wheeled east toward the Grand Canyon while I was at least a couple thousand feet too high to get into position to see a flood. No time for the big pack; it would take too long to lumber that thing down the canyon. I wrapped what I needed into a small waist pack: a bottle to hold some floodwater, a quart of drinking water, some food, tape measure, notes, binoculars, raincoat, knife, and a map. I thought of bringing the webbing to help with climbing, but figured I would avoid that kind of unpleasantness entirely. I left the rim, heading toward low ground for a flood. I felt like one of those people studying tornadoes, driving into the storm while everybody else is hell-bent to get out. But there was no one to come running the other way, calling me crazy.

The storm arrived in half an hour, combing the rims, belting out thunder that sounded like a loose aluminum roof pounding in the wind. Still another fifteen minutes before I reached the upper channel of the canyon below. This was a long, narrow catch basin of a canyon, about fifteen miles from end to end. Down inside, it dug itself into a vast chasm, sawing through the planet to the Colorado River.

Rain began as I jogged across one of the interior rims, passing the lone standing boulders that had tumbled thousands of feet to get this far. I started to run. Cloudbursts pounded into the canyon as lightning began striking open ground. I sprinted down to the channel, just above where it entered the canyon. Rain had filled my boots already.

Here the rock was basalt, a lava flow from about a million years ago. Treated with the same regard as any sandstone or limestone out here, the black basalt had been cut into a wormhole of a channel, smooth and polished. I skittered down its chutes, entering the pit of a canyon tall and narrow like a snake path through high grass. This is when I had to think, when I slowed to check every twenty feet for an escape route, some crack or ledge above the high-water mark. The old high-water mark rose as the canyon tightened—ten feet, sixteen, nineteen, twenty-five feet. From the narrow floor of the canyon I was looking for a good place to bundle up and wait out the storm, a platform as far in as possible, where I could safely sit and watch if a flood should happen through.

Built of constant steep plunges where waterfalls formed during floods, the canyon complicated navigation. One of the descents down the middle was too difficult. A small piece of Kaibab limestone had wedged into a crack over a plunge, making a chockstone, something that sat sturdy enough to use as a hand-hold. Twenty feet below was a plunge pool full of water, its surface jumping like popcorn from the rain. I paced a few times, looking down-canyon, up-canyon. Should have brought the webbing, I thought. I grabbed the chockstone, shook it around to see if it was stable. Good enough. So I got down there, swung my body over the stone, and held on for dear life. I wanted to see if there was a way down. I figured if there was one more hold below the chockstone, I could climb inside just that much farther.

There was not another hold. This was not going to get me anywhere. From my suspended vantage I could see plunge pools lining the canyon from here on down. I pulled myself up to climb out. But I could not get my boots on anything. The angle of the rock was wrong. All I had was this wedged stone to hang from, enough to hold me there but not enough to get me up. I grunted, cursed, squirmed around, and could not get back up. I turned quiet for a second, listening. If the flood came now, it would hit me at just about eye level. I made a trapped animal sound and tried another position. My right arm weakened. The muscles in my chest drew tight. Then I started to kick. The waist pack wedged me in. I forced myself until something popped in my shoulder. Pain shot up my neck. It was a small strap of muscle pulled too far. I could feel my face involuntarily losing composure.

With my free left hand, I reached down and unclipped my pack. I pulled, so I could toss it up, out of my way. As I pulled, the strap wormed from my fingers. The pack fell. I saw it sail for an instant, the straps swinging out. It landed in the pool below like a sack of laundry.

My notes.

That is all I thought, *my notes.*

For two seconds I tried to find an alternative. There was nothing to hold here. I knew this already. I let go. The only thing to do to get my notes back.

Falling took longer than I thought. My legs started kicking unintentionally in the air. Then I hit the pool, chest-deep. I pawed at the gravel, sputtering juniper scales and small, wet twigs from my mouth. I pulled myself out, the pack in my right hand. The canyon echoed with my splashes.

For a moment I stood with my draining pack, listening so hard it hurt. The sound of thunder. Water running from my clothes. My heartbeat.

The world changes colors when you think you might die very soon. Everything stood brilliant. The purple shade of the storm had a thirsty lushness. The rock was smooth as pearl. Even as I stood panicked, listening to water pour through my pants, out of my boots, it was unmistakable that everything I believed was down here. Each part of my faith: the scalloped walls; how each sound was sharply distinguished; the smell of water on stone; the fine patterns left in sand from the last flood. Every last piece of magic and belief. I had spent my life clutched to these canyons. I had always sought this. I could feel lumps of juniper berries down my shirt.

Even if it looked feasible, I could not go downstream from here. That is definitely how people die. From desperation. Bad decisions. If a flood never came, I would be trapped in there like someone stuck down a well peering hopelessly up at a little circle of sunlight. So I turned to the place where I had fallen. I scrambled at the left side, got halfway up and scraped back down into the pool. Skin stripped from my palm like an offering. I sucked on the cut, mumbling obscenities. My flesh for an escape.

Then the right side. A couple of cracks lacing the basalt, part of the jointing that occurs in cooling lava, were exaggerated by erosion. With the pack slung over a shoulder and out of the way, I managed to reach the halfway point, just below where I had jumped. I lay back against the last handhold and rose finger by finger. I used all of my energy, a day's worth just for my fingertips. Then, just for my palms when I ran out of cracks. I used my chin, my right cheekbone, my hip. Anything I could get. It was bad rock. Too slick. My body began to shake, muscles jackhammering.

Rain plucked at my eyes. Skin started to slip, sending my heart jumping. I held to the rock with the side of my face, with my palms flat as palms can lie, the last knuckles in my fingers crimping at the rock. Water started over the edge of the canyon floor above me. It started into a waterfall. Clear water. A small, ornamental flood. *Okay,* I thought, *clear water, just clear water.* The clear water increased, spreading toward me as it ran into the plunge pool with a sluicing sound. *Oh Jesus, not now.* I could not move. If I did I would fall. I let the weight of my body settle on my flesh and the rock. I breathed. The voice of the water grew louder.

I could go down. If I could not get up, I would have to go down. I thought about the circle of sunlight, and the sad, helpless look that would be on my face. I banished the thought and went ahead with my left hand. My body would be sore tonight. Every part of it. I relished the thought. *Tonight. Out of here.* Then the right leg. My left hand drifted over, touched the bottom of the limestone chockstone at a full reach. Fingers crept up its side. I got a hold, my face still flush to the wall. I wrapped fingers around the stone. My entire weight shifted. Water ran down my arm, using my body now as a waterfall. I inched up, boots against one side, hands against the chockstone. When I got high enough, without thinking, I pushed off like a frog, thighs tight, launching my body away and landing with my torso in the gravel and water of the next higher level. My fingers dug in, keeping the dangling half of my body from yanking me off. Gravel let loose and flowed over my shoulders. As fast as I could, I scrambled away from the edge.

I bolted off to one of the walls, climbed up to the rim. Scared enough to have this crisp, anxious stare on my face, I sat in the rain watching the streamflow, which never got bigger, never muddied. It stayed ornamental. Most of the storm had hit lower in the canyon, where I would not have expected it. Big floods down there. The rain stopped. I peeled off my clothes and wrung them out so that murky water spattered the rock, then scooped water in my hands to clean the small debris from my skin and rub clean the abrasions on my palm. Scanning through binoculars (a bit foggy now), I could see water running off the Esplanade sandstone miles below. I sat there naked for a while, thinking I would get up, dress, and walk away soon. But I did not get up. I sat. I watched. The canyon had given me back. There are certain gambles out here. A commodity of value comes into risk. I figure this is why people spend hours in casinos, tossing money down for a sense of immediacy that is often removed from civilization, a sense of wildness perhaps, where loss or gain will be simple, quick, and definitive. That would be my sense of loss at my own death—simple, quick, and definitive. I shook my head, made promises to myself. But I was here to find floods, regardless. I walked around the basalt rim, finding my way into the lower canyon.

Miles inside, the canyon floor burrowed into a corkscrew passage. Eighty-foot boulders lounged along the dry bottom, some wedged between the walls, others perched on top of each other. Walls took directly to the sky, leaving shadows to feast all over each other at the floor. This is what it must have been like, I thought, to be the first to stand beneath the Empire State Building or beside the docked *Titanic*. The canyon was enormous.

By late morning a second storm broke the canyon rim. The sky turned the color of a bruised plum. Ten minutes ago there had been no sign of clouds, straight sunlight, and now the bulk of a thunderstorm shouldered into the canyon. From a small ledge over the dry canyon floor I watched each movement in the sky, my body shifting to whip-cracks in the wind.

This second storm came erratic and elastic, leaning any direction. It was driven from the inside, from descending swells of rain that severed rising heat cells. By now it was certain; the storm had committed itself. It would land here.

I hit the stopwatch when the rain arrived like the dropping of a cement block. No pause, no first raindrops, just suddenly here. A cloudburst. These storms had been liberating forty-ton boulders lately, and I had been arriving days too late, finding downstream carnage, falling clumsily into a pit of old floodwater, panicking even as no flood came. Storms had been swerving drunkenly across the landscape, suddenly expelling into one canyon and not the next.

Now it was here. I jumped from the ledge when a curtain of waterfalls came over me. I landed in the drainage and ran. Rain took the land. Waterfalls stirred down every cliff face. Rain beat at my head.

The flood was here, two minutes after the rain began. It filled the channel with no warning. When you hear tales of desert floods you hear about sudden waves, walls of water. These impulsive walls are deep inside the canyon, down in the menacing constrictions, or out the other side. There came no wave here at the very beginning. This was the place where the wave was constructed, the fingerprint where the storm had landed. A stream assembled, midcalf in some places, deeper behind boulders and in the plunges. And rising. Foam of released air and silt collected in eddies. I could not even track this water's origination. It was simply here, fed from every side, fed from things that were not even canyons, were not even places where water should flow.

Canyons are basically nets that catch water. Branches and fingers and tributaries scour the land above, sending everything down, so that when a storm passes, all of its rainwater is driven toward a single point. Water can run from tens of miles down hundreds of feeder canyons, spilling into deeper and deeper, fewer and fewer canyons until the volume of the flood has jumped exponentially into one final chasm where everything converges. I was in this single point. I slapped through its gathering water, running downstream to glimpse the behavior of each local tributary. Water from one side canyon choked and growled, arcing down and bursting into the main channel. A couple of tributaries added enough to triple the flood's volume, one emerging from a slim crack, ushering the curve of a waterfall. Not water, though. It was something else: half rock, half water. It ran red with Supai and Hermit shale, red like a soup of cayenne and fresh, squashed tomatoes thickened with sand and stones. It threw rocks into the air, plunking them into the flood around my legs.

There is a specific geometry to a canyon floor built by this kind of water. There will be long segments of gentle gradients interrupted by sudden drops and pools, followed by more narrow runways leading to more drops. These narrow flood canyons are built like stairways where, at critical points, the energy of increasing stream-force becomes too much. Turbulence drives water and debris until it fists a hole into the canyon. The cauldron that has now been cut into the floor is called a *hydraulic jump*. It is a method of dissipating the flood's energy into a plunge pool, some ten to twenty feet deep, before the water can resume its downstream travel. Floods spill out of these hydraulic jumps, move downstream, build force, and again reach peak turbulence, carving another bowl. This is followed by the slope, then the waterfall, then the next bowl, on and on down the canyon. The pattern is a way for the flood to shed energy, like pumping the car brakes to keep from going out of control.

Within moving water are an array of genetic instructions, which are driven into stone and passed from one flood to the next. If the water is funneled through a thick forest, say in the Olympic Mountains of Washington, it will make the same matrix of steps and pools, only out of fallen trees and woody debris, not out of bedrock. If the medium is boulders and sand, the final shape will be the same, as if sorted by hand—steps and pools in perfect order. You will see it down a steep street gutter where cigarette butts and pieces of loose asphalt have been arranged to form runs and puddles. Water is not concerned with the setting. It consistently uses this language.

This canyon sank into the Supai Formation and strangled itself with meanders and waterfalls. I found ways around, jumping between backs of boulders to keep pace with the rising water. The flood became dangerous in the constriction, boiling with mud and rocks and smaller parts of trees. Large rocks began surging up from their settings, lumbering half out of the water, then thudding downstream. I dragged my left hand on the wall, scooting far over, remembering how the desert fishes get through these floods by squeezing to the side, by keeping straight. The flood began pushing at my legs, telling me *faster, faster!* Water swelled behind my thighs, rising, causing my feet to fumble, almost knocking me over.

Maybe I had made a mistake. Maybe I shouldn't be here. It was time to get out. The *f*·st exit to higher ground within the canyon, with ledges just barely beyond reach, did not work. I ducked through a culvert of fallen boulders. Rainwater latticed my face. Where the floodwater smacked into obstacles, mud burst into the air and onto me. The rain then washed the mud from my forearms, off my neck. I turned every eight or ten seconds, wiping my face, to glance behind for the infamous wave. With the storm top of me, I figured I was *in* the wave. The wave was building around me. At this point I could not turn around and run back up against the flow. I had to follow or I would be tumbled backward.

There are things one cannot know about canyons and floods. One Arizona flood in August 1971 came from a fairly insignificant drainage and yielded what is clearly the largest known flood for a canyon of its size. In a brief event, Bronco Creek belted out about a thousand tons of water every second. The creek, which drains nineteen square miles, was suddenly as large as the Colorado River, a river born from seven states, draining thirteen hundred times the land of Bronco Creek. You never know what you will get—where the storm will hit, how much rain will fall, or how the canyon will play it.

In general, storms travel over the Grand Canyon from southwest to northeast. For canyons like this that open into the common local path of storms, floods tend to be more numerous and more pronounced. Canyons cutting perpendicular to the path are shielded from the bulk of a thunderhead, which crosses briefly from one side to the next. The volume and frequency of storms can be read in the terraces of flood debris left at the mouths. Canyons facing into the storms have shoveled layer after layer of flood debris out, while those facing other directions have produced more scant debris. Storms happen to track along the pattern of geologic faulting in the Grand Canyon, so that many canyons, which use faults as blueprints, are open like mouths swallowing the weather. The entire Grand Canyon is thus a machine designed to capture and drive flash floods. Every last wrinkle and crack lends itself to this mechanism, showing water the quickest, most efficient way down.

A catwalk of a ledge protruded from one wall and I took it, narrow but elevated enough to be out of reach from the flood. On hands and knees I made the first moves. The canyon floor dropped around me through fallen two-story boulders. Where I had last walked, an acacia tree rattled, then bent as mud slopped through its branches. The water below grew from knee-deep to shoulder-deep. Then shoulder-deep to eye-deep. Then the references were gone.

The ledge became wide enough for me to stand as it hugged the curving east wall. At the junction of several major tributaries, the ledge entered a four-hundred-foot-deep sanctum where floods jumped from each side, spanning well away from their cliffs. Two particular tributaries flowed with unnerving throbs, dropping from canyons that hung a hundred feet above the floor. Shapes were visible in their muddy veils, shadows of large, sailing objects. A newborn waterfall burst off one edge, throwing rocks into the air in its lead. It was as if the scaffolding of the planet was coming down, the bolts and metal sleeves of time and physical structures snapping apart, planks caving in. Wind sheeted up from the canyon floor, propelling mud and mist straight up the wall and against my face, through my soaked clothes.

You could not shout over this sound. It was like gritting teeth and clenching fists. It was the sound angels make as their wings are torn off. Occasionally a single sound stood out: the smack of a boulder, or the sucking of a thousand gallons of water finding a new path. Most individual sounds were felt only through my feet or up the bones of my arms. Breaking boulders made sharp clacks. The low-pitched sounds were those of larger rocks, and when I heard these I backed against the wall in case the earth should split open here. It is simply not possible to stand limp before something like this. The muscles in my neck stood out.

I have often thought that trapped on a shelf in a flood, a person could go insane, waiting for the flood to lift and take the ledge. I remembered a story from Havasu Canyon, when a twenty-foot wall of water came down on the village of Supai in 1910. Charles Coe, the Indian Service superintendent, was found around noon the next day with his wife and their Havasupai cook, huddled on the roof of their house. Theirs was one of only two structures left standing. The three people clung to each other, wearing nightclothes and a few blankets they had salvaged, while the flood growled around them, carrying off horses and cottonwood trees. From the roof, they had witnessed other buildings collapsing into the flood while somehow, theirs stood. But the fear. The endless fear. During the night they had listened to the world crumble around them, to lumber splitting as roofs buckled. I imagined the fear of waiting for their house to topple beneath them. As soon as Coe was rescued and got out of the canyon, he never checked on his responsibilities to the Havasupai people he had been serving. He left Arizona and did not return.

To my back I could see the scours of old floods against the wall, over my head. How old? A hundred years? A thousand years? It became difficult to carry a thought for more than a couple of seconds. My senses jerked back and forth as if I were being dragged.

What was most remarkable in this flood was not the force or the sound, but the overwhelming smell. It was the smell of drowned pocket mice, sage, newborn canyon tree frogs and sun-heated rocks doused in ice water, the same smell as rain on a hot sidewalk. The bold, musty smell of sacred datura leaves and seepwillows. It was the smell of raw oxygen foamed into the finest silt this planet produces, and the methane of rotting cactus burped through the mud. The dissolving endosperm of acacia seeds. The damp underbelly of a red-spotted toad. Old, rank feathers of ravens, wings of cicadas, and bones of a black-tailed jackrabbit washed from the rim. It was the stench of everything living and dead.

An entire oak tree paused at the margin of a falls, then tumbled, branches prying away as I watched. The main trunk, as thick as my chest, cantilevered over space, caught on a ledge, and shuttered down ladder rungs of exposed boulders. At the base, small rocks, most the size of kneecaps, jetted into the air. They took odd trajectories, pelting anything nearby, breaking into shrapnel. I could not count fast enough. Maybe ten rocks a second, six hundred rocks a minute, into the air. The tree was pulverized at the bottom.

Any jag or protrusion was beaten down. If I were to stick my hand in there, my bones would splinter. The flood pummeled impurities out of this canyon, ridding the place of friction and awkward shapes, taking it down to an archetypal form—that of a smooth, carved canyon. Every physical element of a canyon network is mercurial, with no hard givens, no solid obstacles. These seemingly unflagging walls of the Supai Formation were simply another moving part. This is how canyons are formed, by the sway of the earth against floods, where the shape is defined by an alertness to even the most trivial tension. If a boulder falls in, everything adjusts. Channel cobbles shift as floodwater shunts to one side, beating a hollow into the wall, while the offending boulder rapidly erodes into a hydraulic shape like the nose of a speedboat. Any interruption alters the hydraulics. The flood might change its mind and a new canyon will be built to reach a new equilibrium. The equilibrium ends up looking like a house of cards, a succession of pits and shells and sudden turns.

Flood researcher Luna Leopold called the flexible aspects of a flood *degrees of freedom*. Degrees of freedom measure the rates at which objects give way to pressure: the quick erosion of sand, the steady wearing back of stone walls, and the instant recoil of water hitting a boulder. From his technical descriptions of research sites, each item in a flood like this is a degree of freedom. Everything changes shape.

Leopold, witnessing numerous floods in New Mexico, tromping the Arroyo Caliente, Arroyo de los Frijoles, and Arroyo San Cristobal in search of flash floods, had time in his life to decipher the motion of water through the desert, watching banks of mud caving in behind him while rocks battered his legs. In his scientific language, the relationship between a desert's geometry and its floods seems organic: "If the degrees of freedom of the [water] are reduced, the remaining factors [sand, canyon walls, cottonwood trees, and so on] tend toward a mutual accommodation." Meaning, the more durable and deeper the canyon, the more resistance is given to a flood. The more resistance that is given, the more the canyon wears into the shape of water, and water takes on the shape of the canyon.

I stared into the melee below. The flood bounded over immovable boulders, churning into whirlpools. It had a texture like a rapid boil, sending debris up, sucking it down, each roil a barrel rising to the surface. Nothing stayed on top for more than a couple of seconds. The trunk of a cottonwood tree showed through. Smaller boulders, three feet across, stabbed and rolled against the larger ones.

About forty-five minutes after the start, the flood began receding. The storm abandoned the canyon entirely, leaving the high sun to bake my head. A few more flood pulses arrived, latecomer tributaries finally sending water down, altering the flood by only a matter of inches. I climbed off the ledge and found a wide stretch in the channel where the water was not so deep. When I reached in to touch the edge of the bed, my arm quivered at the impact. There was no bed. Everything was moving. My skin stung with driven sand. A comparison of sediment loads of a desert canyon, dry all but a few hours of the year, and a year-round stream in Oregon shows that even with so much less flow time, the desert carries a million times more debris. Oregon creek beds are armored with cobblestones packed around each other, accustomed to a constant wash of water. Here, everything is angled for motion. A few of the seepwillows might stay. Half the cottonwoods in a grove may hold their ground. But everything else, the sand and boulders, is primed for momentum. You could close your eyes and run your hands across the stones in the floor of a canyon like this to tell which way the water last moved. It is called *imbrication,* the particular way water stacks objects in a downstream direction. Each rock leans against the next, placed in the position of least resistance, always the same position pointing the way down the canyon, so that if you turn and walk upcanyon, all the shapes are against you. Here and there are imbricate clusters of rocks and boulders; they look like stacked books, so uniform that you will swear someone has been emphatically arranging the local stones.

When I handled a rock large enough that it might be stationary in the water, it rotated from my hand and was dragged downstream. Large rocks actually appeared *above* the surface, tossed up for a moment as if the water had run out of room. Downstream from here, where I would not even think of going, was even more of a keyhole of a passage. The flood down there would become catastrophically huge, soon to burst onto the Colorado River like a bomb.

It would be simple enough to say that there is no grace to a flood, that it is nothing but uncooked power. That is what I saw today, the heedless battering against sandstone, against time, and against my most precious of sensibilities. But what was left behind—this entire canyon—is not graceless, not haphazard. I could see it in the camber of bedrock that the flood chose as a course. Each rock was left in a deliberate fashion. Passageways were left shaped like blown glass. The intentions of floods are expertly refined. The shape of the canyon is the shape of moving water, and the shape of water, like the canyon, will amend to the slightest bias. While resisting and accommodating each other, water and canyon both become patterns of the same intelligence.

I found a place to sit, squatting in a patch of boulder shade where I could listen to the roar come down, watching the flood dwindle. The water finally stopped. It took two minutes to arrive, then two hours and seven minutes to leave. I expected hissing, some sound of decompression. At least the isolated clatter of cobbles settling into each other. But there was nothing. I did not know how to handle the silence. The simple aspects of the environment I had admired in past days—shadows beneath a western redbud tree, the intense blue of the sky, bighorn tracks across an upper level—now seemed inappreciable. I was standing weak-limbed, uncertain of what to do. There was no evidence that it had ever happened. I picked up a cobble, something that had sailed here from miles away, an integral part of motion and violence. It was now as inert as the rest of the desert. The flood had abandoned me. I walked back to my camp to put notes together, to prove to myself that it happened.

BRIGHT ANGEL TRAIL

Ann Zwinger

In more than a dozen works of nature writing published over four decades, naturalist Ann Zwinger has been an even-tempered guide to the ecology of the West. Her work is uniquely modest: rather than focus on her own adventures or her own feelings about nature, she relies on close observation, detailed description, and clear scientific explanation to help her readers both understand and appreciate the places she studies. "More than anything," she writes, "I hope to leave trails by which every person can find a binding relationship to the natural world." Her 1995 book *Downcanyon* weaves stories of her many exploratory hikes and river trips in the Grand Canyon together with richly detailed descriptions of its natural and human history. In this selection, she hikes the park's most popular trail and meditates on the lessons to be learned from the ancestral Puebloan people's attempt to settle the harsh inner gorge.

. . .

For Christmas my eldest daughter, Susan, and I give each other a hike down the Bright Angel Trail, a couple of nights at Phantom Ranch. We will walk back up the South Kaibab Trail on winter solstice, the end of autumn, the beginning of winter, the rounding of the year when Sun prepares to leave his Winter House. We start down, knowing a major snow is coming in on a huge outbreak of polar air. Scathing winds. A wind chill factor of ten below. I question my good sense in going. There may not be enough clothes in the world to keep me warm.

The Bright Angel Trail follows the Bright Angel Fault, a fault that simply on the basis of accessibility is the best-known in the Grand Canyon. Walking inside it helps one understand the other great fault systems to which there is no easy access. Once below the rim the wind mercifully abates. Sun lights the Coconino Sandstone and snow outlines ledges on the damp Hermit Shale like chalk lines on a blackboard. Not quite ten miles from rim to river, the elevation drops from 6,860 feet at the South Rim to 2,400 feet at river's edge. With each footstep, we go back 20,000 to 30,000 years in time.

Because the path is so narrow, hikers must flatten against the cliff wall while the "scrawniest Rosinantes and wizened-rat mules," as Muir described them, pass by. The eighteen miles of trail that the mules travel are doused yearly with 8,000 gallons of mule urine and 117 tons of road apples. I shouldn't grouse: Charles Silver Russell, trying to do a photographic run of the river in 1915, had a steel boat built, which he and his helpers loaded on a dolly to cart it down the Bright Angel Trail. Every time the mules came by, the men had to jockey dolly and boat off to the side and cover them with canvas so as not to scare the mules. It took a week to get it down and then Russell wrecked it at Crystal. Twice.

Even in December the cottonwoods at Indian Gardens hold their leaves, although most fade to dirty yellow. They were planted by Emery Kolb, who maintained a darkroom here to avoid having to pay for pumping water to the South Rim (water issues from Roaring Springs, just below the North Rim, and runs by gravity to Indian Gardens). After taking pictures of tourists on their mules, Kolb would race down the trail to Indian Gardens, develop and make prints, and sprint back up to the top by the time the riders returned, all prints seventy-five cents each, thank you very much.

Clouds begin to filter across the sky. Sunlight washes the far buttes but shadows wallow in the canyon. We've picked up six more degrees. Even in December while snow garnishes the Kaibab, brittlebushes and one sweetbush bloom, both cheerful brassy yellow. The change from prehistoric path to commercial trail transpired in 1891, when miner Ralph Cameron and others improved it to allow access to copper mining claims. Cameron (it was originally called Cameron Trail) operated it as a toll trail. When the courts declared his claims invalid, the trail became, in one instant, the property of Coconino County, Arizona, and *its* toll road.

In 1902 the U.S. Geological Survey established a trail from the North Rim down to the river, connecting with the Bright Angel Trail, and called it the North Kaibab Trail. One crossed the river in a boat "lent by a friendly prospector" at the only crossing between Lees Ferry, eighty-nine miles upstream, and the Bass Trail, thirty-five miles west. By 1903 the trails had become such a regular route that the county upgraded the river crossing to a steel rowboat.

After the National Park Service took over administration of the Grand Canyon in 1919, it decided to replace the boat with a steel suspension bridge. Harriet Chalmers Adams, on assignment for the *National Geographic*, came down on mule back to write about its construction. Getting building materials down was a logistical nightmare. Eight mules carried the twelve-hundred-pound cables that were anchored into the walls eighty feet up. As today, wooden planking floors the bridge, and wire mesh cages the sides for protection. Adams took a canvas boat across to "Roosevelt camp" (now Phantom Ranch, which got its name from early surveyors who noticed a ghostly haze that often hung in the canyon in late afternoon), and exited by mule up the North Kaibab Trail.

Failing in its first attempts to acquire the Bright Angel Trail from Coconino County, the Park Service, from 1924 to 1928, built its own toll-free trail and crossing: the South Kaibab Trail, which connects with the North Kaibab Trail via the bridge. Upon completion of the South Kaibab, Coconino County, scarcely in a spate of public dedication, sold the Bright Angel Trail, which it had gotten for nothing, to the Park Service for $100,000, a *very* tidy profit.

We lunch at the top of a series of switchbacks called the Devil's Staircase, relishing the last sunlight before we enter the shadowy murk along Pipe Creek. Across the way the line of the Great Unconformity bears witness to what the earth did with its yesterdays, Tapeats against Vishnu, sandstone against schist, a familiar, friendly juxtaposition that has come to mark my eons in the Inner Gorge.

Pipe Creek chortles down the Pipe Creek Fault, a branch of the Bright Angel Fault system. The trail crosses a vein of salmon-pink Zoroaster Granite with big chunks of milky quartz, one of the proliferation of Zoroaster dikes and sills in the Bright Angel section. Lichens spatter paint a swath of deep red granite. Being damp intensifies the lichens' color, rendering them vivid gray green against the darker rock, ruffled edges markedly brighter with new growth. Scraps of brilliant chartreuse map lichen vibrating with color on this cloudy day, scabbing the surface with a near Day-Glo brilliance, growing above a webbing of cracks vivid with moss.

As Pipe Creek nears the river, Vishnu Schist begins to look like marble cake batter, swirled in ribbons and stripes: the Pipe Creek migmatites, a transitional stage between metamorphic and igneous rock. White lines swirl into dark gray rock with overtones of purple, undertones of navy blue, no orderly layers like a sandstone or a shale, but rock molded and welded, puddled and re-reworked, sunbaked and frostsplit. Bands of white quartz flecked with red outline rounded knobs, and wider bands of crimson beribbon it. Sometimes the lighter lines are as steady as a stretched string, other times as quirky as a corkscrew, recording in turn a white quartz lizard, a red granite ankh, a silvery snake, a gray sneeze, a purple sniffle.

Wind shoots off the river and whips every bush and grass stem with a vicious, malevolent intensity, seeming to come from everywhere and all at once. Clouds bullet across the sky. I start across the old foot bridge over the river at Bright Angel Creek. Despite the cold I stop at midcrossing. The river makes a big curve downstream, posing that old evocative river question: what's around the bend? Horn Creek Rapid, that's what. For some peculiar satisfaction, I'm glad I know.

Susan and I hurry along Bright Angel Creek, eyes tearing from the wind, too chilled to talk. Bright Angel was originally called Silver Creek for the silver "float," although the source of the silver was never found. Trout are spawning, a month or so earlier than those in Nankoweap Creek, just forty miles upstream. Two ouzels fly along the creek, darting and jabbering. Despite the presence of ouzels in almost every tributary stream in the canyon, it is still a treat to see them parading underwater as easily and perkily as other birds do on the bank. Snow flares through the cottonwood leaves, flakes the size of chads. Chicken wire wraps many of the big cottonwood trees along Bright Angel Creek to protect them from beavers—by the time Phantom Ranch was established in 1922, beavers had pretty well cleared them out.

We straggle into Phantom Ranch in day-darkening, spitting rain, altogether foreboding weather. After dinner, the wind tunes up to gale force, a wild Walpurgis Night. The cottonwoods clatter. Wind shrieks in uneven pulses and jagged crescendos. The ragged intervals between blasts create an erratic, irrational, breath-holding tempo that breaks the easy rhythm of nightfall. The latest weather forecast comes in with the last hiker: a foot of snow on the rim, blizzard conditions, all roads closed in and out of the park. That night winter knocks on the doors of consciousness, flaunting all its chill and bleakness, darkness and bitter corners, full of vindictive winds and treachery.

Two mornings later, still afflicted with truculent skies, belligerent wind, and clanging cold, we start up the South Kaibab Trail, leaving the river as the Anasazi did, on foot. Just before the Kaibab Bridge, some Anasazi tucked a small living space between wall and river. When Powell stopped here looking for wood from which to carve replacements for his eternally broken oars, he noted this site and wondered "why these ancient people sought such inaccessible places for their homes." The answer is, of course, that these were no "inaccessible places" to the Anasazi, who traveled this canyon freely and easily. Constructed on a talus slope about thirty feet directly above the river, the site has the highest elevation available of any place on the delta of Bright Angel Creek, the first space along the river downstream from Unkar Delta amenable to settlement.

Twice between A.D. 1050 and 1150 small groups of Anasazi farmers located here, encouraged by the same temporary increase in annual rainfall that allowed marginal agricultural land to be taken up elsewhere along the river. Although the steepness presented some leveling problem for the builders, siting here substantially reduced the chance of being flooded out by living too close to the creek. They situated carefully to take advantage of solar radiation and to free up the largest amount of potential farming area. Even the floods of 1983 did not reach its masonry walls. But the benches they farmed a quarter-mile down the creek no longer exist, having been modified when Phantom Ranch was built as well as by the December 1966 flood that also created Crystal Rapid. At its peak, the population here never exceeded fifteen or sixteen people, still a group large enough to build their own kiva.

When I take my gloves off to take notes, my fingers sting with the cold. In this confined chasm, the lack of sunlight and warmth congeal my marrow. Focused on my own discomfort, I recall the miseries registered in one of the two skeletons found here, that of a middle-aged Anasazi woman of my stature. The burial, rare in the Grand Canyon, was unearthed quite by accident when a construction crew was working at Bright Angel Creek in 1982. Typical of this egalitarian Anasazi society, only two artifacts accompanied the bodies: a Tusayan Corrugated jar, a cooking vessel of no special or decorative significance, and a bracelet on the arm of the juvenile.

The woman's skeleton bore marks of unusual trauma and degeneration. The atlas, named after Atlas, the Greek Titan who carried the heavens on the back of his neck, and the base of her skull were fused at the junction of the first cervical vertebra and the backbone. This fusion, a birth defect known today as Klippel-Feil Syndrome, is often hereditary and accompanied by other physical anomalies. In addition, the second and third cervical vertebrae were frozen into a single unit (now called a block vertebra), which put greater than normal stress on the neck, surely exacerbated if she used a tumpline. These fusions can reduce the size of the neural canal, allowing bone to impinge directly upon the spinal cord, which normally causes numbness and pain in the arms, weakness in the legs, sometimes muscle control problems, headaches, and blurring or doubling of vision.

Her left leg showed two fractures, one a stress fracture, probably from a fall while the left leg was extended, such as might have happened by losing her balance and pitching forward while stepping off a height. The full impact of the shock traveled through the knee while it was in an extremely vulnerable position, and when it healed with only yucca poultices to damp the pain, although movement was probably restored, osteoarthritic degeneration set in.

All her life she must have lived in pain, unsure of her balance, always walking in a blurred landscape. She bore pain without medication, misery without surcease, no hope of feeling better tomorrow, a bitter lot in this place of cold leavings. And yet, my instinct tells me that somehow she was a useful working member of her family group and did the work that she could do. I give her honor.

A short way up the trail I turn and look back down across the river to that small site squeezed in between river and cliff. Its emptiness on this chilling day epitomizes for me the Anasazi's final exodus from the Grand Canyon, for by A.D.

1200 there were no beginnings, only endings. Land expansion ended. The Virgin Anasazi branch disappeared. The uplands were virtually abandoned. Because there *was* someplace else to go, the whole population picked up and filtered eastward to the Rio Grande drainage, where their ancestors still live today.

The Southwest is unique in having a body of data—geological, climatological, palynological, tree-ring, and radiometric—that establishes in extraordinary detail the fabric of prehistoric climate unavailable elsewhere. A preponderance of the Anasazi movements on the Colorado Plateau neatly match known environmental changes, and all evidence verifies the hypothesis that environmental stress combined with overpopulation *does* trigger the kind of socioeconomic change and population dislocation that beset the Anasazi in the middle of the twelfth century. No evidence of warfare or aggression, no massive epidemics, no other catastrophic causes can be documented. The massive movement eastward ties clearly and directly to environmental deterioration exacerbated by too many people.

When the climate turns bad, no one then or now can make an arroyo carry more water, no one can lengthen a growing season, or raise a water table, no one can gentle violent summer storms. Arroyo cutting destroyed fields and pulled chunks of arable land into the river, lowered the water table, and left remaining lands high and dry. In most canyon tributaries debris caught high in shrubs and trees tells of fearful and fast torrents that reamed out a creek bed, clawed out the banks, and rattled the cobbles, destructive rampages against which, even today, there is no protection.

The Anasazi already employed strategies to deal with a falling water table, such as more rigorous use of agricultural ground, and soil and water control features to curtail erosion and conserve summer's rains. Anasazi farmers engineered a more drought-resistant maize, incorporated more fields of more aspects into their system. Their technology produced reliable yields in places that cannot support agriculture today. The failure of prehistoric Southwestern farmers was not for lack of ingenuity or expertise but simply tells that the problems they faced were unsolvable.

Good times in the Southwest have a way of not lasting long; change blew in on a cruel, dry wind. Arroyo cutting begins when groundwater depletion is rapid, where valley floors are narrow and stream gradients high, a good description of most of the Colorado's tributaries here. No rain gauge recorded fewer tenths of inches over time, no data bank furnished comparative data, no climatologists forecast oncoming disaster or disagreed about global warming or global cooling. Tree rings narrowed in response to a less benevolent climate, a lowering water table paralleled diminishing rainfall, and an arroyo's steepening sides told of unmanageable erosion, narrowing the dry-farm belt to zero.

The mechanics of leaving, the breaking down of a settlement system, are complex. If enough people leave, the remaining population may be small enough now to be compatible with what the area can support, and those who remain gain more mobility, more territory, more lands upon which to hunt or gather. But there may be a point of no return beyond which a settlement cannot be maintained, when families choose not to be separated, when social relationships that depend upon contiguity cannot be held together long distance, when not enough people remain to carry out the necessary ceremonial roles, and when the exodus of people frays local exchange networks.

The casual nature of their leaving, taking some goods with them, leaving others, suggests an intent to return when conditions bettered as they had time and again in the past. But this departure was different. Even during short wetter intervals no one ventured back, perhaps because most arable lands were too damaged or were simply gone, washed down the river, along with a way of life.

Today is the winter solstice. Somewhere, far away, Sun begins a slow turn to the north, but here my boots squeak on the powdery snow. Body heat drains into an encompassing shuffling coldness, miles of growing cold, ascending into a colder, rougher-edged world, a shivered dark, always framed by those continuing icy vistas of such brutal starkness and terrible beauty.

The interminable zigzags of miles of trail unwind upward to a rim eternally out of sight, elusive, dangerously distant, perhaps unattainable. Blowing snow bites like pulverized diamonds across my face. The views build, illustrations in a wondrous fairy story of ice castles with cut-crystal spires, scrims of spun snow for ballets of ice crystals. Clouds canter into the canyon and out again with cymbal-clashing grandeur. Cold hones the world to a hypersharpness, as if it inhales the atmosphere and leaves this transparency, a gelid nothingness, the clarity of a vacuum.

We flatten against the cliff as the ascending mule garbage train passes us. For once I am thankful to see them. Their trail-breaking saves us from having to struggle through crusted snow drifted hip-deep. How such large four-footed animals make such a narrow track is beyond me. To stay in their path I mince and teeter, awkwardly placing one foot directly in front of the other.

At Cedar Ridge, a mile and a half from the top, a demonic wind explodes, unleashing razor blades of ice, ready to flash freeze a face on the instant. I jockey on a windbreaker over my down jacket. At the top when I take it off a quarter-inch of frost coats it inside like a frozen fleece lining. The temperature is 6°F.

I drop my pack and step to the edge of the canyon for one last look down into its shrouded silence. The sky dims early and the landscape shimmers with tender pinks and blues and whites. Frosty mists powder every turret. A stately pavane of snowshowers threads among farther buttes. Cold stings my nose and my eyes. In this terrible silence I see below me no silly lizards doing push-ups, no springtime bloom of redbuds, no little tree frog smiling smugly like a miniature Buddha, no bald eagle with a fierce yellow eye nailing a fat trout, no humpback chub ferreting out an existence between fast water and slow water, none of the animation of the canyon, only a final stillness, only a beckoning, deepening cold, an absence, beyond which there is no more beyond, and I step back, uneasy: in this terrible clarity of pure white light there is some kind of clarion warning.

Yet hypnotized by the singular beauty of the view, once more I step to the edge, wanting to make contact with the river just one more time. With the river out of sight and only this uncharacteristic preternatural silence, it takes an act of faith to believe that it even exists. Yet I know it is there, curling into back-eddies that chase upstream, nibbling at sandbars and rearranging beaches, always sculpting the perfect river cobble and fluting the limestones, dancing with raindrops, multiplying the sun in its ripples, taking its tolls and levies against the cliffs, pounding and pulsing with life that vitalizes anyone who rows and rides it, yesterday left upstream with a sixteen-hour lag, tomorrow waiting at the bottom of a rapid, today an intensity of being that runs with the river.

Into my cold-impaired memory flashes the picture of another ascent. One November, after two weeks on the river, I hiked out alone up the Bright Angel Trail. To keep warm I wore an outlandish assortment of layers, walked in scuffed boots, and labored under an ugly, bulging daypack. As I gained the asphalt walk at the top of the trail, the number of people dismayed me. After an idyllic two weeks spent at only two campsites, with time to wander far and alone every day, I felt as bewildered as Rip van Winkle must have: the world had gone on and left me behind. Maybe I didn't know how things like light switches and faucets and computers worked anymore. My head, my heart, my psyche lagged a dozen miles down in the canyon. I remembered John Burroughs quoting a lady tourist's comment that the canyon had been built a little too near to the lodge.

Out of one of the clusters of people stepped a nice-looking, neatly dressed, middle-aged woman, a question obvious in her face. I paused, uncomfortably conscious of how derelict I must appear. "Excuse me," she began, "is there anything down there?"

Sensing the sincerity in the question and wanting to be courteous, but overwhelmed by trying to put the richness I had always been blessed with "down there" into quick words, I could only mumble something about yes, there's a beautiful river down there, although the question so unseated me I'm not sure what I said.

The question haunted me, as questions like that often do, and the real answer came, as answers often do, not in the canyon but at an unlikely time and in an unexpected place, flying over the canyon at thirty thousand feet on my way to be a grandmother. My mind on other things, intending only to glance out, the exquisite smallness and delicacy of the river took me completely by surprise. In the hazy light of early morning, the canyon lay shrouded, the river flecked with glints of silver, reduced to a thin line of memory, blurred by a sudden realization that clouded my vision. The astonishing sense of connection with *that* river and *that* canyon caught me completely unaware, and in a breath I understood the intense, protective loyalty so many people feel for the Colorado River in the Grand Canyon. With that came the answer: there *is* something down there, and it cannot be explained in a listing of its parts. It has to do with truth and beauty and love of this earth, the artifacts of a lifetime, and the descant of a canyon wren at dawn.

Sometimes the "down there" is so huge and overpowering, the river so commanding, walled with rock formations beyond time, that one feels like a mite on a lizard's eyelid. And at other times it is so close and intimate: a tree lizard pattering little chains of prints in the sand around my ground cloth, a soldier beetle traipsing the margin of my notepad as I write by firelight, the trilling of redspotted toads in iambic pentameter, cicadas singing a capella, the mathematical precision of leaf-cutter bees, a limestone cavern measureless to man swathed with yards of gauzy webs woven by tiny spiders. Often the "down there" encompasses contrasts between minute midge and pounding waterfall, between eternity in an ebony schist and the moment in the pulsing vein in a dragonfly's wing, a delicate shard lost in an immensity of landscape, all bound together by the time to observe, question, presume, enjoy, exaltate. The "down there" is bound up with care and solicitude, sunlight on scalloped ripples, loving life and accepting death, all tied to a magnificent, unforgiving, and irrevocable river, a river along which I wandered for a halcyon while, smelled the wet clay odor of the rapids, listened to the dawns, and tasted the sunsets.

Some of the things I know about the river are undefined, as amorphous as the inexplicable connection that seeps into my bones while leaning against a warming sandstone wall on an early spring afternoon, or the ominous rockfalls on a winter night giving notice of a canyon under construction, the ragged pound of a rapid that matches no known rhythm but has lodged in my head like an old familiar song, the sheer blooming, healthy joy of the river's refrain.

But one thing is defined and clear: the terrible life-dependent clarity of one atom of oxygen hooked to two of hydrogen that ties us as humans to the only world we know.

HAVASU

Edward Abbey

Desert Solitaire, Edward Abbey's 1968 book about his year working at Arches National Monument, helped his generation fall in love with the canyon country of the Colorado Plateau. But Abbey also railed against the "industrial tourism" that was transforming the remotest places in the West into intensively managed parks where a true wilderness experience was almost impossible to find. His next major book, *The Monkey Wrench Gang,* convinced many desert lovers that it was both necessary and morally right to take direct action in defense of wilderness. For Abbey, wilderness was not only a place to experience pristine nature; it was also a space of freedom from the restrictions and oppressions of a bureaucratic world dominated by the military-industrial complex. This essay from *Desert Solitaire* describes Abbey's first encounter with Grand Canyon. Soon after arriving in the West, Abbey hiked into Havasu Canyon and discovered a freedom so total that he nearly lost his mind and then his life.

• • •

One summer I started off to visit for the first time the city of Los Angeles. I was riding with some friends from the University of New Mexico. On the way we stopped off briefly to roll an old tire into the Grand Canyon. While watching the tire bounce over tall pine trees, tear hell out of a mule train and disappear with a final grand leap into the inner gorge, I overheard the park ranger standing nearby say a few words about a place called Havasu, or Havasupai. A branch, it seemed, of the Grand Canyon.

What I heard made me think that I should see Havasu immediately, before something went wrong somewhere. My friends said they would wait. So I went down into Havasu—fourteen miles by trail—and looked things over. When I returned five weeks later I discovered that the others had gone on to Los Angeles without me.

That was fifteen years ago. And still I have not seen the fabulous city on the Pacific shore. Perhaps I never will. There's something in the prospect southwest from Barstow which makes one hesitate. Although recently, driving my own truck, I did succeed in penetrating as close as San Bernardino. But was hurled back by what appeared to be clouds of mustard gas rolling in from the west on a very broad front. Thus failed again. It may be however that Los Angeles will come to me. Will come to all of us, as it must (they say) to all men.

But Havasu. Once down in there it's hard to get out. The trail led across a stream wide, blue and deep, like the pure upper reaches of the River Jordan. Without a bridge. Dripping wet and making muddy tracks I entered the village of the Havasupai Indians where unshod ponies ambled down the only street and the children laughed, not maliciously, at the sight of the wet white man. I stayed the first night in the lodge the people keep for tourists, a rambling old bungalow with high ceilings, a screened verandah and large comfortable rooms. When the sun went down the village went dark except for kerosene lamps here and there, a few open fires, and a number of lightning bugs or fireflies which drifted aimlessly up and down Main Street, looking for trouble.

The next morning I bought a slab of bacon and six cans of beans at the village post office, rented a large comfortable horse and proceeded farther down the canyon past miniature cornfields, green pastures, swimming pools and waterfalls to the ruins of an old mining camp five miles below the village. There I lived, mostly alone except for the ghosts, for the next thirty-five days.

There was nothing wrong with the Indians. The Supai are a charming cheerful completely relaxed and easygoing bunch, all one hundred or so of them. But I had no desire to live *among* them unless clearly invited to do so, and I wasn't. Even if invited I might not have accepted. I'm not sure that I care for the idea of strangers examining my daily habits and folkways, studying my language, inspecting my costume, questioning me about my religion, classifying my artifacts, investigating my sexual rites and evaluating my chances for cultural survival.

So I lived alone.

The first thing I did was take off my pants. Naturally. Next I unloaded the horse, smacked her on the rump and sent her back to the village. I carried my food and gear into the best-preserved of the old cabins and spread my bedroll on a rusty steel cot. After that came a swim in the pool beneath a great waterfall nearby, 120 feet high, which rolled in mist and thunder over caverns and canopies of solidified travertine.

In the evening of that first day below the falls I lay down to sleep in the cabin. A dark night. The door of the cabin, unlatched, creaked slowly open, although there was no perceptible movement of the air. One firefly flickered in and circled my bacon, suspended from the roofbeam on a length of baling wire. Slowly, without visible physical aid, the door groaned shut. And opened again. A bat came through one window and went out another, followed by a second firefly (the first scooped up by the bat) and a host of mosquitoes, which did not leave. I had no netting, of course, and the air was much too humid and hot for sleeping inside a bag.

I got up and wandered around outside for a while, slapping at mosquitoes, and thinking. From the distance came the softened roar of the waterfall, that "white noise" as soothing as hypnosis. I rolled up my sleeping bag and in the filtered light of the stars followed the trail that wound through thickets of cactus and up around ledges to the terrace above the mining camp. The mosquitoes stayed close but in lessening numbers, it seemed, as I climbed over humps of travertine toward the head of the waterfall. Near the brink of it, six feet from the drop-off and the plunge, I found a sandy cove just big enough for my bed. The racing creek as it soared free over the edge created a continuous turbulence in the air sufficient to keep away all flying insects. I slept well that night and the next day carried the cot to the place and made it my permanent bedroom for the rest of July and all of August.

What did I do during those five weeks in Eden? Nothing. I did nothing. Or nearly nothing. I caught a few rainbow trout, which grew big if not numerous in Havasu Creek. About once a week I put on my pants and walked up to the Indian village to buy bacon, canned beans and Argentine beef in the little store. That was all the Indians had in stock. To vary my diet I ordered more exotic foods by telephone from the supermarket in Grand Canyon Village and these were shipped to me by U.S. Mail, delivered twice a week on muleback down the fourteen-mile trail from Topocoba Hilltop. A little later in the season I was able to buy sweet corn, figs and peaches from the Supai. At one time for a period of three days my bowels seemed in danger of falling out, but I recovered. The Indians never came down to my part of the canyon except when guiding occasional tourists to the falls or hunting a stray horse. In late August came the Great Havasupai Sacred Peach Festival and Four-Day Marathon Friendship Dance, to which I was invited and in which I did participate. There I met Reed Watahomagie, a good man, and Chief Sinyala and a fellow named Spoonhead who took me for five dollars in a horse race. Somebody fed my pick a half-bushel of green figs just before the race. I heard later.

The Friendship Dance, which continued day and night to the rhythm of drums made of old inner tube stretched over #10 tomato cans while ancient medicine men chanted in the background, was perhaps marred but definitely not interrupted when a drunken free-for-all exploded between Spoonhead and friends and a group of visiting Hualapai Indians down from the rim. But this, I was told, happened every year. It was a traditional part of the ceremony, sancti-fied by custom. As Spoonhead told me afterwards, grinning around broken teeth, it's not every day you get a chance to wallop a Hualapai. Or skin a paleface, I reminded him. (Yes, the Supai are an excellent tribe, healthy, joyous and clever. Not only clever but shrewd. Not only shrewd but wise: e.g., the Bureau of Indian Affairs and the Bureau of Public Roads, like most government agencies always meddling, always fretting and itching and sweating for something to do, last year made a joint offer to blast a million-dollar road down into Havasu Canyon at no cost whatsoever to the tribe, thus opening their homeland to the riches of motor-ized tourism. The people of Supai or at least a majority of them voted to reject the proposal.) And the peach wine flowed freely, like the water of the river of life. When the ball was over I went home to my bunk on the verge of the waterfall and rested for two days.

On my feet again, I explored the abandoned silver mines in the canyon walls, found a few sticks of dynamite but no caps or fuses. Disappointing; but there was nothing in that area anyway that required blowing up. I climbed through the caves that led down to the foot of Mooney Falls, 200 feet high. What did I do? There was nothing that had to be done. I listened to the voices, the many voices, vague, distant but astonishingly human, of Havasu Creek. I heard the doors creak open, the doors creak shut, of the old forgotten cabins where no one with tangible substance or the property of reflecting light ever entered, ever returned. I went native and dreamed away days on the shore of the pool under the waterfall, wandered naked as Adam under the cottonwoods, inspecting my cactus gardens. The days became wild, strange, ambiguous—a sinister element pervaded the flow of time. I lived narcotic hours in which like the Taoist Chuang-tse I worried about butterflies and who was dreaming what. There was a serpent, a red racer, living in the rocks of the spring where I filled my canteens; he was always there, slipping among the stones or pausing to mesmerize me with his suggestive tongue and cloudy haunted primeval eyes. Damn his eyes. We got to know each other rather too well I think. I agonized over the girls I had known and over those I hoped were yet to come. I slipped by degrees into lunacy, me and the moon, and lost to a certain extent the power to distinguish between what was and what was not myself: looking at my hand I would see a leaf trembling on a branch. A *green* leaf. I thought of Debussy, of Keats and Blake and Andrew Marvell. I remembered Tom o'Bedlam. And all those lost and never remembered. Who would return? To be lost again? I went for walks. I went for walks. I went for walks and on one of these, the last I took in Havasu, regained everything that seemed to be ebbing away.

Most of my wandering in the desert I've done alone. Not so much from choice as from necessity—I generally prefer to go into places where no one else wants to go. I find that in contemplating the natural world my pleasure is greater if there are not too many others contemplating it with me, at the same time. However, there are special hazards in traveling alone. Your chances of dying, in case of sickness or accident, are much improved, simply because there is no one around to go for help.

Exploring a side canyon off Havasu Canyon one day, I was unable to resist the temptation to climb up out of it onto what corresponds in that region to the Tonto Bench. Late in the afternoon I realized that I would not have enough time to get back to my camp before dark, unless I could find a much shorter route than the one by which I had come. I looked for a shortcut.

Nearby was another little side canyon which appeared to lead down into Havasu Canyon. It was a steep, shadowy, extremely narrow defile with the usual meandering course and overhanging walls; from where I stood, near its head, I could not tell if the route was feasible all the way down to the floor of the main canyon. I had no rope with me   only my walking stick. But I was hungry and thirsty, as always. I started down.

For a while everything went well. The floor of the little canyon began as a bed of dry sand, scattered with rocks. Farther down a few boulders were wedged between the walls; I climbed over and under them. Then the canyon took on the slickrock character—smooth, sheer, slippery sandstone carved by erosion into a series of scoops and potholes which got bigger as I descended. In some of these basins there was a little water left over from the last flood, warm and fetid water under an oily-looking scum, condensed by prolonged evaporation to a sort of broth, rich in dead and dying organisms. My canteen was empty and I was very thirsty but I felt that I could wait.

I came to a lip on the canyon floor which overhung by twelve feet the largest so far of these stagnant pools. On each side rose the canyon walls, roughly perpendicular. There was no way to continue except by dropping into the pool. I hesitated. Beyond this point there could hardly be any returning, yet the main canyon was still not visible below. Obviously the only sensible thing to do was to turn back. I edged over the lip of stone and dropped feet first into the water.

Deeper than I expected. The warm, thick fluid came up and closed over my head as my feet touched the muck at the bottom. I had to swim to the farther side. And here I found myself on the verge of another drop-off, with one more huge bowl of green soup below.

This drop-off was about the same height as the one before, but not overhanging. It resembled a children's playground slide, concave and S-curved, only steeper, wider, with a vertical pitch in the middle. It did not lead directly into the water but ended in a series of steplike ledges above the pool. Beyond the pool lay another edge, another drop-off into an unknown depth. Again I paused, and for a much longer time. But I no longer had the option of turning around and going back. I eased myself into the chute and let go of everything—except my faithful stick.

I hit rock bottom hard, but without any physical injury. I swam the stinking pond dog-paddle style, pushing the heavy scum away from my face, and crawled out on the far side to see what my fate was going to be.

Fatal. Death by starvation, slow and tedious. For I was looking straight down an overhanging cliff to a rubble pile of broken rocks eighty feet below.

After the first wave of utter panic had passed I began to try to think. First of all I was not going to die immediately, unless another flash flood came down the gorge; there was the pond of stagnant water on hand to save me from thirst and a man can live, they say, for thirty days or more without food. My sun-bleached bones, dramatically sprawled at the bottom of the chasm, would provide the diversion of the picturesque for future wanderers—if any man ever came this way again.

My second thought was to scream for help, although I knew very well there could be no other human being within miles. I even tried it but the sound of that anxious shout, cut short in the dead air within the canyon walls, was so inhuman, so detached as it seemed from myself, that it terrified me and I didn't attempt it again.

I thought of tearing my clothes into strips and plaiting a rope. But what was I wearing?—boots, socks, a pair of old and ragged blue jeans, a flimsy T-shirt, an ancient and rotten sombrero of straw. Not a chance of weaving such a wardrobe into a rope eighty feet long, or even twenty feet long.

How about a signal fire? There was nothing to burn but my clothes; not a tree, not a shrub, not even a weed grew in this stony cul-de-sac. Even if I burned my clothing the chances of the smoke being seen by some Hualapai Indian high on the south rim were very small; and if he did see the smoke, what then? He'd shrug his shoulders, sigh, and take another pull from his Tokay bottle. Furthermore, without clothes, the sun would soon bake me to death.

There was only one thing I could do. I had a tiny notebook in my hip pocket and a stub of pencil. When these dried out I could at least record my final thoughts. I would have plenty of time to write not only my epitaph but my own elegy.

But not yet.

There were a few loose stones scattered about the edge of the pool. Taking the biggest first, I swam with it back to the foot of the slickrock chute and placed it there. One by one I brought the others and made a shaky little pile about two feet high leaning against the chute. Hopeless, of course, but there was nothing else to do. I stood on the top of the pile and stretched upward, straining my arms to their utmost limit and groped with fingers and fingernails for a hold on something firm. There was nothing. I crept back down. I began to cry. It was easy. All alone, I didn't have to be brave.

Through the tears I noticed my old walking stick lying nearby. I took it and stood it on the most solid stone in the pile, behind the two topmost stones. I took off my boots, tied them together and hung them around my neck, on my back. I got up on the little pile again and lifted one leg and set my big toe on the top of the stick. This could never work. Slowly and painfully, leaning as much of my weight as I could against the sandstone slide, I applied more and more pressure to the stick, pushing my body upward until I was again stretched out full length above it. Again I felt about for a fingerhold. There was none. The chute was smooth as polished marble.

No, not quite that smooth. This was sandstone, soft and porous, not marble, and between it and my wet body and wet clothing a certain friction was created. In addition, the stick had enabled me to reach a higher section of the S-curved chute, where the angle was more favorable. I discovered that I could move upward, inch by inch, through adhesion and with the help of the leveling tendency of the curve. I gave an extra little push with my big toe—the stones collapsed below, the stick clattered down—and crawled rather like a snail or slug, oozing slime, up over the rounded summit of the slide.

The next obstacle, the overhanging spout twelve feet above a deep plunge pool, looked impossible. It *was* impossible, but with the blind faith of despair I slogged into the water and swam underneath the drop off and floundered around for a while, scrabbling at the slippery rock until my nerves and tiring muscles convinced my numbed brain that *this was not the way.* I swam back to solid ground and lay down to rest and die in comfort.

Far above I could see the sky, an irregular strip of blue between the dark, hard-edged canyon walls that seemed to lean toward each other as they towered above me. Across that narrow opening a small white cloud was passing, so lovely and precious and delicate and forever inaccessible that it broke the heart and made me weep like a woman, like a child. In all my life I had never seen anything so beautiful.

The walls that rose on either side of the drop-off were literally perpendicular. Eroded by weathering, however, and not by the corrasion of rushing floodwater, they had a rough surface, chipped, broken, cracked. Where the walls joined the face of the overhang they formed almost a square corner, with a number of minute crevices and inch-wide shelves on either side. It might, after all, be possible. What did I have to lose?

When I had regained some measure of nerve and steadiness I got up off my back and tried the wall beside the pond, clinging to the rock with bare toes and fingertips and inching my way crabwise toward the corner. The watersoaked, heavy boots dangling from my neck, swinging back and forth with my every movement, threw me off balance and I fell into the pool. I swam out to the bank, unslung the boots and threw them up over the drop-off, out of sight. They'd be there if I ever needed them again. Once more I attached myself to the wall, tenderly, sensitively, like a limpet, and very slowly, very cautiously, worked my way into the corner. Here I was able to climb upward, a few centimeters at a time, by bracing myself against the opposite sides and finding sufficient niches for fingers and toes. As I neared the top and the overhang became noticeable I prepared for a slip, planning to push myself away from the rock so as to fall into the center of the pool where the water was deepest. But it wasn't necessary. Somehow, with a skill and tenacity I could never have found in myself under ordinary circumstances, I managed to creep straight up that gloomy cliff and over the brink of the drop-off and into the flower of safety. My boots were floating under the surface of the little puddle above. As I poured the stinking water out of them and pulled them on and laced them up I discovered myself bawling again for the third time in three hours, the hot delicious tears of victory. And up above the clouds replied—thunder.

I emerged from that treacherous little canyon at sundown, with an enormous fire in the western sky and lightning overhead. Through sweet twilight and the sudden dazzling flare of lightning I hiked back along the Tonto Bench, bellowing the *Ode to Joy*. Long before I reached the place where I could descend safely to the main canyon and my camp, however, darkness set in, the clouds opened their bays and the rain poured down. I took shelter under a ledge in a shallow cave about three feet high—hardly room to sit up in. Others had been here before: the dusty floor of the little hole was littered with the droppings of birds, rats, jackrabbits and coyotes. There were also a few long gray pieces of scat with a curious twist at one tip—cougar? I didn't care. I had some matches with me, sealed in paraffin (the prudent explorer); I scraped together the handiest twigs and animal droppings and built a little fire and waited for the rain to stop.

It didn't stop. The rain came down for hours in alternate waves of storm and drizzle and I very soon had burnt up all the fuel within reach. No matter. I stretched out in the coyote den, pillowed my head on my arm and suffered through the long long night, wet, cold, aching, hungry, wretched, dreaming claustrophobic nightmares. It was one of the happiest nights of my life.

THE MAN WHO
WALKED THROUGH TIME

Colin Fletcher

Colin Fletcher taught America how to go backpacking. His first book, *The Thousand-Mile Summer,* describes a 1958 walk from the Mexican border to Oregon through the Sonoran Desert, across Death Valley, and along the High Sierra. Five years later, he became the first person to traverse the entire length of Grand Canyon below the rim, linking routes pioneered by Grand Canyon hiking legend Harvey Butchart. Fletcher tells the story of that trek in *The Man Who Walked through Time,* which was published in 1968, the same year as his best-selling how-to book, *The Complete Walker.* For Fletcher, hiking was always about more than a physical challenge: it also offered the chance to experience moments of heightened awareness of the kind that come when we lose ourselves in wilderness. In this chapter from *The Man Who Walked through Time,* he describes his first week in Grand Canyon, when he became hardened to the trail and began gradually to awaken to the beauty of his surroundings. Fletcher's book is a lasting favorite among canyon hikers, in part because his writing so faithfully captures the winding stream of thought that runs through a walker's mind on a long solo journey.

. . .

When I stepped up out of a sidecanyon onto a rock terrace, thirteen hundred feet above Supai, I knew at once that along the Esplanade I faced no trial of the spirit. Not, at least, a trial by enclosure. For my map showed that this terrace was a preview of the Esplanade; and I had stepped up into a country of space and light. A country that stirred in me, after a week in constricting sidecanyons, the pleasure of open vision. Now I could look far out across flat red rock and watch the long, swift flight of a cloud shadow. And I found that it was a joy and a release to watch one of these shadows dissolve for a moment as it crossed a sidecanyon, then reappear and race onward, diminishing, until it accelerated up a distant talus slope, vaulted a cliff face, and vanished over the Canyon's Rim, five or eight or even ten miles away.

The discovery of this airy and open and quite unexpected world left me feeling surprisingly well informed about what I could expect to find during the week that lay ahead. For I already knew in considerable detail most of the really critical facts.

That I knew anything at all was due almost entirely to one man.

At the very start of my year of waiting I had begun trying to gather information about foot travel through those parts of the Canyon away from the river and the Rim-to-Rim tourist trail. I inquired of park rangers, packers, geologists, and men who had "run" the river several times. But before long it dawned on me that when it came to extensive hiking in remote parts of the Canyon, none of them really knew what he was talking about. So I set about tracking down the experts on foot travel. In the end I discovered that they totaled one: a math professor at Arizona State College in Flagstaff. But Dr. Harvey Butchart, I was relieved to find, knew exactly what he was talking about. He had been learning for seventeen years.

If I had known seventeen years earlier that I would try to walk through the Canyon when I did I would no doubt have arranged for someone with an inquiring and well-trained mind to move immediately to some place close by. Someone like a math professor, say, to move to Arizona State College. I would have arranged for this man to fall under the Canyon's spell. And I would have had him see the Canyon as a natural obstacle course and an irresistible challenge. I would have tempted him down long disused trails. Then out into the wild places. And before long he would decide that one of the things he wanted most in life was to cover, in a series of three- and four-day trips strung out over many years, the entire length of his obstacle course of a National Park. He would mark the route of each trip on a topographic map. Mark it with mathematical care. He would write accurate notes, too, and record in his well-trained mind a mass of trustworthy information that never got into the notes.

When the seventeen years were nearly up I would no doubt have had this man write an article on the Canyon's trails in *Appalachia* magazine. Then I would have arranged for that particular copy of the magazine to be tucked under the arm of a friend of mine when, a week after I saw the Canyon for the first time, I expressed a guarded interest in the place. And finally, I would have arranged for my mathematical explorer to be so generously motivated that when I revealed my plans he would invite me to be his house guest in Flagstaff so that he could more easily pass on his hard-won information.

As things turned out it did not matter in the least that seventeen years earlier no such unlikely project as walking through Grand Canyon had entered my young head. It had all happened anyway.

Today, Harvey Butchart is a compact, coiled-spring fifty-five—and a happy and devoted schizophrenic. Teaching mathematics is only one of his worlds. At intervals he lives in a quite different reality. His three-year-old grandson, a young man of perception, recently heard someone use the words "Grand Canyon." "Where Grandpa lives?" he asked, just to make sure.

Harvey fed me a stream of accurate information, first by letter, then on the phone, and finally in person.

To my first question—whether it was indeed possible to traverse the Canyon on foot—he did not quite have a definitive answer. But he came close. Over the years, the ink lines he had drawn on the map to represent his short trips from the Rim had consolidated into a tortuous blue snake that ran almost from one end of the Park to the other. Only one gap remained: a four- or five-mile traverse along a narrow hanging terrace below Great Thumb Point, at the far end of the Esplanade. The Havasupai still had a tradition that this stretch was impassable. But Harvey had stood at each end of it and had looked into two of the three precipitous canyon heads that the map suggested were the ultimate barriers. Each curving canyon head was a natural amphitheater, lacking only the flat central arena.

"They're steep, those amphitheaters," Harvey told me. "Very steep. But I'd guess that they're both passable. Still, you can never really tell with these things until you give them a try. And as for that middle one—I guess we'll just have to wait and see."

Harvey confirmed the tentative ideas I had formed about routes. You could usually, he said, find a way along the hanging terraces. But if the one you were following petered out (as quite often happened to the narrowest of them) you could very rarely climb up or down onto the next terrace. From a mile or two away you might see what looked like a gap in the intervening cliff face, with only a few feet of deeply seamed rock separating two terraces. But you were almost certainly in for one of the Canyon's continual surprises. The scale of the sculpture had unhinged your sense of proportion. Close up, you were likely to find it was not "a few feet" but fifty or a hundred. And although the helpful-looking seams did exist, they ran fifteen or twenty feet apart. In between stretched smooth, unclimbable rock. Almost the only place you had a chance of changing levels was where a section of cliff had collapsed and so much rubble had tumbled down that it had buried the next cliff under continuous talus. Such ramps often looked, as one ranger put it, "as though they only need a man's footstep to start the whole place sliding." Actually, the weight of a man, or even of a battalion, is so insignificant compared with the forces of rock and gravity involved that the danger is negligible.

Harvey gave me all this hard-won information, and much more, quite un-grudgingly. There was only one moment when he seemed to have second thoughts. It happened just after I went to stay with him and his wife, Roma, in Flagstaff, before I drove up to Grand Canyon Village.

"I'm sure you realize," Harvey had said, "that it's one thing to take on the Canyon the way I do, in a series of small bites from the Rim, but quite another to swallow it whole. Frankly, I'm not at all sure I ought to be encouraging you." He hesitated. "One thing that worries me is that you're not really the right build for the desert."

It wasn't only, I knew, that beside his greyhound of a figure I loomed rather bulky. I was undeniably out of condition. In other words, fat. But I also knew that by the end of the week's shakedown cruise I would have fined down appreciably. "Bet you a nickel I make it," I said. "A brand-new nickel that I can mount as a souvenir."

Harvey grinned. "Okay," he said. "I'll just keep hoping you win. Hoping hard."

And I never heard another word of doubt.

From all that Harvey had said, and also from my understanding of the paradox of outdoor living, I felt that I knew just about how the journey would go in the week beyond Supai, the week that would culminate in the airdrop. Above all, I knew that at this early stage of my journey I should not expect to do more than glimpse, at the very most, the things I hoped to find in the end.

My forecast proved all too accurate. Right from the start, the week developed into a heads-down struggle with the physical and the present. I found little time to consider the 200-million-year span of a rock's existence or even the decades of an Indian tribe's decline. All week I grappled with the day and the hour and the minute; and at the very end, with slow, tantalizing seconds. The Canyon had its moments, but they were desperately rare.

Yet when I stepped up out of the sidecanyon above Supai at the very start of the week and discovered the openness and the racing cloud shadows, it was without question one of those moments, and I sat quietly on the lip of the rock terrace for almost half an hour and watched the cloud shadows and the rock and the light. I would have liked to sit there much longer. But I knew that this was no day for sightseeing. It was the day that Harvey Butchart regarded as the first test of my ability to tackle the Canyon.

The terrace I sat on twisted northward to Mount Sinyala and the beginning of the Esplanade; and not until I had passed Mount Sinyala and reached Sinyala Canyon would I find water. On the map it did not look like much of a day's jour-ney. My map measurer, wheeled sinuously around the many canyon heads that cut into the terrace, had recorded barely seven miles.

But that "seven miles" meant next to nothing.

Cross-country on foot, miles are always misleading: the hours are what count. In the Canyon, miles become virtually meaningless. From start to finish of my journey I would cover, in a straight line, only forty-three. The river mileage came to one hundred and four. When I ran the map measurer from one end to the other of my proposed route, carefully following each winding contour, it registered just two hundred. But I felt sure, and Harvey Butchart agreed, that I would walk at least four hundred miles as the foot slogs. And there were times when I would be lucky to travel half a mile in an hour.

Harvey had confirmed my doubts about those "seven miles" for the first day's journey out of Supai.

"I went around that way only last year," he said. "And from Sinyala Canyon to Supai was a full day. Even when you're fit it takes eight hours of hard, fast traveling with a thirty-pound pack. A good eight hours. Equal to every step of twenty miles on the flat."

Now, Harvey had a local reputation for prodigious feats of sustained speed (he has been called The Flagstaff Flyer even in print), and I was still by no means fit enough for real Butcharting. Even more to the point was my pack. It now held a full week's food and two gallons of water, and just before I left Supai it had pulled the arm on the store's scale down to sixty-six and a half pounds. I was prepared for quite a day.

It had begun well, though, and as I turned northward along the terrace and settled down to the long, steady grind toward Sinyala Canyon and water I calculated that I had eleven hours of daylight left and only six Butchart-hours of actual walking to go. Even allowing for rests, it seemed a comfortable balance.

The day turned out to be a curious blend of stupidity and satisfaction.

Almost at once I hit a trail, thick with the prints of horses' hooves. And for an hour the trail turned what would have been slow and sweaty scrambling into fast, easy going. One hour, almost one straight-line mile. Ten hours of daylight left, and only five hours to go. I began to relax.

It was then that the stupidities began. Not to mention the mischances.

First I met the horse. It stood fifty yards ahead; motionless; head hanging dejectedly, like a man dozing his woes away after a bad day at the races. It was sway-backed and stark-ribbed but not, to my surprise, particularly small. I suspected it, therefore, of being a Supai stray; but I also knew that it might be one of the so-called little horses of the Esplanade.

Stupidly, I decided that there was plenty of time for me to photograph this miserable but intriguing specimen of a horse. I clamped binoculars in front of my camera lens with a flash bracket, and moved in. Any photographer will understand why, by the time the animal finally bolted, a dozen meticulous shots later, my watch showed that almost an hour had passed. Nine left and still five to go.

The trail promptly petered out. Immediately, my first canyon head: a fan of ravines slashing into the terrace. I found myself edging forward over steep and unstable talus, scrambling up and around one house-size boulder, then easing past another's undercut basement. At last, back onto solid rock. But only four hundred yards in the hour. Lunch and a rest. Seven left now, and three or four to go.

An hour's fast walking over solid rock. Then, as I passed a small bush, a violent pain above my left ankle. Half an hour, and the final extraction of a broken twig-end that had driven in beside my shinbone, firm as a pier piling. Another hour, and thousand-foot Mount Sinyala jutting up at last from the flat mesa ahead like a huge molar tooth.

The sight took some of the pressure off, made me forget that I had begun to feel footsore and a little tired. Sinyala Canyon was just around the corner now, perhaps two hours away. And still four hours of daylight left.

Fifteen minutes later I saw a rainpocket. It was no bigger than a good-sized frying pan, but it seemed the final assurance of success.

While I stood looking down at the rainpocket I noticed that the adhesive tape covering the twig puncture on my leg had worked loose. I swung the pack off my back and unzipped a side pocket.

The moment I saw that the first-aid kit was missing, I knew what had happened.

By the time I had made up my mind, had propped pack against walking staff on top of a prominent rise and begun to hurry back southward, another fifteen minutes had slipped away. An hour of fast, packless walking. And there, exactly where I had sat and extracted the twig, lay the little plastic bag with its roll of tape showing through. Another hour, faster, back to the pack. Almost six o'clock. Two left now, and two to go.

As I moved ahead again, beyond the rainpocket, a heavy cloud bank doused the sun like a candle snuffer. All at once the evening was prematurely cold and daunting. But an hour's determined walking brought the molar silhouette of Mount Sinyala level with my left shoulder. The grayness began to seem less daunting. Only an hour to Sinyala Canyon. With luck, even less.

And then another stupidity. The final canyon head cut deep into the terrace, back to the very foot of the bounding cliffs. But the canyon itself looked very easy to cross, and I chose the direct route. Hidden drop-offs; overhangs; rock faces seven times as high as they had looked. By the time I climbed onto the far rim another half hour had dribbled away.

But at last, with the day almost dead, I came to the slot that was the beginning of Sinyala Canyon. Five minutes later, clambering down the canyon's floor, I glimpsed a string of palenesses ahead. And then my flashlight was shining into water a foot deep.

I camped at once, there beside the biggest rainpocket. Soon I was sitting up in my sleeping bag, shielding stove and dinner from a cold, blustering wind. I felt well satisfied. Although nothing much had happened, it had been a long day for someone still in pulpy shape, and I felt no more than reasonably tired. And now that I had time to look back at the day I saw that the stupidities had helped to make it a success. It was like getting 100 per cent in a driving test that you were stupid enough to take with a hangover. I felt I had passed Harvey Butchart's qualifying exam with something to spare. And that, after all, was what the day had been for.

In spite of Harvey's briefings I had formed no very clear impression of what the Esplanade would be like. It usually happens this way, I think: you wait for the reports of your own eyes and ears and nose and skin before you construct a coherent picture of a place. But in all my planning the one salient fact about the Esplanade had been that it was enclosed by impassable cliffs; and although I had not really stopped to consider the matter, I think I had connected the terrace, vaguely, with words like "constricted" and "shut in" and even "cramped." Crowded map contours, representing the network of sidecanyons that seam it like gaping cracks in a mud flat, had tended to confirm the impression.

But the Esplanade turned out to be a broad and open place. A country of air and light and distance. An even more spacious land than the open rock terrace that had surprised and delighted me above Supai. For now the cloud shadows raced over red rock for ten, twenty, and sometimes thirty miles before they vaulted out of sight over distant cliffs that were the North Rim of the Canyon.

This airy openness of the Esplanade has a quality that is lacking in the openness of an ordinary plain. Your eye passes smoothly across the rock and joins one flat mesa to the next; but your mind remembers the sidecanyons. It remembers their thin fingers that reach out and isolate the mesas, slicing down into the rock for a hundred, five hundred, a thousand feet. Your mind even remembers, from time to time, the Inner Gorge. You find it difficult, though, to grasp the reality. To accept that off to the left—two miles away, or three, or five—your eye passes without recording it across a gap broad enough to contain the Colorado, across an incision more than two thousand feet deep. But the knowledge is there, somewhere. And it pollinates the Esplanade with hints and possibilities.

You know too that your eye is suffering another illusion. An illusion of space and texture. For the Esplanade is above all a land of textures. Of textures and colors. You live under a smooth blue sky. Raised white clouds scurry across it. Off to the left your world is bounded by fine-grained cliffs, white and far away. Below them curves burlap talus. Then the red rock begins. First, as fine-grained as the cliffs. Then, when distance no longer hides the whole truth, coarsening. And finally, in the last half mile, slashed and fissured and crumbled into a chaos of ledges and clefts and massive boulders. And this final close-up reveals how smoothly the distant textures have lied.

The Esplanade, I decided at last, was an island in reverse. Not land raised above the sea, but space engraved into the land. Yet it remained an open, not a constricted, place. It just existed within the two bounding lines of cliffs, one close above my right shoulder, the other far away across the red rock. And I accepted the limits. I do not think I was yet aware of how completely they had cut off the reality of the outside world. That awareness did not come until later, much later, when I was almost ready to leave the Canyon. At the time I inquired no further than a continual but fluctuating roar that came from the nearby cliffs, as though waterfalls were cascading down their pale walls. At first I found it difficult to believe that such a solid sound was only the wail of wind tearing at stone buttresses.

The Esplanade, then, was a pleasant place. But it remained a stern and insistent challenge. Above all, every hour of every day, there was the water problem.

Harvey had promised only two or three unreliable seeps and rainpockets before I reached the far end of the Esplanade. But there I would almost certainly find a spring—though even that had gone dry at least once in the past ten summers.

It was this spring, close under Great Thumb Mesa, that I had chosen as the site for my first airdrop; but we had also arranged an alternate site at a deep rainpocket that Harvey Butchart had recently discovered near the head of Fossil Bay. This rainpocket lay a long day-and-a-half's journey beyond Great Thumb Spring. Naturally, I was hoping to take the drop at Fossil Bay. For one thing, I wanted to push as far ahead as possible while the weather was on my side. Pride came into it too: Harvey had seemed convinced that Great Thumb Spring was as far as I could hope to go in a week. And at first there had been another spur, a severely practical one: at Fossil Bay I would be safely past my route's biggest question mark—the four or five miles of unknown country, with its three steep natural amphitheaters, that Harvey had never crossed. But just before I left Supai a verbal message had reached me that Harvey had succeeded in negotiating these amphitheaters. Although I felt some sense of loss—a certain slackening in the challenge—it was a relief to know that if the message had not been garbled, as verbal messages routinely are, my way was clear. I felt pleased, too, for quite a different reason. Without Harvey's help I could never have planned a route. Not with confidence, anyway. And it was only right that he should be the first man through. I think I already knew, in any case, that although I would still be bound tight by the trivia for at least another week, the physical challenge was no longer what mattered.

But, at least on the surface of my mind, the target for the week remained, quite clearly, one or other of the airdrop sites.

I knew, of course, that everything depended on water. And the water depended on the weather.

"Before you take off from Sinyala Canyon," Harvey had said, "make dead sure there's been enough rain. You could easily get just enough to make you feel safe out on the Esplanade and then run into a spell of hot weather that would dry everything up fast—including you. I can't imagine a neater trap."

By the time I reached Sinyala Canyon at the end of that long day of blended stupidity and satisfaction, seventy-two hours had passed since the rain that fell on the evening of my Gorge reconnaissance, and I felt by no means sure that there was enough water along the Esplanade for safety.

Partly because of this doubt (and partly because the second day out nearly always seems the hardest on feet and muscles), I had planned something close to a rest day. I would do no more than make a leisurely reconnaissance of a long and apparently unexplored rock fault that looked as though it might be a major short cut. But I would also check, very carefully, how much water the storm had left in the Esplanade's smaller rainpockets.

When I woke beside the big rainpocket in Sinyala Canyon, one day out from Supai, the blustering wind of the night before had honed itself a cutting edge. By the time I struck camp, rain was falling. Not heavily, but with malice. And I had hardly climbed up onto the broad, flat terrace that was the beginning of the Esplanade and begun to look for the unexplored rock fault—with no very great determination—when the raindrops began to shiver themselves into snowflakes.

The flakes never really got a grip on the wet ground, but for long, muffled minutes I would walk imprisoned. The pale brown stalk of a century plant might stand out for a moment, erect and tasseled, like a windswept Maypole. Otherwise there was only a small, flat disk of rock around me, and a vague gray-white outer encirclement. Then the squall would pass. And when I looked back westward I could see faintly, as if through a lace curtain, the thrusting molar shape of Mount Sinyala. But soon another gray-white blanket would swoop down and imprison me once more.

After half an hour, one squall seemed to leave the Esplanade unnaturally bright. Now, when I looked westward, Mount Sinyala stood out sharp and clear, like a floodlit castle. Above it, streaks of blue had begun to partition clouds that were no longer leaden. And then, all around me, the sun was flashing celebration signals from a hundred little pools in the red rock.

It was these temporary rainpockets that reminded me of Harvey Butchart's "no neater trap." The biggest of them looked as if they would hold the trap door open for a week. And suddenly I saw that a rest day had become an unforgivable luxury. Although the rock fault might just possibly conceal a short cut, searching for it would most likely do nothing but waste valuable time. I decided, there and then, that while the going was good I would make a break for it along the known Butchart-route that skirted the bounding cliffs of the Esplanade.

It was from that moment of decision—the final taking of the bit between my teeth—that the week's real business began.

All week I made steady progress. Progress in many things.

Most obviously, there was measurable progress in space. It was very simply measured progress. In the first two days, for example, I went exactly three straight-line miles. But the straight line crossed a deep, many-armed monster called Matkatamiba Canyon. And I could not. I spent the whole of those first two days skirting its outstretched fingertips, back at the very base of the cliffs.

The first day, the sixty pounds on my back felt more like a hundred, and by dusk I had barely passed the main head canyon of Matkatamiba. In a straight line (a line that ran almost at right angles to the two-day straight line) I had come just two and a half miles. But the apparently flat Esplanade imposed a consistently serpentine route. Every step was zig or zag: zig along a sidecanyon; zig again for a side-sidecanyon; then zag along its far side to resume the first zig; almost at once, a new zig for a new side-sidecanyon; and then another zig up a side-side-sidecanyon. And the going was almost never level. All day I kept having to cross or to detour laboriously around little tributary gullies that were hardly deeper than suburban living rooms.

The second day, zagging back along the far side of Matkatamiba Canyon, I went almost three straight-line miles. And that brought me to a seep spring near Chikapanagi Point. It was the last water I could be reasonably sure of finding before Great Thumb Spring, and when I walked away from it early on the third morning out of Supai I knew that I had to put a lot of miles behind me before dark. I succeeded. And surprisingly easily. For although I did not know it yet, the worst of the zigging and zagging was past.

Each day, from the moment of my decision to press ahead, I made progress in other things too, apart from space. Most notably, I made progress in my war with the trivia.

It is often difficult to remember, when conditions have radically changed, what occupied your thoughts most at a certain time. A notebook is the surest guide. My notebook shows, quite luminously, what the important things were in those first days across the Esplanade. It makes sparkling reading: "Tea time: wash sox, fill canteens"; and "Wearing long pants all day, so it *must* be cold"; and "Dawn 4:45, ground temp 32°, sox frozen solid (drying on pack). Frost on sleeping bag, but slept only very slightly cold, naked. No wind, and really very pleasant weather"; and next day: "Lunch 1:30: Shade temperature 76°, in sun 102°." Neck and neck with these weighty matters ran the medical reports: "Twig-puncture nerve still stiff, but seems getting better"; and "Don't altogether like feel of deepish blister forming near ball of left foot"; and "Two travertine cuts on right foot now septic"; and even "Chapped inner thighs, partly heritage from lime of Havasu Creek. Try coconut oil on one, fly dope on other. Dope better." In these early days, then, I still labored along under the burden of the stubborn and obtrusive paradox of "simple living."

But even in this tight little world of trivia, things were getting better. Each day my muscles responded more readily to the pack's dead weight. "Chapped thighs" and "twig-puncture nerve" grew less painful. Above all, my feet held out—under a growing patchwork of those oddly miraculous adhesive felt pads called Moleskins. The Moleskins, marked forty cents, were the most precious commodity in my pack. One day I found a five-dollar bill I had tucked into their package for use in Supai and forgotten about. But the useless scrap of paper hardly seemed heavy enough, even by my dram-paring standards, to throw away; and there was always the chance it might come in handy for lighting a fire.

It was the same with camping and cooking and the rest of the daily routine. I still did the same things. But I hardly noticed what I was doing. When I propped up my pack at dusk, when I rolled out the blue groundsheet and inflated the little green air mattress, and when I lit the stove and stirred the stew, the physical acts touched little more than the skin of my mind. The rest of me, the part where the answers can begin, was already part way free to wander and observe and record and ruminate.

As the days passed there was progress, too, in what I can only call "confidence."

It may seem ridiculous for an experienced walker to feel ill at ease about routine matters almost every time he starts a major journey. But more is involved than experience. Whether you like it or not, the occasion tells: most people, I think, suffer some degree of stage fright on their first day at a new job. The sidecanyon up and away from Supai had been in a sense the real beginning of my journey, and I had duly suffered stage fright. Within a mile of the village, traveling too fast over rough ground and moving about as nimbly as a no-toed sloth, I twice stumbled and almost sprawled full length. And the rest of that "Butchart test day" to Sinyala Canyon had hardly been a model of efficiency. Then, out on the Esplanade two days later, I left my pack on the lip of a sidecanyon and went down to look for a seep spring that Harvey had reported; and when I climbed back up there was no sign of the pack. For three or four racking minutes, cursing myself for not checking landmarks, I searched among the rock chaos. Then I came around a boulder I had already passed twice—and there, fifteen feet away, stood the pack. But that was about the end of my elementary lapses.

The really critical progress, though, came in route-finding. And it was the route-finding, more than anything else, that at first kept my mind screwed tight to the present.

The Esplanade, for all its flat and open aspect, is a maze. All along it you face a choice of two routes: rock terrace or talus. The rock terraces mean relatively level going, and they often open up into broad boulevards. But they are not only consistently serpentine—as I discovered around Matkatamiba Canyon—they also keep petering out. And then you have to decide whether to climb ten, twenty, or thirty feet up or down onto the next ledge. You base your choice on the look of the ledges on the far side of the subcanyon you are zigging and zagging along. And this raises one of the scale problems that the Canyon is always posing. A rockface that from a distance looks like something you might have to lift your pack over turns out to be high as a house. As compensation, though, a ledge that promises no more than a handhold may be wide enough to drive a bus along.

But at each major canyon head the rockledges vanish. Rubble from the cliffs has spilled down over the bedrock. To cross these steep talus slides in the least horrifying places you have to climb high; and on the far side of the canyon head you find yourself part way up the talus that always skirts the cliff. The first rock terrace may be a hundred feet below. Or two hundred. And because head and legs both kept reminding you of the old adage, "Never lose elevation unnecessarily," you usually decide to stay up on the talus.

The talus is the direct route. For each mile on the map you only walk about one and a half. But it is slow and sweaty walking. No striding out, now, along flat bedrock. Instead, weave and detour in and out of low, leg-scratching scrub. Strain and pant along loose gravel slopes. Then struggle and grunt across deep-cut gullies. And still, at every big canyon head, the slides.

At each canyon head you look back. If you have kept low, along the sinuous ledges, you can see that the talus route would have cut miles of meandering and saved a good half hour. If, on the other hand, you have come along the talus you can always see quite clearly that the ledge route would have been only a kickshaw longer and would have saved at least an hour in time and a full pint in sweat.

But after two days I had grasped the pattern of this maze, and my route-finding began to improve. Along the ledges I found myself picking the right levels more often, then holding them more accurately across talus overspills. In time, I realized that the spiky leaves of century plants, which tended to grow about three feet tall, provided a rough-and-ready scale for judging the height of distant rockfaces. And along the talus I began to strike the right line: neither so high that every yard was a scramble nor so low that every gully had dug itself into a gorge. I knew I was doing better because I found myself, more and more often, following faint game trails. For the first two and a half days "game trail" meant only vague indications that several deer had been that way; but at least it was comforting to find myself following in the experts' footsteps.

And then, about noon on the third day, revolution.

All morning the going had been as rough and slow as ever. I had covered barely a third of the final, vital leg to Great Thumb Spring. Then, quite suddenly, I was walking along a trail. A clear, well-traveled horse trail.

This time the trail did not peter out. It intensified. It ran high on the talus, not twisting and turning too tortuously, and along its well-beaten surface I could stride out as fast as along bedrock. And now I could leave the route-finding to the horses.

The difference was critical. It was like driving mile after mile across a strange city on back streets studded with stop signs and then hitting a six-lane boulevard with synchronized traffic lights.

When I looked back later I could see that hitting the horse trail was the turning point. Was the beginning of the end of the paradox of simple living.

But I must not mislead you into believing that even in those first three days of earthbound effort I was totally imprisoned by the brutal immediacies of the physical world. The Canyon, as I have said, had its moments. Deep in a sidecanyon, a Sphinx overhang, massive with hints of wisdom, brooded above a seep spring. A torch cactus, angling out from its crevice, cocked a slyly humorous snook. I lay on naked rock, sipping nectar that an hour earlier had been snow, and all around me the sun distilled voluptuous scents. A whiskered ground squirrel bounced onto a rock, froze, blurred, and was gone. Beyond shadow that still belonged to the night, a day's incoming sunlight streamed across the rock reefs. Noon pressed down onto the Esplanade, hotter each day, more ponderously silent. Evening came, and a softer, richer silence

Such moments held the promise of progress. Of real progress. Of progress in my pilgrimage. But they never lasted long.

Then, late on the evening of the third day, as I hurried along the horse trail toward Great Thumb Spring (knowing I could not reach it before dark, but confident now for the morning), my eye caught brown movement away to the right. Suddenly, close and electric, the thunder of hooves. Almost at once, the thundering died. The horse stood facing me, curious, its white blaze like a torch in the evening shadow. Then it was once more thundering up and away across the talus, back into the lingering sunset. Its hoofbeats grew fainter. Its dark shape began to merge with the shadows. And then, as it crossed the skyline, it stopped and looked back at me. To its left, the cliff was a black wall against red sky. The skirting talus swept down and away, paused, then curved upward again to an isolated hillock. The horse stood framed between cliff and hillock, etched against the sun's afterglow. I could see its pricked ears, feel their nervousness. As I stood watching, with the horse poised and tense, a hummingbird whirred brief greetings a foot from my eyes. I found myself smiling at it. When it dipped away my eyes followed its flight and I saw beyond it the white cliffs of Great Thumb Mesa. But the cliffs were no longer white. They burned now with the deep red sunset glow of the desert, the glow that catches your breath and quietens the striving and makes you want to manacle time so that the beauty can go on and on and on. For long moments I stood watching the cliffs. At last I glanced back over my shoulder. The horse had gone. And when I looked at the cliffs again the glow had already begun to die. But it did not matter now. The moment would always be there.

I walked on a little way down the trail, then camped inside the radiating warmth of a huge boulder. And soon after sunrise next morning I came to Great Thumb Spring.

The trail dipped down into a gully. All at once, thirty feet ahead, a trickle of water gleamed on red rock. And suddenly the sun was shining through a clump of scarlet Indian paintbrush and cool air was brushing over my skin and birds were murmuring in the foliage of a cottonwood tree. And at that moment I knew again—differently from the moment of the wild horse in the half-light, but with the same sure promise—that, given time, I would find in the Canyon the things I had come for.

When I reached Great Thumb Spring there were still more than three days left to the airdrop, and there was never really much doubt in my mind that I would take the drop in Fossil Bay, beyond the three critical amphitheaters. At first, faint question marks hung over feet and weather. But by the evening of the second day that I rested at the spring I could walk in something bordering on comfort (thanks largely to my having brought soft moccasins for wear around camp); and light rain showers were cooling the air and filling new rainpockets. By nine thirty on the third morning, in weather still pleasantly crisp and promisingly unsettled, I stood on the lip of the first amphitheater.

It was an impressive place. The Esplanade tapered abruptly to a narrow terrace that hung between two cliffs as if it had merely paused there, waiting for a heavy storm to send it crashing on downward. The scrub-covered talus sloped at a horrifying angle. And below its lip the rock plunged almost sheer for fifteen hundred feet. Now that I had seen the place I understood why the far side of the amphitheater was bighorn-sheep country.

Now, it is one thing to be the first man somewhere and quite another to know, or to be almost sure, that you are only the second. I knew, or half-knew, that one man had already crossed that forbidding amphitheater. Had crossed it only a week earlier. But I don't think I realized until afterward what a difference the knowledge made. Instead of hanging back on my mental heels and wondering if the thing were really possible I just checked the route through binoculars and then moved out onto the terrace.

For a hundred yards the talus sloped quite gently. A faint horse trail still wound through the sparse scrub. Then, abruptly, the talus steepened. The trail vanished. Almost at once I found myself crossing a bright red gully. Slowly, I eased forward across its eroded wall, kicking shallow footholds. Fragments of damp dirt and gravel bounced away below. They gathered noisy speed, then vanished over the lip, suddenly and ominously silent.

At its center the gully had worn down to hard red earth, steep as the walls of a cutting on a mountain road. The only holds were a few half-embedded stones. I hesitated. Then, remembering Harvey Butchart, I began to ease forward again. I was agonizingly conscious now of the terrace lip, down below my feet, and of the silent space beyond it. For three or four yards each delicately balanced step was a tense and breathless movement—the kind of movement that opens up, if you are as timid a climber as I am, a trap door in the floor of your stomach. Then the red earth was past. And then the gully was past. And instead of reaching out with tense fingertips I could keep on balance merely by digging my staff into the loose talus.

I did not know at the time, of course, that the red gully was the worst of it. But nothing else quite matched those few yards across its center. All morning, though, I had to move slowly. Very slowly. Each step was the kind you took no chances with. By the time I climbed clear of the first amphitheater it was almost one o'clock.

But long before that I found myself relaxed enough to notice much more than the way ahead. To notice that horse tracks had finally given way to the scattered imprints of cloven feet. To pause after an unexpected hailstorm and find myself seeing new rainpockets on a distant rock terrace less as safety markers than as the essential elements in a cool and beautiful blue pattern. Not merely to register, when for the first time in a week I glimpsed the Colorado two thousand feet below, that some engineering manipulation at the distant upstream dam must account for the dramatic change in its color but also to feel deep pleasure at the way its sullen brown surface had been transformed into a brilliant blue. To rest beside a precariously balanced boulder and contemplate the huge, harmonic sweep of rock that plunged down to the river, paused, and then swept up again in gigantic counterstatement. To find myself, long after the halt should have ended, still sitting beside the boulder and fondling with the fingertips of my mind the texture and color and tilted pattern of cliff and hanging terrace and then cliff again. And to find that soon afterward I had stopped deep in the inner recesses of the amphitheater to admire a fragile white desert primrose that thrust up at my feet from a desolation of rubble. The need to hurry kept trying to brush aside these softer moments, but its success remained marginal.

After the red gully there were only two more really big moments that day. Neither was quite the kind I had expected.

The first lasted barely fifteen seconds.

I was walking along an easy rock terrace that led to the second amphitheater. Swirling cloud had closed down, obliterating another magnificent, plunging view of the Inner Gorge and leaving me to pick my way forward among shadowy rock shapes. It was like tramping across a Scottish moor in midwinter.

I think I saw movement first. Anyway, I know that suddenly I was peering at a vague form that stood forty or fifty yards away, on the brink of the precipice. For an instant the animal was peering back at me, tense and expectant. But almost at once it bounded away.

Then I saw something else.

It was closer than the other had been. Barely thirty yards away. Motionless on the brink of the precipice, silhouetted against swirling cloud, it seemed less an animal than a presence. A magnificent green presence. A stately, sculptured statue. For a long time we stared at each other, the statue and I, and I had time to understand that the greenness was in the massive horns that curled almost full circle. Had time to grasp that the dignity came from the horns too. From the horns and from the superb set of the head. Very slowly, I began to reach for my binoculars. Unhurriedly, the bighorn turned. After that magnificent head, its white rump looked rather ridiculous. But the beast moved with unruffled dignity, with a slow and liquid grace. It moved away from me for three or four yards. And then it was gone. Not helter-skelter gone but fading-and-merging gone, so that it was there one moment and somehow not there the next, and once more I stood alone in the swirling Scottish gloom.

The other big moment of the day had something eerie about it too.

I had crossed the second amphitheater, and then the third. Both were steep, but neither was as difficult as the first. All day, rain squalls and hailstorms had been sweeping down from the northwest. In mid-afternoon the air began to grow colder. And as I came out at last, about five o'clock, onto the broad rock terrace that led to Fossil Bay, snow began to fall.

Snowflakes quickly covered the sandy, chocolate-brown earth that lined the bigger rock basins. Soon the flakes were beginning to settle on the wet rock too. Once again, as had happened in the morning beyond Mount Sinyala, I found myself walking through a hushed white world of vague shapes and muffled horizons.

And then, as I padded on half an inch of snow across one of the earth-filled basins, beginning to feel a little tired at last, I stopped dead. Ahead of me across the snow, dark and definite and impossible, stretched a line of human footprints. Each print stood out sharp and clear. And the line cut straight and purposeful, like a pre-echo of my own trail, out and away into the gloom.

I stood motionless in the thickly falling snow, staring, trying to reconcile what I saw with what I knew. The footprints were undeniable. But it seemed impossible that someone was walking just ahead of me across that remote and desolate rock terrace. Was walking such a short way ahead that the snow had not even begun to dull the outline of his tracks. I peered into the whiteness, trying to push back the horizon. All day I had been savoring the knowledge that I was the second man to pass this way. Perhaps even the first. And now, it seemed, the place was public.

I knelt down and examined one of the footprints. It was genuine enough. But almost at once I understood. All around the imprint, minute pinnacles formed the surface of the undisturbed earth. The snowflakes were straddling the peaks of these pinnacles and building into a thick white carpet. But within the imprint the boot's weight had compacted the earth into a hard and relatively smooth pan. This pan tended to hold the recent rain, and as each snowflake landed the collected moisture dissolved it. I examined the edges of the footprint. Wind and water had dulled their definition. Had, perhaps, been eroding the outline for a week.

I stood up, smiling. When I walked on through the snowstorm, following the dark imprints into the gloom, I found that my tiredness had gone. It was good to know, beyond any real shadow of doubt, that I was following, with a most artistic symbolism, the footsteps of the man who had blazed my trail and who had, a week before, fulfilled a seventeen-year ambition. But there was more to it, I think, than feeling glad for Harvey's sake. I found something obscurely yet warmly companionable about these footsteps. And their meaning was so delayed that they did not even begin to blur the solitude.

My exhilaration outlasted the snowstorm and then the sleet that was falling two hours later when I holed up at dusk under an overhang, within easy striking distance of Fossil Bay. It was still there next morning when I swung around into the bay in brilliant sunshine that had quickly canceled the overnight snow. And it was still there, reinforced by anticipation, when I began, about nine thirty, to prepare for the airdrop.

First I spread out my bright-orange sleeping bag, which Ranger Jim Bailey and the pilot would be looking for. Then I collected firewood and filled two of my cooking pots with water for making smoke signals to indicate which way the wind was blowing. And finally, in the suddenly tense minutes that were left, I practiced yet again the technique of sighting my extended thumb on a distant object (representing the plane) and with a small mirror aiming the sun's reflected rays partly onto the thumbtip, partly into thin air. I had never taken an airdrop before, but back in Flagstaff the pilot had shown me how to signal this way. In sunny weather, he said, he would see the flashes from miles away. It was partly his confidence in the mirror that made me decide at the last minute to take the drop two miles short of the proposed alternate site at the head of Fossil Bay, at a place that was not only more convenient for me—because I wanted to make a reconnaissance from that point, down into Fossil Canyon—but also seemed much safer for the plane's low approach run.

The zero hour I had arranged with Jim Bailey was ten o'clock. At one minute to zero I heard the sound of a motor. The little Cessna—silvery, with unmistakable red wing tips—came in higher than I had expected. I began to flash with the mirror. The plane came on. Came on. Came on. It passed directly overhead, still high, without a recognition rock of its wing tips. And then it was droning on and away and I was standing, astonished, on the red rock terrace.

The plane passed over Great Thumb Mesa and began to circle, slowly losing height. I could imagine Jim Bailey peering down at the cottonwood tree that marked Great Thumb Spring—the spring I had camped beside two nights before, the spring that was our primary dropping site. The plane vanished behind the mesa, but I could still hear it circling. And I could imagine Jim Bailey shouting at the pilot: "Looks like he hasn't made it!"

I waited, pacing up and down the red rock terrace.

Ten minutes, and they were back. They passed high above the head of Fossil Bay, then banked toward me. The plane droned overhead, ignored my frantic flashing, then began to skirt Great Thumb Point, following the rock terrace and amphitheaters that I had crossed the day before. Soon it vanished again.

For a while I could still hear its faint drone. Then the Canyon was silent with the silence I had grown used to and I knew they were searching along the Esplanade. They would probably go as far back as Supai. I no longer cared to think about what Jim Bailey was saying.

The minutes dragged by. Ten. Twenty. Thirty. The sun beat down on the red rock. I tried not to think about the sparse food reserves in my pack.

They came back at last, still high. The moment they cleared Great Thumb Mesa I lit the fire. The plane droned on, apparently heading for Grand Canyon Village and home. When the fire was burning briskly enough, I poured on the two waiting pots of water. A plume of smoke rose into the clear air. Then I was once more flashing furiously with the mirror, willing the sunlight into the pilot's eye. For long, tantalizing seconds the plane held course. Then it banked toward me. Minutes later its wings rocked the recognition signal.

The plane made three trial runs, low enough for me to see that one door had been removed to make the drop easier. On the fourth, something tumbled out of the blank door space. A bright-orange parachute cracked open. For brief seconds it was floating, full and calm and beautiful, against blue sky. Then the cardboard-wrapped can that hung from it touched down, barely a hundred feet from my sleeping bag. The chute collapsed. I ran toward it.

The plane came back once more, still low. I butterflied "All's well" with my arms. Wing tips rocked. Then the little Cessna was dwindling into the distance and I stood alone once more in the sunshine and the silence.

WHERE SOLITUDE IS EASY TO FIND

Joseph Wood Krutch

During a long career as an art critic at the *Nation* and as a professor at Columbia University, Joseph Wood Krutch became well known for his ideas about the psychology of modern life. In the book that made his reputation, *The Modern Temper,* he argues that science and technology have destroyed traditional religious and moral beliefs, but offer nothing to replace them. In 1952, at the age of sixty, Krutch left New York City and retired to Tucson, Arizona, then a small desert town; there, he began writing about the spiritual healing he found in his new home. Just then, many Americans were celebrating their new prosperity, as well as the end of World War II, by hitting the road for vacations in the family car. Krutch introduced this new generation of tourists to the Southwest with several volumes of nature writing, including *The Desert Year, The Voice of the Desert,* and his most successful effort, *The Grand Canyon: Today and All Its Yesterdays* (1958), from which this selection is taken. In these quiet, wise books, he helped readers see deserts not as a barren wastelands but as clean and timeless refuges from the pressures and anxieties of modern life.

· · ·

Twenty years ago I was one of the tourist thousands who saw Grand Canyon for the first time. In those days, travelers approaching from the south by car or bus had no warning until they stood actually upon the brink. Usually they descended at the front door of Bright Angel Lodge, passed through the lobby, and wandered across the terrace at the other side, wondering as they went where the Canyon was. Then, suddenly, they were at the brink with only a low parapet between them and a vast abyss.

First there is the sheer drop of several thousand feet, then the wide Tonto Plateau, then another sheer drop to an invisible bottom whose depth the visitor can only guess. Apparently this was the way [García López de] Cárdenas, the first white man to see the Canyon, came upon it in 1540. Since then thousands of men and women have shared his wonder and delight. Though I have made many visits since my first, I still get a real if diminished shock.

Today a new road, built only a few years ago, gives automobilists a glimpse into the chasm as they approach. That spoils a bit of the drama; but perhaps it is just as well. On my first visit a fellow traveler took one look and then ran back to throw his arms around a tree. When I saw him last, he was desperately resisting the efforts of two women companions to pry him loose.

At first glance the spectacle seems too strange to be real. Because one has never seen anything like it, because one has nothing to compare it with, it stuns the eye but cannot really hold the attention. For one thing, the scale is too large to be credited. The Canyon is ten miles across from rim to rim at the point where one usually sees it first and almost exactly a mile deep. But we are so accustomed to thinking of skyscrapers as high and of St. Peter's or the Pentagon as massive that we can hardly help misinterpreting what the eye sees; we cannot realize that the tremendous mesas and curiously shaped buttes which rise all around us are the grandiose objects they are. For a time it is too much like a scale model or an optical illusion. One admires the peep show and that is all. Because we cannot relate ourselves to it, we remain outside; very much as we remain outside the frame of a picture. And though we may come back to a picture again and again, we cannot look at it continuously for any considerable period of time. To pass on to another picture is the almost inevitable impulse. And this is the reaction of a majority of visitors to the Canyon.

To get into the picture one must relate one's self to it somehow and that is not easy to do in a short time. A few of the more hardy take the daylong journey on muleback to the bottom and return. A few of the more foolhardy brush warnings aside and plunge gaily downward on foot only to discover—unless they are seasoned hikers—that they have to be rescued in a state of exhaustion from an illusory panorama through which, as in a dream, they seem unable to make any progress. They have related themselves, but the relation is one of frustration and defeat.

A more sensible procedure for those willing to take the time is to allow the relationship to establish itself gradually. After a few days well but quietly spent, one begins to lose the sense of unreality and to come to terms with a scale of magnitude and of distance which could not at first be taken in. And it is only then that the spectacle, even as mere spectacle, makes its full impression or that one begins to have some dim sense of what the geologists mean when they talk of the millions of years during which the Canyon was cut and of the billions during which the rocks were prepared for the cutting. The Canyon requires what we call in the lingo of our day "a double take." Only that way does its size, its antiquity or the grandioseness of the forces which made it become real. Moreover, as I have learned from many visits, the process has to be repeated every time. First there is the impression of some sort of man-made diorama trying to fool the eye. Only later comes the gradual acceptance of the unbelievable fact.

Hendrik van Loon once remarked—I have not checked his figures—that the entire human population of the earth could be packed in a box only a mile wide, deep, and high. He then went on to add that if such a box were dropped into the middle of Grand Canyon, it would just about reach the rim but be not much more conspicuous than many of the mesas which here and there rise almost as high. Only a confirmed misanthropist will feel that the experiment would be worth making, but the visitor is soon struck by a more benign demonstration. This is that men—even hordes of men—cannot fill the Canyon sufficiently to detract from the sense of vast emptiness.

This is, after all, one of the most visited spots on the face of the earth. As the Swiss hotel is said to have boasted, "Thousands come here from all parts of the world seeking solitude." But at Grand Canyon at least they can find it. They form their little knot, of course, around the hotel and its terrace. But one can lose them very easily and then literally have a whole landscape to oneself. Even from the terrace of Bright Angel Lodge the Canyon itself is so empty that a little flurry of excitement arises when someone spots through his binoculars a speck moving up the side or across a plateau and when it can be assumed, though not actually seen, that the speck is a man or perhaps a man and a mule. The rim itself, except for the short stretch on either side of the main tourist area, is equally deserted. A few miles away—indeed within easy walking distance—one finds without looking a hundred perches where one may sit in absolute solitude, looking across a vista of many miles in which there is neither a human being nor any sign that any human being was ever there. And it is from such a perch that those who wish to take the Canyon in should begin to make its acquaintance.

Actually, of course, there are many areas in the Southwest a great deal farther from the conveniences and inconveniences of civilization—places hundreds of miles from a railroad and scores from a paved or even graded road; places where no man may come for months or even years. One knows that this is so and when one visits such a region the knowledge has its effect upon the imagination. But I cannot say that I ever looked upon any scene which, on the basis of what the eye could see, appeared to be more completely out of the world of man and modernity, although actually my perch was perhaps half a mile from a paved highway along which cars were passing at the rate of a hundred an hour, and only two or three miles from a crowded resort hotel. It is a pity—or perhaps it isn't—that so few visitors realize how close they are to an experience not elsewhere easy to have in the twentieth century, and the fact that one can have it so easily here reminds one again of the scale of this landscape. If, as Mr. van Loon said, the entire population of the earth could be all but lost in the Canyon, it is no wonder that a few thousands leave lots of unoccupied space.

Not very long ago, and after an absence of several years, I again took up my position on one of the little promontories which jut out from the rim. It was past the middle of June, and in the thin air of seven thousand feet even visitors from the southern Arizona desert are burned one tone deeper. But in the shade of a piñon pine the air still hints of the nights which can be almost cold, even at that season.

I looked across the ten miles to the opposite rim, down the successive terraces to the inner gorge at whose invisible bottom the great river still runs after having cut through a mile of stone, and then at the wall of an opposite promontory on my own side. I checked where I could the dividing lines between the successive formations of the geological ages—the Permian limestone on which I sat, the hundreds of feet of sandstone below it, the great Redwall of the Carboniferous age, the resisting plateau of Cambrian sediments, and finally the black wall of Archean schist. I made, in other words, a brief attempt at adjustment to the world of time as well as of space. But for the moment I was less interested in what the Canyon had been than in what it is at this moment and has been able to remain. It is not often that twentieth-century man has so much space to himself.

Here and there near the rim and below its edge there are scattered evidences that Indians inhabited the area—as one tribe still inhabits a section of the Canyon itself. But no evidence of even long past occupation was visible from where I sat, and indeed it nowhere appears that many men ever lived very long or very well here. This is dry country with thin soil or none, and also, perhaps, as one may at least fancy, a little too disconcerting in the immensities of its vistas. Yet it is by no means lifeless and now, as in the past, various small creatures find it very much to their liking. Violet green swallows dip and swerve, now above, now below the rim. Ravens soar above, nonchalantly putting another few hundred feet between them and the bottom a mile below where I sit. And if they seem to take the abyss with the casualness inspired by confidence in their strong wings and the solidity of the air for those who know how to navigate it, there are many other creatures obviously unaware of the terrible chasm open at their feet. Chipmunks and rock squirrels scamper a few feet below the edge; lizards dart here and there; a small gopher snake, apparently stalking some game, wiggles slowly across a piece of crumbling stone which a slight push would send hurtling below. Little junipers anchored at the very edge dangle bare roots over the side. And there, two feet below the rim, a penstemon waves a red wand over nothingness.

Despite all these living things so obviously at home here, there is absolutely no sign from which I would be able to deduce that any man besides myself had ever been here or, for that matter, that he had ever existed at all. This scene, I say to myself, would be exactly what it is if he never had. It is not quite the world before man came, because too many other living things have disappeared since then. But otherwise it is still the world as though man had never been.

At least there is absolutely nothing to remind me of all that he has done in (and to) the globe he lives on. The tamer of fire and the inventor of the wheel might never have existed—to say nothing of Newton and Watt and Faraday. Neither is there anything to remind me of the less dubious human achievements with which I have been concerned for most of my life. Plato and Shakespeare and Mozart also might never have existed, and if I had never come in contact with anything not visible here, I can hardly imagine what my life would have been like or what the character of my consciousness would be.

Here, so I am tempted to say, are the eternal hills without the eternal thoughts with which we have clothed them. Yet actually the hills are not eternal, whether the thoughts are or are not. In half a dozen places I can see the still visible evidences of recent rockfalls where great slabs of stone have broken loose and gone hurtling down. The widening of the Canyon is going on visibly, its deepening invisibly and no doubt much more slowly. One does not have to think in terms of geological time to realize that even the Canyon is changing. It is wider than it was a century ago and will inevitably be wider still after another has passed.

Man changes the face of the earth much more rapidly than nature does and he is creeping up on this area. Just out of sight are the tumbled-down remains of a miner's cabin. The miner came, scratched the surface a little and dug a few insignificant holes. Then he and the others like him admitted defeat, though this one has left a name and a bit of a legend behind him.

> They say the Lion and the Lizard keep
> The Courts where Jamshyd gloried and drank deep . . . .

Well, I don't know how much John Hance gloried or how deep he drank. I do know that the mountain lion does not keep court there because the lion has been all but exterminated in the area and his extermination has not been an unmixed blessing, even for man. But the lizard eludes us, and when I visited Hance's cabin a few minutes before taking up my perch, a lizard was sunning himself on the sagging door Hance had built for himself.

Modern man will not give up so easily. Scarcely a mile from where I sat a paved road was carrying cars to a village from which telegraph and telephone reach out. Magazines and newspapers are delivered. Occasionally an airplane hurtling across the continent passes overhead. A year or two ago two of them collided improbably above the Canyon and fell into its depths. These—or at least

some of them—are good things to have but not unmitigated comforts. They suggest by what a narrow margin (and possibly for how short a time) such primitive,
isolated spots as my perch may continue to exist.

How many more generations will pass before it will have become nearly
impossible to be alone even for an hour, to see anywhere nature as she is without
man's improvements upon her? How long will it be before—what is perhaps
worse yet—there is no quietness anywhere, no escape from the rumble and the
crash, the clank and the screech which seem to be the inevitable accompaniment
of technology? Whatever man does or produces, noise seems to be an unavoid-
able by-product. Perhaps he can, as he now tends to believe, do anything. But he
cannot do it quietly.

Perhaps when the time comes that there is no more silence and no more aloneness, there will also be no longer anyone who wants to be alone. If man is the
limitlessly conditionable creature so many believe him to be, then inevitably the
desire for a thing must disappear when it has become no longer attainable. Even
now fewer and fewer are *aware* of any desire to escape from crowds, and most
men and women who still make traditional excursions to beach or picnic grounds
unpack their radios without delay and turn on a noise to which they do not listen.
But it is not certain that this is not a morbid appetite rather than one which has
become normal or that it, any more than any other morbid appetite, brings real
satisfaction when it is gratified.

There is also another aspect to the situation. At least a few do still consciously
seek quietness and some degree of solitude; a great many more seek it less consciously, but seek it nonetheless. If this were not so, the various national parks
would not be so persistently visited. When all possible discount has been allowed
for the irrelevant motives, for the frequent failure to get what the visitor presum-
ably came for, and for the perverseness of many who try to avoid the very things
which the parks have to offer, the fact still remains that many find (and many
others do not find only because they do not know how to find it) that brief experience with solitude, silence, and a glimpse of nature herself which, to some greater
or less degree, they do feel the need of.

As a matter of fact, the deliberate search for them is a modern phenomenon
not, I think, because they were never before enjoyed but because they were taken
for granted. Only when they began to be scarce, only after the natural rather
than the man-made, and solitude rather than company had to be sought after,
did the great empty spaces become attractive or, indeed, other than alarming.
Man's place in nature was precarious long before the situation was reversed and
it became nature rather than man whose survival seemed uncertain.

If the first white man ever to see the Canyon felt anything except frustration
when he came upon this great barrier he saw no hope of crossing, his journal

gives no hint of the fact. Cárdenas had been dispatched by Coronado on a side trip in order to scout out a part of the region where they were searching for the seven Golden Cities that did not exist, and Cárdenas was in no mood to look at scenery or to indulge the luxury of wonder. He had had more than enough of empty, inhospitable spaces. He had had hardships and "adventures" aplenty. He had made almost impossible journeys overcoming almost unconquerable impediments. And here was a difficulty which could not be overcome. He had been led on and on in the hope that the difficulties were almost over. Now, after all he had gone through, nature laughed and said, "Thus far shalt thou go and no farther." In his day even the Alps were still regarded almost universally as "horrid"—a barrier to be dreaded before one came upon it and to be looked back upon with shuddering after it had been conquered.

The white men known to have seen the Canyon during the next three centuries can be counted on the fingers of one hand. And when in 1857 Lieutenant Joseph C. Ives made for the United States Government an extensive reconnaissance in the region of its western end, he wrote in his report: "Ours has been the first and will doubtless be the last party of whites to visit this profitless locality. It seems intended by nature that the Colorado river, along the greater portion of its lonely and majestic way, shall be forever unvisited and undisturbed."

Forgivable, perhaps, since Lieutenant Ives could hardly be expected to know either how transportation would increase the mobility of men or, what is perhaps more important, that the America which was even in his day still largely wilderness, was so soon to become the America in which wilderness is a rarity.

Forgivable or not, this was certainly one of the unluckiest prophecies ever made, and Ives would be hardly less astonished than Cárdenas to be told that this region "destined to be forever unvisited and undisturbed" is actually one of the most frequently visited on earth—at least if one uses the word "visited" to mean sought out purely in order to be looked at. Yet two of the words he used do nevertheless suggest the beginning of the change in man's attitude toward the more grandiose and least conquerable aspects of the natural world. Cárdenas would not have spoken of the Colorado as "majestic." That word could have been used only by a man upon whose sensibilities a new attitude had already taken some effect. Ives was echoing the changed language of Europeans to whom "horrid mountains" had become "awful mountains" and the once merely terrifying had become "sublime." Three centuries had been required to change Cárdenas' dismay into the reaction which Ives revealed not only in the word "majestic" but almost equally in the word "lonely," which is already touched with a romantic aura. Hardly more than half a century later this area destined to be "forever unvisited" was a national park preserved for its own "awful" sake.

Another change equally significant in its different way is evident in the report of a scientific member of the Ives party. Cárdenas had no curiosity concerning the origin or meaning of the Canyon. He would never have asked (or cared) what could be learned from it about the history of the earth. He would have liked to be able to get to the other side and he would have liked to get there only because gold might be found there. At least that would have been the only reason he could have given, though one may guess that the desire for gold, like its companion motive, the desire to save Indian souls, may have sometimes been partly a rationalization of the desire for adventure. Such a desire seemed less readily understandable then than now, because one did not then have to go as far as one has to go today to find novel and testing experiences. John S. Newberry, who was Ives' geologist, had on the other hand the advantage of living in an age when one could ask and get some answer to the question "What does this Canyon mean?" and he sketched out a broadly accurate account of the Canyon's geological significance.

By 1890, C. Hart Merriam, who made for the Department of Agriculture the first "Biological Survey of the San Francisco Region and Desert of the Little Colorado, Arizona" could state the third reason why the Canyon repays study—namely that it is a self-contained biological unit. "In short," so he wrote, "the Grand Canyon of the Colorado is a world in itself, and a great fund of knowledge is in store for the philosophic biologist whose privilege it is to study exhaustively the problems there presented."

On my own first visit twenty years ago I think I had no more definite idea of what had brought me, no more knowledge of the various kinds of things which the Canyon region is and has to offer, than the average tourist. To me also it was then little more than "spectacle," one of "the wonders of the world" which one feels some vague obligation to see and gets some vague pride out of having seen. Like everybody else, I took a few pictures and probably dispatched a few post cards. Then I departed, taking little more with me than what a post card will hold.

I did not then recognize more than very dimly the need or the desire for that experience of a world we did not make which was later to become so important to me. Neither was I aware of more than a very casual interest in what is known about the way in which the Canyon was made or what it reveals of time and history. Yet there was just enough recognition of the one and interest in the other to bring me back. And even for those whose attitude is still what mine then was, a *part* of the half-understood fascination is the result of a vaguely perceived sense that the spectacle represents something the imagination could feed upon and that it is ready to tell a story to those who will listen.

A COUGAR HUNT ON
THE RIM OF THE GRAND CANYON

Theodore Roosevelt

President Theodore Roosevelt first visited Grand Canyon in 1903, the same year he camped in the Yosemite backcountry with John Muir. While at the South Rim, Roosevelt called on the people of the Arizona Territory to protect what was still only a forest preserve open to grazing, mining, and other kinds of development. "Leave it as it is," he said "You cannot improve on it. The ages have been at work on it, and man can only mar it." Roosevelt established Grand Canyon National Monument in 1908, setting the stage for its eventual designation as a national park. After his presidency, Roosevelt turned his attention to outdoor travel and writing. He crossed the globe in pursuit of big game, making several hunting expeditions to the Kaibab Plateau. He wrote many popular essays about his adventures, including this one, which was first published in the magazine *Outlook* in 1913 and then included in his 1916 collection, *A Book-Lover's Holidays in the Open.*

· · ·

On July 14, 1918, our party gathered at the comfortable El Tovar Hotel, on the edge of the Grand Canyon of the Colorado, and therefore overlooking the most wonderful scenery in the world. The moon was full. Dim, vast, mysterious, the canyon lay in the shimmering radiance. To all else that is strange and beautiful in nature the Canyon stands as Karnak and Baalbec, seen by moonlight, stand to all other ruined temples and palaces of the bygone ages.

With me were my two younger sons, Archie and Quentin, aged nineteen and fifteen respectively, and a cousin of theirs, Nicholas, aged twenty. The cousin had driven our horses, and what outfit we did not ourselves carry, from southern

Arizona to the north side of the canyon, and had then crossed the canyon to meet us. The youngest one of the three had not before been on such a trip as that we intended to take; but the two elder boys, for their good fortune, had formerly been at the Evans School in Mesa, Arizona, and among the by-products of their education was a practical and working familiarity with ranch life, with the round-up, and with travelling through the desert and on the mountains. Jesse Cummings, of Mesa, was along to act as cook, packer, and horse-wrangler, helped in all three branches by the two elder boys; he was a Kentuckian by birth, and a better man for our trip and a stancher friend could not have been found.

On the 15th we went down to the bottom of the canyon. There we were to have been met by our outfit with two men whom we had engaged; but they never turned up, and we should have been in a bad way had not Mr. Stevenson, of the Bar Z Cattle Company, come down the trail behind us, while the foreman of the Bar Z, Mr. Mansfield, appeared to meet him, on the opposite side of the rushing, muddy torrent of the Colorado; Mansfield worked us across on the trolley which spans the river; and then we joined in and worked Stevenson, and some friends he had with him, across. Among us all we had food enough for dinner and for a light breakfast, and we had our bedding. With characteristic cattleman's generosity, our new friends turned over to us two pack-mules, which could carry our bedding and the like, and two spare saddle-horses—both the mules and the spare saddle-horses having been brought down by Mansfield because of a lucky mistake as to the number of men he was to meet.

Mansfield was a representative of the best type of old-style ranch foreman. It is a hard climb out of the canyon on the north side, and Mansfield was bound that we should have an early start. He was up at half-past one in the morning; we breakfasted on a few spoonfuls of mush; packed the mules and saddled the horses; and then in the sultry darkness, which in spite of the moon filled the bottom of the stupendous gorge, we started up the Bright Angel trail. Cummings and the two elder boys walked; the rest of us were on horseback. The trail crossed and recrossed the rapid brook, and for rods at a time went up its boulder-filled bed; groping and stumbling, we made our blind way along it; and over an hour passed before the first grayness of the dawn faintly lighted our footsteps.

At last we left the stream bed, and the trail climbed the sheer slopes and zigzagged upward through the breaks in the cliff walls. At one place the Bar Z men showed us where one of their pack-animals had lost his footing and fallen down the mountainside a year previously. It was eight hours before we topped the rim and came out on the high, wooded, broken plateau which at this part of its course forms the northern barrier of the deep-sunk Colorado River. Three or four miles farther on we found the men who were to have met us; they were two days behindhand, so we told them we would not need them, and reclaimed what horses, provisions, and other outfit were ours. With Cummings and the two elder boys we were quite competent to take care of ourselves under all circumstances, and extra men, tents, and provisions merely represented a slight, and dispensable, increase in convenience and comfort.

As it turned out, there was no loss even of comfort. We went straight to the cabin of the game warden, Uncle Jim Owens; and he instantly accepted us as his guests, treated us as such, and accompanied us throughout our fortnight's stay north of the river. A kinder host and better companion in a wild country could not be found. Through him we hired a very good fellow, a mining prospector, who stayed with us until we crossed the Colorado at Lee's Ferry. He was originally a New York State man, who had grown up in Montana, and had prospected through the mountains from the Athabaska River to the Mexican boundary. Uncle Jim was a Texan, born at San Antonio, and raised in the Panhandle, on the Goodnight ranch. In his youth he had seen the thronging myriads of bison, and taken part in the rough life of the border, the life of the cow-men, the buffalo-hunters, and the Indian fighters. He was by instinct a man of the right kind in all relations; and he early hailed with delight the growth of the movement among our people to put a stop to the senseless and wanton destruction of our wild life. Together with his—and my—friend Buffalo Jones he had worked for the preservation of the scattered bands of bison; he was keenly interested not only in the preservation of the forests but in the preservation of the game. He had been two years buffalo warden in the Yellowstone National Park. Then he had come to the Colorado National Forest Reserve and Game Reserve, where he had been game warden for over six years at the time of our trip. He has given zealous and efficient service to the people as a whole; for which, by the way, his salary has been an inadequate return. One important feature of his work is to keep down the larger beasts and birds of prey, the arch-enemies of the deer, mountain sheep, and grouse; and the most formidable among these foes of the harmless wild life are the cougars. At the time of our visit he owned five hounds, which he had trained especially, as far as his manifold duties gave him the time, to the chase of cougars and bobcats. Coyotes were plentiful, and he shot these wherever the chance offered; but coyotes are best kept down by poison, and poison cannot be used where any man is keeping the hounds with which alone it is possible effectively to handle the cougars.

At this point the Colorado, in its deep gulf, bends south, then west, then north, and incloses on three sides the high plateau which is the heart of the forest and game reserve. It was on this plateau, locally known as Buckskin Mountain, that we spent the next fortnight. The altitude is from eight thousand to nearly ten thousand feet, and the climate is that of the far north. Spring does not come until June; the snow lies deep for seven months. We were there in midsummer, but the thermometer went down at night to 36, 34, and once to 33 degrees Fahrenheit; there was hoarfrost in the mornings. Sound was our sleep under our blankets, in the open, or under a shelf of rock, or beneath a tent, or most often under a thickly leaved tree. Throughout the day the air was cool and bracing.

Although we reached the plateau in mid-July, the spring was but just coming to an end. Silver-voiced Rocky Mountain hermit-thrushes chanted divinely from the deep woods. There were multitudes of flowers, of which, alas! I know only a very few, and these by their vernacular names; for as yet there is no such handbook for the flowers of the southern Rocky Mountains as, thanks to Mrs. Frances Dana, we have for those of the Eastern States, and, thanks to Miss Mary Elizabeth Parsons, for those of California. The sego lilies, looking like very handsome Eastern trilliums, were as plentiful as they were beautiful; and there were the striking Indian paint-brushes, fragrant purple locust blooms, the blossoms of that strange bush the plumed acacia, delicately beautiful white columbines, bluebells, great sheets of blue lupin, and the tall, crowded spikes of the brilliant red bell—and innumerable others. The rainfall is light and the ground porous; springs are few, and brooks wanting; but the trees are handsome. In a few places the forest is dense; in most places it is sufficiently open to allow a mountain-horse to twist in and out among the tree trunks at a smart canter. The tall yellow pines are everywhere; the erect spires of the mountain-spruce and of the blue-tipped Western balsam shoot up around their taller cousins, and the quaking asps, the aspens with their ever-quivering leaves and glimmering white boles, are scattered among and beneath the conifers, or stand in groves by themselves. Blue grouse were plentiful—having increased greatly, partly because of the war waged by Uncle Jim against their foes the great horned owls; and among the numerous birds were long-crested, dark-blue jays, pinyon-jays, doves, band-tailed pigeons, golden-winged flickers, chickadees, juncos, mountain-bluebirds, thistle-finches, and Louisiana tanagers. A very handsome cock tanager, the orange yellow of its plumage dashed with red on the head and throat, flew familiarly round Uncle Jim's cabin, and spent most of its time foraging in the grass. Once three birds flew by which I am convinced were the strange and interesting evening grosbeaks. Chipmunks and white-footed mice lived in the cabin, the former very bold and friendly; in fact, the chipmunks, of several species, were everywhere; and there were gophers or rock-squirrels, and small tree-squirrels, like the Eastern chickarees, and big tree-squirrels—the handsomest squirrels I have ever seen—with black bodies and bushy white tails. These last lived in the pines, were diurnal in their habits, and often foraged among the fallen cones on the ground; and they were strikingly conspicuous.

We met, and were most favorably impressed by, the forest supervisor, and some of his rangers. This forest and game reserve is thrown open to grazing, as with all similar reserves. Among the real settlers, the home-makers of sense and farsightedness, there is a growing belief in the wisdom of the policy of the preservation of the national resources by the National Government. On small, permanent farms, the owner, if reasonably intelligent, will himself preserve his own patrimony; but everywhere the uncontrolled use in common of the public domain has meant reckless, and usually wanton, destruction. All the public domain that is used should be used under strictly supervised governmental lease; that is, the lease system should be applied everywhere substantially as it is now applied in the forest. In every case the small neighboring settlers, the actual home-makers, should be given priority of chance to lease the land in reasonable sized tracts. Continual efforts are made by demagogues and by unscrupulous agitators to excite hostility to the forest policy of the government; and needy men who are short-sighted and unscrupulous join in the cry, and play into the hands of the corrupt politicians who do the bidding of the big and selfish exploiters of the public domain. One device of these politicians is through their representatives in Congress to cut down the appropriation for the forest service; and in consequence the administrative heads of the service, in the effort to be economical, are sometimes driven to the expedient of trying to replace the permanently employed experts by short-term men, picked up at haphazard, and hired only for the summer season. This is all wrong: first, because the men thus hired give very inferior service; and, second, because the government should be a model employer, and should not set a vicious example in hiring men under conditions that tend to create a shifting class of laborers who suffer from all the evils of unsteady employment, varied by long seasons of idleness. At this time the best and most thoughtful farmers are endeavoring to devise means for doing away with the system of employing farm-hands in mass for a few months and then discharging them; and the government should not itself have recourse to this thoroughly pernicious system.

The preservation of game and of wild life generally—aside from the noxious species—on these reserves is of incalculable benefit to the people as a whole. As the game increases in these national refuges and nurseries it overflows into the surrounding country. Very wealthy men can have private game-preserves of their own. But the average man of small or moderate means can enjoy the vigorous pastime of the chase, and indeed can enjoy wild nature, only if there are good general laws, properly enforced, for the preservation of the game and wild life, and if, furthermore, there are big parks or reserves provided for the use of all our people, like those of the Yellowstone, the Yosemite, and the Colorado.

A small herd of bison has been brought to the reserve; it is slowly increasing. It is privately owned, one-third of the ownership being in Uncle Jim, who handles the herd. The government should immediately buy this herd. Everything should be done to increase the number of bison on the public reservations.

The chief game animal of the Colorado Canyon reserve is the Rocky Mountain blacktail, or mule, deer. The deer have increased greatly in numbers since the reserve was created, partly because of the stopping of hunting by men, and even more because of the killing off of the cougars. The high plateau is their summer range; in the winter the bitter cold and driving snow send them and the cattle, as well as the bands of wild horses, to the lower desert country. For some cause, perhaps the limestone soil, their antlers are unusually stout and large. We found the deer tame and plentiful, and as we rode or walked through the forest we continually came across them—now a doe with her fawn, now a party of does and fawns, or a single buck, or a party of bucks. The antlers were still in the velvet. Does would stand and watch us go by within fifty or a hundred yards, their big ears thrown forward; while the fawns stayed hid near by. Sometimes we roused the pretty spotted fawns, and watched them dart away, the embodiments of delicate grace. One buck, when a hound chased it, refused to run and promptly stood at bay; another buck jumped and capered, and also refused to run, as we passed at but a few yards' distance. One of the most beautiful sights I ever saw was on this trip. We were slowly riding through the open pine forest when we came on a party of seven bucks. Four were yearlings or two-year-olds; but three were mighty master bucks, and their velvet-clad antlers made them look as if they had rocking-chairs on their heads. Stately of port and bearing, they walked a few steps at a time, or stood at gaze on the carpet of brown needles strewn with cones; on their red coats the flecked and broken sun-rays played; and as we watched them, down the aisles of tall tree trunks the odorous breath of the pines blew in our faces.

The deadly enemies of the deer are the cougars. They had been very plentiful all over the table-land until Uncle Jim thinned them out, killing between two and three hundred. Usually their lairs are made in the well-nigh inaccessible rugged-ness of the canyon itself. Those which dwelt in the open forest were soon killed off. Along the part of the canyon where we hunted there was usually an upper wall of sheer white cliffs; then came a very steep slope covered by a thick scrub of dwarf oak and locust, with an occasional pinyon or pine; and then another and deeper wall of vermilion cliffs. It was along this intermediate slope that the cougars usually passed the day. At night they came up through some gorge or break in the cliff and rambled through the forests and along the rim after the deer. They are the most successful of all still-hunters, killing deer much more easily than a wolf can; and those we killed were very fat.

Cougars are strange and interesting creatures. They are among the most successful and to their prey the most formidable beasts of rapine in the world. Yet when themselves attacked they are the least dangerous of all beasts of prey, except hyenas. Their every movement is so lithe and stealthy, they move with such sinuous and noiseless caution, and are such past masters in the art of concealment, that they are hardly ever seen unless roused by dogs. In the wilds they occasionally kill wapiti, and often bighorn sheep and white goats; but their favorite prey is the deer.

Among domestic animals, while they at times kill all, including, occasionally, horned cattle, they are especially destructive to horses. Among the first bands of horses brought to this plateau there were some of which the cougars killed every foal. The big males attacked full-grown horses. Uncle Jim had killed one big male which had killed a large draft-horse, and another which had killed two saddle-horses and a pack-mule, although the mule had a bell on its neck, which it was mistakenly supposed would keep the cougar away. We saw the skeleton of one of the saddle-horses. It was killed when snow was on the ground, and when Uncle Jim first saw the carcass the marks of the struggle were plain. The cougar sprang on its neck, holding the face with the claws of one paw, while his fangs tore at the back of the neck, just at the base of the skull; the other fore paw was on the other side of the neck, and the hind claws tore the withers and one shoulder and flank. The horse struggled thirty yards or so before he fell, and never rose again. The draft-horse was seized in similar fashion. It went but twenty yards before falling; then in the snow could be seen the marks where it had struggled madly on its side, plunging in a circle, and the marks of the hind feet of the cougar in an outside circle, while the fangs and fore talons of the great cat never ceased tearing the prey. In this case the fore claws so ripped and tore the neck and throat that it was doubtful whether they, and not the teeth, had not given the fatal wounds.

We came across the bodies of a number of deer that had been killed by cougars. Generally the remains were in such condition that we could not see how the killing had been done. In one or two cases the carcasses were sufficiently fresh for us to examine them carefully. One doe had claw marks on her face, but no fang marks on the head or neck; apparently the neck had been broken by her own plunging fall; then the cougar had bitten a hole in the flank and eaten part of one haunch; but it had not disembowelled its prey, as an African lion would have done. Another deer, a buck, was seized in similar manner; but the death-wound was inflicted with the teeth, in singular fashion, a great hole being torn into the chest, where the neck joins the shoulder. Evidently there is no settled and invariable method of killing. We saw no signs of any cougar being injured in the struggle; the prey was always seized suddenly and by surprise, and in such fashion that it could make no counter-attack.

Few African leopards would attack such quarry as the big male cougars do. Yet the leopard sometimes preys on man, and it is the boldest and most formidable of fighters when brought to bay. The cougar, on the contrary, is the least dangerous to man of all the big cats. There are authentic instances of its attacking man; but they are not merely rare but so wholly exceptional that in practise they can be entirely disregarded. There is no more need of being frightened when sleeping in, or wandering after nightfall through, a forest infested by cougars than if they were so many tom-cats. Moreover, when itself assailed by either dogs or men the cougar makes no aggressive fight. It will stay in a tree for hours, kept there by a single dog which it could kill at once if it had the heart—and this although if hungry it will itself attack and kill any dog, and on occasions even a big wolf. If the dogs—or men—come within a few feet, it will inflict formidable wounds with its claws and teeth, the former being used to hold the assailant while the latter inflict the fatal bite. But it fights purely on the defensive, whereas the leopard readily assumes the offensive and often charges, at headlong, racing speed, from a distance of fifty or sixty yards. It is absolutely safe to walk up to within ten yards of a cougar at bay, whether wounded or unwounded, and to shoot it at leisure.

Cougars are solitary beasts. When full-grown the females outnumber the males about three to one; and the sexes stay together for only a few days at mating-time. The female rears her kittens alone, usually in some cave; the male would be apt to kill them if he could get at them. The young are playful. Uncle Jim once brought back to his cabin a young cougar, two or three months old. At the time he had a hound puppy named Pot—he was an old dog, the most dependable in the pack, when we made our hunt. Pot had lost his mother; Uncle Jim was raising him on canned milk, and, as it was winter, kept him at night in a German sock. The young cougar speedily accepted Pot as a playmate, to be enjoyed and tyrannized over. The two would lap out of the same dish; but when the milk was nearly lapped up, the cougar would put one paw on Pot's face, and hold him firmly while it finished the dish itself. Then it would seize Pot in its fore paws and toss him up, catching him again; while Pot would occasionally howl dismally, for the young cougar had sharp little claws. Finally the cougar would tire of the play, and then it would take Pot by the back of the neck, carry him off, and put him down in his box by the German sock.

When we started on our cougar hunt there were seven of us, with six pack-animals. The latter included one mule, three donkeys—two of them, Ted and Possum, very wise donkeys—and two horses. The saddle-animals included two mules and five horses, one of which solemnly carried a cow-bell. It was a characteristic oldtime Western outfit. We met with the customary misadventures of such a trip, chiefly in connection with our animals. At night they were turned loose to feed, most of them with hobbles, some of them with bells. Before dawn, two or three of the party—usually including one, and sometimes both, of the elder boys—were off on foot, through the chilly dew, to bring them in. Usually this was a matter of an hour or two; but once it took a day, and twice it took a half-day. Both breaking camp and making camp, with a pack-outfit, take time; and in our case each of the packers, including the two elder boys, used his own hitch—single-diamond, squaw hitch, cow-man's hitch, miner's hitch, Navajo hitch, as the case might be. As for cooking and washing dishes—why, I wish that the average tourist-sportsman, the city-hunter-with-a-guide, would once in a while have to cook and wash dishes for himself; it would enable him to grasp the reality of things. We were sometimes nearly drowned out by heavy rain-storms.

We had good food; but the only fresh meat we had was the cougar meat. This was delicious; quite as good as venison. Yet men rarely eat cougar flesh.

Cougars should be hunted when snow is on the ground. It is difficult for hounds to trail them in hot weather, when there is no water and the ground is dry and hard. However, we had to do the best we could; and the frequent rains helped us. On most of the hunting days we rode along the rim of the canyon and through the woods, hour after hour, until the dogs grew tired, or their feet sore, so that we deemed it best to turn toward camp; having either struck no trail or else a trail so old that the hounds could not puzzle it out. I did not have a rifle, wishing the boys to do the shooting. The two elder boys had tossed up for the first shot, Nick winning. In cougar hunting the shot is usually much the least interesting and important part of the performance. The credit belongs to the hounds, and to the man who hunts the hounds. Uncle Jim hunted his hounds excellently. He had neither horn nor whip; instead, he threw pebbles, with much accuracy of aim, at any recalcitrant dog—and several showed a tendency to hunt deer or coyote. "They think they know best and needn't obey me unless I have a nose-bag full of rocks," observed Uncle Jim.

Twice we had lucky days. On the first occasion we all seven left camp by sunrise with the hounds. We began with an hour's chase after a bobcat, which dodged back and forth over and under the rim rock, and finally escaped along a ledge in the cliff wall. At about eleven we struck a cougar trail of the night before. It was a fine sight to see the hounds running it through the woods in full cry, while we loped after them. After one or two checks, they finally roused the cougar, a big male, from a grove of aspens at the head of a great gorge which broke through the cliffs into the canyon. Down the gorge went the cougar, and then along the slope between the white cliffs and the red; and after some delay in taking the wrong trail, the hounds followed him. The gorge was impassable for horses, and we rode along the rim, looking down into the depths, from which rose the chiming of the hounds. At last a change in the sound showed that they had him treed; and after a while we saw them far below under a pine, across the gorge, and on the upper edge of the vermilion cliff wall. Down we went to them, scrambling and sliding; down a break in the cliffs, round the head of the gorge just before it broke off into a side-canyon, through the thorny scrub which tore our hands and faces, along the slope where, if a man started rolling, he never would stop until life had left his body. Before we reached him the cougar leaped from the tree and tore off, with his big tail stretched straight as a bar behind him; but a cougar is a short-winded beast, and a couple of hundred yards on, the hounds put him up another tree. Thither we went.

It was a wild sight. The maddened hounds bayed at the foot of the pine. Above them, in the lower branches, stood the big horse-killing cat, the destroyer of the deer, the lord of stealthy murder, facing his doom with a heart both craven and cruel. Almost beneath him the vermilion cliffs fell sheer a thousand feet without a break. Behind him lay the Grand Canyon in its awful and desolate majesty.

Nicholas shot true. With his neck broken, the cougar fell from the tree, and the body was clutched by Uncle Jim and Archie before it could roll over the cliff—while I experienced a moment's lively doubt as to whether all three might not waltz into the abyss together. Cautiously we dragged him along the rim to another tree, where we skinned him. Then, after a hard pull out of the canyon, we rejoined the horses; rain came on; and, while the storm pelted against our slickers and down-drawn slouch hats, we rode back to our water-drenched camp.

On our second day of success only three of us went out—Uncle Jim, Archie, and I. Unfortunately, Quentin's horse went lame that morning, and he had to stay with the pack-train.

For two or three hours we rode through the woods and along the rim of the canyon. Then the hounds struck a cold trail and began to puzzle it out. They went slowly along to one of the deep, precipice-hemmed gorges which from time to time break the upper cliff wall of the canyon; and after some busy nose-work they plunged into its depths. We led our horses to the bottom, slipping, sliding, and pitching, and clambered, panting and gasping, up the other side. Then we galloped along the rim. Far below us we could at times hear the hounds. One of them was a bitch, with a squealing voice. The other dogs were under the first cliffs, working out a trail, which was evidently growing fresher. Much farther down we could hear the squealing of the bitch, apparently on another trail. However, the trails came together, and the shrill yelps of the bitch were drowned in the deeper-toned chorus of the other hounds, as the fierce intensity of the cry told that the game was at last roused. Soon they had the cougar treed. Like the first, it was in a pine at the foot of the steep slope: just above the vermilion cliff wall. We scrambled down to the beast, a big male, and Archie broke its neck; in such a position it was advisable to kill it outright, as, if it struggled at all, it was likely to slide over the edge of the cliff and fall a thousand feet sheer.

It was a long way down the slope, with its jungle of dwarf oak and locust, and the climb back, with the skin and flesh of the cougar, would be heart-breaking. So, as there was a break in the cliff line above, Uncle Jim suggested to Archie to try to lead down our riding animals while he, Uncle Jim, skinned the cougar. By the time the skin was off, Archie turned up with our two horses and Uncle Jim's mule—an animal which galloped as freely as a horse. Then the skin and flesh were packed behind his and Uncle Jim's saddles, and we started to lead the three animals up the steep, nearly sheer mountainside. We had our hands full. The horses and mule could barely make it. Finally the saddles of both the laden animals slipped, and Archie's horse in his fright nearly went over the cliff—it was a favorite horse of his, a black horse from the plains below, with good blood in it, but less at home climbing cliffs than were the mountain horses. On that slope anything that started rolling never stopped unless it went against one of the rare pine or pinyon trees. The horse plunged and reared; Archie clung to its head for dear life, trying to prevent it from turning down-hill, while Uncle Jim sought to undo the saddle and I clutched the bridle of his mule and of my horse and kept them quiet. Finally the frightened black horse sank on his knees with his head on Archie's lap; the saddle was taken off—and promptly rolled down-hill fifty or sixty yards before it fetched up against a pinyon; we repacked, and finally reached the top of the rim.

Meanwhile the hounds had again started, and we concluded that the bitch must have been on the trail of a different animal, after all. By the time we were ready to proceed they were out of hearing, and we completely lost track of them. So Uncle Jim started in the direction he deemed it probable they would take, and after a while we were joined by Pot. Evidently the dogs were tired and thirsty and had scattered. In about an hour, as we rode through the open pine forest across hills and valleys, Archie and I caught, very faintly, a far-off baying note. Uncle Jim could not hear it, but we rode toward the spot, and after a time caught the note again. Soon Pot heard it and trotted toward the sound. Then we came over a low hill crest, and when half-way down we saw a cougar crouched in a pine on the opposite slope, while one of the hounds, named Ranger, uttered at short intervals a husky bay as he kept his solitary vigil at the foot of the tree. Archie insisted that I should shoot, and thrust the rifle into my hand as we galloped down the incline. The cougar, a young and active female, leaped out of the tree and rushed off at a gait that for a moment left both dogs behind; and after her we tore at full speed through the woods and over rocks and logs. A few hundred yards farther on her bolt was shot, and the dogs, and we also, were at her heels. She went up a pine which had no branches for the lower thirty or forty feet. It was interesting to see her climb. Her two fore paws were placed on each side of the stem, and her hind paws against it, all the claws digging into the wood; her body was held as clear of the tree as if she had been walking on the ground, the legs being straight, and she walked or ran up the perpendicular stem with as much daylight between her body and the trunk as there was between her body and the earth when she was on the ground. As she faced us among the branches I could only get a clear shot into her chest where the neck joins the shoulder; down she came, but on the ground she jumped to her feet, ran fifty yards with the dogs at her heels, turned to bay in some fallen timber, and dropped dead.

The last days before we left this beautiful holiday region we spent on the table-land called Greenland, which projects into the canyon east of Bright Angel. We were camped by the Dripping Springs, in singular and striking surroundings. A long valley leads south through the table-land; and just as it breaks into a sheer walled chasm which opens into one of the side loops of the great canyon, the trail turns into a natural gallery along the face of the cliff. For a couple of hundred yards a rock shelf a dozen feet wide runs under a rock overhang which often projects beyond it. The gallery is in some places twenty feet high; in other places a man on horseback must stoop his head as he rides. Then, at a point where the shelf broadens, the clear spring pools of living water, fed by constant dripping from above, lie on the inner side next to and under the rock wall. A little beyond these pools, with the chasm at our feet, and its opposite wall towering immediately in front of us, we threw down our bedding and made camp. Darkness fell; the stars were brilliant overhead; the fire of pitchy pine stumps flared; and in the light of the wavering flames the cliff walls and jutting rocks momentarily shone with ghastly clearness, and as instantly vanished in utter gloom.

From the southernmost point of this table-land the view of the canyon left the beholder solemn with the sense of awe. At high noon, under the unveiled sun, every tremendous detail leaped in glory to the sight; yet in hue and shape the change was unceasing from moment to moment. When clouds swept the heavens, vast shadows were cast; but so vast was the canyon that these shadows seemed but patches of gray and purple and umber. The dawn and the evening twilight were brooding mysteries over the dusk of the abyss; night shrouded its immensity, but did not hide it; and to none of the sons of men is it given to tell of the wonder and splendor of sunrise and sunset in the Grand Canyon of the Colorado.

THE GRAND CAÑON OF THE COLORADO

John Muir

John Muir, founder of the Sierra Club, was his generation's most powerful advocate for the preservation of nature. His spiritually intense writings about the mountains of the West were widely read during his lifetime and have since achieved the status of scripture among lovers of wilderness. Through his many books and essays, he changed the way Americans thought about their public lands. He showed them that nature is not simply a store of economic resources, but that it also is, and should be, a sustaining home for our souls. Muir was most deeply attached to the Yosemite Valley and the Sierra Nevada of California, but he traveled widely. In 1902, just a year after the opening of the line, he rode the Santa Fe Railroad to the South Rim, where he spent much of his time observing his fellow tourists. In this essay, published later that year in the *Century Illustrated Monthly,* Muir struggles to decide whether easy access via modern transportation has cheapened travelers' experiences of the wild.

. . .

Happy nowadays is the tourist, with earth's wonders, new and old, spread invitingly open before him, and a host of able workers as his slaves making everything easy, padding plush about him, grading roads for him, boring tunnels, moving hills out of his way, eager, like the Devil, to show him all the kingdoms of the world and their glory and foolishness, spiritualizing travel for him with lightning and steam, abolishing space and time and almost everything else. Little children and tender, pulpy people, as well as storm-seasoned explorers, may now go almost everywhere in smooth comfort, cross oceans and deserts scarce accessible to fishes and birds, and, dragged by steel horses, go up high mountains, riding gloriously beneath starry showers of sparks, ascending like Elijah in a whirlwind and chariot of fire.

First of the wonders of the great West to be brought within reach of the tourist were the Yosemite and the Big Trees, on the completion of the first transcontinental railway; next came the Yellowstone and icy Alaska, by the northern roads; and last the Grand Cañon of the Colorado, which, naturally the hardest to reach, has now become, by a branch of the Santa Fé, the most accessible of all.

Of course, with this wonderful extension of steel ways through our wildness there is loss as well as gain. Nearly all railroads are bordered by belts of desolation. The finest wilderness perishes as if stricken with pestilence. Bird and beast people, if not the dryads, are frightened from the groves. Too often the groves also vanish, leaving nothing but ashes. Fortunately, nature has a few big places beyond man's power to spoil—the ocean, the two icy ends of the globe, and the Grand Cañon.

When I first heard of the Santa Fé trains running to the edge of the Grand Cañon of Arizona, I was troubled with thoughts of the disenchantment likely to follow. But last winter, when I saw those trains crawling along through the pines of the Coconino Forest and close up to the brink of the chasm at Bright Angel, I was glad to discover that in the presence of such stupendous scenery they are nothing. The locomotives and trains are mere beetles and caterpillars, and the noise they make is as little disturbing as the hooting of an owl in the lonely woods.

In a dry, hot, monotonous forested plateau, seemingly boundless, you come suddenly and without warning upon the abrupt edge of a gigantic sunken landscape of the wildest, most multitudinous features, and those features, sharp and angular, are made out of flat beds of limestone and sandstone forming a spiry, jagged, gloriously colored mountain-range countersunk in a level gray plain. It is a hard job to sketch it even in scrawniest outline; and, try as I may, not in the least sparing myself, I cannot tell the hundredth part of the wonders of its features— the side-cañons, gorges, alcoves, cloisters, and amphitheaters of vast sweep and depth, carved in its magnificent walls; the throng of great architectural rocks it contains resembling castles, cathedrals, temples, and palaces, towered and spired and painted, some of them nearly a mile high, yet beneath one's feet. All this, however, is less difficult than to give any idea of the impression of wild, primeval beauty and power one receives in merely gazing from its brink. The view down the gulf of color and over the rim of its wonderful wall, more than any other view I know, leads us to think of our earth as a star with stars swimming in light, every radiant spire pointing the way to the heavens. . . .

Of all the various kinds of ornamental work displayed—carving, tracery on cliff-faces, moldings, arches, pinnacles—none is more admirably effective or charms more than the webs of rain-channeled taluses. Marvelously extensive, without the slightest appearance of waste or excess, they cover roofs and dome-tops and the base of every cliff, belt each spire and pyramid and massy, towering temple, and in beautiful continuous lines go sweeping along the great walls in and out around all the intricate system of side-cañons, amphitheaters, cirques, and scallops into which they are sculptured. From one point hundreds of miles of this fairy embroidery may be traced. It is all so fine and orderly that it would seem that not only had the clouds and streams been kept harmoniously busy in the making of it, but that every raindrop sent like a bullet to a mark had been the subject of a separate thought, so sure is the outcome of beauty through the stormy centuries. Surely nowhere else are there illustrations so striking of the natural beauty of desolation and death, so many of nature's own mountain buildings wasting in glory of high desert air—going to dust. See how steadfast in beauty they all are in their going. Look again and again how the rough, dusty boulders and sand of disintegration from the upper ledges wreathe in beauty the next and next below with these wonderful taluses, and how the colors are finer the faster the waste. We oftentimes see Nature giving beauty for ashes—as in the flowers of a prairie after fire—but here the very dust and ashes are beautiful.

Gazing across the mighty chasm, we at last discover that it is not its great depth nor length, nor yet these wonderful buildings, that most impresses us. It is its immense width, sharply defined by precipitous walls plunging suddenly down from a flat plain, declaring in terms instantly apprehended that the vast gulf is a gash in the once unbroken plateau, made by slow, orderly erosion and removal of huge beds of rocks. Other valleys of erosion are as great—in all their dimensions some are greater—but none of these produces an effect on the imagination at once so quick and profound, coming without study, given at a glance. Therefore by far the greatest and most influential feature of this view from Bright Angel or any other of the cañon views is the opposite wall. Of the one beneath our feet we see only fragmentary sections in cirques and amphitheaters and on the sides of the out-jutting promontories between them, while the other, though far distant, is beheld in all its glory of color and noble proportions—the one supreme beauty and wonder to which the eye is ever turning. For while charming with its beauty it tells the story of the stupendous erosion of the cañon—the foundation of the unspeakable impression made on everybody. It seems a gigantic statement for even nature to make, all in one mighty stone word, apprehended at once like a burst of light, celestial color its natural vesture, coming in glory to mind and heart as to a home prepared for it from the very beginning. Wildness so godful, cosmic, primeval, bestows a new sense of earth's beauty and size. Not even from high mountains does the world seem so wide, so like a star in glory of light on its way through the heavens.

I have observed scenery-hunters of all sorts getting first views of yosemites, glaciers, White Mountain ranges, etc. Mixed with the enthusiasm which such scenery naturally excites, there is often weak gushing, and many splutter aloud like little waterfalls. Here, for a few moments at least, there is silence, and all are in dead earnest, as if awed and hushed by an earthquake—perhaps until the cook cries "Breakfast!" or the stable-boy "Horses are ready!" Then the poor unfortunates, slaves of regular habits, turn quickly away, gasping and muttering as if wondering where they had been and what had enchanted them.

Roads have been made from Bright Angel Hotel through the Coconino Forest to the ends of outstanding promontories, commanding extensive views up and down the cañon. The nearest of them, three or four miles east and west, are O'Neill's Point and Rowe's Point; the latter, besides commanding the eternally interesting cañon, gives wide-sweeping views southeast and west over the dark forest roof to the San Francisco and Mount Trumbull volcanoes—the bluest of mountains over the blackest of level woods.

Instead of thus riding in dust with the crowd, more will be gained by going quietly afoot along the rim at different times of day and night, free to observe the vegetation, the fossils in the rocks, the seams beneath overhanging ledges once inhabited by Indians, and to watch the stupendous scenery in the changing lights and shadows, clouds, showers, and storms. One need not go hunting the so-called "points of interest." The verge anywhere, everywhere, is a point of interest beyond one's wildest dreams. . . .

The dawn, as in all the pure, dry desert country is ineffably beautiful; and when the first level sunbeams sting the domes and spires, with what a burst of power the big, wild days begin! The dead and the living, rocks and hearts alike, awake and sing the new-old song of creation. All the massy headlands and salient angles of the walls, and the multitudinous temples and palaces, seem to catch the light at once, and cast thick black shadows athwart hollow and gorge, bringing out details as well as the main massive features of the architecture; while all the rocks, as if wild with life, throb and quiver and glow in the glorious sunburst, rejoicing. Every rock temple then becomes a temple of music; every spire and pinnacle an angel of light and song, shouting color hallelujahs.

As the day draws to a close, shadows, wondrous, black, and thick, like those of the morning, fill up the wall hollows, while the glowing rocks, their rough angles burned off, seem soft and hot to the heart as they stand submerged in purple haze, which now fills the cañon like a sea. Still deeper, richer, more divine grow the great walls and temples, until in the supreme flaming glory of sunset the whole cañon is transfigured, as if all the life and light of centuries of sunshine stored up and condensed in the rocks was now being poured forth as from one glorious fountain, flooding both earth and sky.

Strange to say, in the full white effulgence of the midday hours the bright colors grow dim and terrestrial in common gray haze; and the rocks, after the manner of mountains, seem to crouch and drowse and shrink to less than half their real stature, and have nothing to say to one, as if not at home. But it is fine to see how quickly they come to life and grow radiant and communicative as soon as a band of white clouds come floating by. As if shouting for joy, they seem to spring up to meet them in hearty salutation, eager to touch them and beg their blessings. It is just in the midst of these dull midday hours that the cañon clouds are born.

A good storm-cloud full of lightning and rain on its way to its work on a sunny desert day is a glorious object. Across the cañon, opposite the hotel, is a little tributary of the Colorado called Bright Angel Creek. A fountain-cloud still better deserves the name "Angel of the Desert Wells"—clad in bright plumage, carrying cool shade and living water to countless animals and plants ready to perish, noble in form and gesture, seeming able for anything, pouring life-giving, wonder-working floods from its alabaster fountains, as if some sky-lake had broken. To every gulch and gorge on its favorite ground is given a passionate torrent, roaring, replying to the rejoicing lightning—stones, tons in weight, hurrying away as if frightened, showing something of the way Grand Cañon work is done. Most of the fertile summer clouds of the cañon are of this sort, massive, swelling cumuli, growing rapidly, displaying delicious tones of purple and gray in the hollows of their sun-beaten houses, showering favored areas of the heated landscape, and vanishing in an hour or two. Some, busy and thoughtful-looking, glide with beautiful motion along the middle of the cañon in flocks, turning aside here and there, lingering as if studying the needs of particular spots, exploring side cañons, peering into hollows like birds seeking nest places, or hovering aloft on outspread wings. They scan all the red wilderness, dispensing their blessings of cool shadows and rain where the need is the greatest, refreshing the rocks, their offspring as well as the vegetation, continuing their sculpture, deepening gorges and sharpening peaks. Sometimes, blending all together, they weave a ceiling from rim to rim, perhaps opening a window here and there for sunshine to stream through, suddenly lighting some palace or temple and making it flare in the rain as if on fire.

Sometimes, as one sits gazing from a high, jutting promontory, the sky all clear, showing not the slightest wisp or penciling, a bright band of cumuli will appear suddenly, coming up the cañon in single file, as if tracing a well-known trail, passing in review, each in turn darting its lances and dropping its shower, making a row of little vertical rivers in the air above the big brown one. Others seem to grow from mere points, and fly high above the cañon, yet following its course for a long time, noiseless, as if hunting, then suddenly darting lightning at unseen marks, and hurrying on. Or they loiter here and there as if idle, like laborers out of work, waiting to be hired.

Half a dozen or more showers may oftentimes be seen falling at once, while far the greater part of the sky is in sunshine, and not a raindrop comes nigh one. These thundershowers from as many separate clouds, looking like wisps of long hair, may vary greatly in effects. The pale, faint streaks are showers that fail to reach the ground, being evaporated on the way down through the dry, thirsty air, like streams in deserts. Many, on the other hand, which in the distance seem insignificant, are really heavy rain, however local; these are the gray wisps well zigzagged with lightning. The darker ones are torrent rain, which on broad, steep slopes of favorable conformation give rise to so-called "cloud-bursts"; and wonderful is the commotion they cause. The gorges and gulches below them, usually dry, break out in loud uproar, with a sudden downrush of muddy, boulder-laden floods. Down they all go in one simultaneous gush, roaring like lions rudely awakened, each of the tawny brood actually kicking up a dust at the first onset.

During the winter months snow falls over all the high plateau, usually to a considerable depth, whitening the rim and the roofs of the cañon buildings. But last winter, when I arrived at Bright Angel in the middle of January, there was no snow in sight, and the ground was dry, greatly to my disappointment, for I had made the trip mainly to see the cañon in its winter garb. Soothingly I was informed that this was an exceptional season, and that the good snow might arrive at any time. After waiting a few days, I gladly hailed a broad-browed cloud coming grandly on from the west in big promising blackness, very unlike the white sailors of the summer skies. Under the lee of a rim-ledge, with another snow-lover, I watched its movements as it took possession of the cañon and all the adjacent region in sight. Trailing its gray fringes over the spiry tops of the great temples and towers, it gradually settled lower, embracing them all with ineffable kindness and gentleness of touch, and fondled the little cedars and pines as they quivered eagerly in the wind like young birds begging their mothers to feed them. The first flakes and crystals began to fly about noon, sweeping straight up the middle of the cañon, and swirling in magnificent eddies along the sides. Gradually the hearty swarms closed their ranks, and all the cañon was lost in gray gloom except a short section of the wall and a few trees beside us, which looked glad with snow in their needles and about their feet as they leaned out over the gulf. Suddenly the storm opened with magical effect to the north over the cañon of Bright Angel Creek, inclosing a sunlit mass of the cañon architecture, spanned by great white concentric arches of cloud like the bows of a silvery aurora. Above these and a little back of them was a series of upboiling purple clouds, and high above all, in the background, a range of noble cumuli towered aloft like snow-laden mountains, their pure pearl bosses flooded with sunshine. The whole noble picture, calmly glowing, was framed in thick gray gloom, which soon closed over it; and the storm went on, opening and closing until night covered all. . . .

Walking quietly about in the alleys and byways of the Grand Cañon city, we learn something of the way it was made; and all must admire effects so great from means apparently so simple; rain striking light hammer-blows or heavier in streams, with many rest Sundays; soft air and light, gentle sappers and miners, toiling forever; the big river sawing the plateau asunder, carrying away the eroded and ground waste, and exposing the edges of the strata to the weather; rain torrents sawing cross-streets and alleys, exposing the strata in the same way in hundreds of sections, the softer, less resisting beds weathering and receding faster, thus undermining the harder beds, which fall, not only in small weathered particles, but in heavy sheer-cleaving masses, assisted down from time to time by kindly earthquakes, rain torrents rushing the fallen material to the river, keeping the wall rock constantly exposed. Thus the cañon grows wider and deeper. So also do the side-cañons and amphitheaters, while secondary gorges and cirques gradually isolate masses of the promontories, forming new buildings, all of which are being weathered and pulled and shaken down while being built, showing destruction and creation as one. We see the proudest temples and palaces in stateliest attitudes, wearing their sheets of detritus as royal robes, shedding off showers of red and yellow stones like trees in autumn shedding their leaves, going to dust like beautiful days to night, proclaiming as with the tongues of angels the natural beauty of death.

Every building is seen to be a remnant of once continuous beds of sediments,— sand and slime on the floor of an ancient sea, and filled with the remains of animals,—and every particle of the sandstones and limestones of these wonderful structures to be derived from other landscapes, weathered and rolled and ground in the storms and streams of other ages. And when we examine the escarpments, hills, buttes, and other monumental masses of the plateau on either side of the cañon, we discover that an amount of material has been carried off in the general denudation of the region compared with which even that carried away in the making of the Grand Cañon is as nothing. Thus each wonder in sight becomes a window through which other wonders come to view. In no other part of this continent are the wonders of geology, the records of the world's auld lang syne, more widely opened, or displayed in higher piles. The whole cañon is a mine of fossils, in which five thousand feet of horizontal strata are exposed in regular succession over more than a thousand square miles of wall-space, and on the adjacent plateau region there is another series of beds twice as thick, forming a grand geological library—a collection of stone books covering thousands of miles of shelving, tier on tier, conveniently arranged for the student. And with what wonderful scriptures are their pages filled—myriad forms of successive floras and faunas, lavishly illustrated with colored drawings, carrying us back into the midst of the life of a past infinitely remote. And as we go on and on, studying this old, old life in the light of the life beating warmly about us, we enrich and lengthen our own.

THE GRAND CAÑON OF THE COLORADO

Harriet Monroe

Harriet Monroe was a hardworking and high-minded poet, playwright, journalist, art critic, literary traveler, and editor who founded *Poetry,* the most influential American magazine of verse in the twentieth century. She was working as a freelance writer when she traveled by train from Chicago to Flagstaff and then by stagecoach to the Bright Angel Hotel in Grand Canyon National Forest Preserve. The canyon had been the subject of a growing stream of articles in American and European newspapers and magazines, but Monroe felt none had yet done justice to the unique grandeur of the landscape. Her glowingly romantic essay about her visit described the canyon as a sacred and inspiring space, not just a giant curiosity. It was published in December 1899 in *Atlantic Monthly,* one of the most widely read and respected magazines of the time. Over the next few years, national interest in the canyon exploded. In 1901, the Santa Fe Railroad completed a rail spur to the South Rim and eastern tourists began to arrive by the thousands.

. . .

The earth grew bold with longing
    And called the high gods down;
Yea, though ye dwell in heaven and hell,
    I challenge their renown.
Abodes as fair I build ye
    As heaven's rich courts of pearl.
And chasms dire where floods like fire
    Ravage and roar and whirl.

Come, for my soul is weary
    Of time and death and change;
Eternity doth summon me,—
    With mightier worlds I range.
Come, for my vision's glory
    Awaits your songs and wings;
Here on my breast I bid ye rest
    From starry wanderings.

The sun-browned miner who sat opposite me in the dusty stage talked of our goal to shorten the long hours of the journey, and of the travelers who had preceded us over that lonely trail to the edge of the Grand Cañon of the Colorado River. "Yes, I have been in and out of the cañon for twenty years," he said, "and I haven't begun to understand it yet. The Lord knows, perhaps, why he gave it to us; I never felt big enough to ask." And he told the story of a young English preacher whom he once picked up near the end of the road; who, too poor to pay stage fares, was walking to the cañon; who, after two days and nights in the thirsty wastes, his canteen empty and only a few biscuits left in his pouch, was trudging bravely on, with blistered feet and aching body, because he "must see" the mighty miracle beyond.

We were out in the open endless desert, the sunburned desolate waste. Our four horses kicked up the dust of the road, and the wind whirled it into our faces and sifted it through our clothes. We had passed the halfway house, where, finding the shanty too hot, we had unpacked and eaten our luncheons out in the sun and wind. It was just at the weary moment of the long, hot drive when the starting place seemed lost in the past, and the goal still far ahead; but the thought of the preacher's ardor made us ashamed to be tired, gave us back the beauty of the day. All the morning we had driven through forests of tall pines and bare white aspens, watching the changing curves of San Francisco Mountain, whose lofty head rose streaked with white against the blue; until at last, as we rounded its foothills, the desert lay below us like a sea, and we descended to the magic shore and took passage over the billows of silver and amethyst that foamed and waved beyond and afar. Lines of opalescent light grew into rocky mesas rising steep and formidable out of the barren plain. Silvery vistas widened into deserts so barren that even sagebrush and dwarfish cactus choked there; and the only signs of life, paradoxically, were the chalk-white skeletons of animals that lay collapsing into dust beside the road. All day long we were alone with the world's immensity,—no human face or voice breaking the wastes of forest and plain, except when our tired horses thrice gave way to fresh ones, and their keepers came out from little shacks to unbuckle the harness and hear the news.

The immense and endless desolation seemed to efface us from the earth. What right had we there, on those lofty lands which never since the beginning of time had offered sustenance to man? Since first the vast plain with its mighty weight of mountains arose far out of the waters, no kindly rill or fountain had broken the silence and invited life. What hidden wells would feed the prairie dogs, what rains would slake the large thirst of the pines, while now for months the aching land must parch and burn under a cloudless sky? It was May, and yet the summer had begun in these high places of the earth, and the last flecks of snow were fading from the peaks. Following slowly the gentle grades of the road, we tried to appreciate the altitude. Was it possible that these long levels lay a mile and a half above the ocean; that this barren slope, where the wind blew keen, was only a thousand feet nearer earth than the crest of the Dent du Midi, whose notched and snowy peak dominates Lac Léman? No wonder the waters leave the great plateau to the sun, and hurl themselves against mountainous barriers, and carve out gorges and cañons in their wild eagerness to find the sea!

At last we reach the third relay station, and take on six horses instead of four, for the final pull uphill. We alight, and run up and down the shaggy little slope, and free our bodies from the long strain. We reflect that as we are traveling now, even in this primitive slavery to beasts of burden, so for many centuries our fathers had traversed the earth, knowing no swifter way. All day for seventy-five miles,—what a tyrannous abuse of time! And yet through ages and ages the lords of the earth had been so deaf to its voices that not one secret of nature's power had escaped to help them conquer her. We had left the nineteenth century behind; we were exploring the wilderness with the pioneers. We were unaware of the road, of the goal; we were pushing out into the unknown, buffeted by its denials, threatened by its wars, lured by its mysteries. The desert lay behind us now; once more the quiet forest for miles on miles. So still and sweet and sylvan were its smooth brown slopes; the tallest pines whose vision overtopped their neighbors were all unsuspicious of nature's appalling and magnificent intention. And we, we could not believe that the forest would not go on forever, even when vistas of purple began to open through the trees, even when the log-cabin hotel welcomed us to our goal.

It was like sudden death,—our passing round the corner to the other side of that primitive inn; for in a moment we stood at the end of the world, at the brink of the kingdoms of peace and pain. The gorgeous purples of sunset fell into darkness and rose into light over mansions colossal beyond the needs of our puny unwinged race. Terrific abysses yawned and darkened; magical heights glowed with iridescent fire. The earth lay stricken to the heart, her masks and draperies torn away, confessing her eternal passion to the absolving sun. And even as we watched and hearkened, the pitiful night lent deep shadows to cover her majesty and hide its awful secrets from the curious stars.

In the morning, when I went out to verify the vision, to compass earth's revelation of her soul, the sun fell to the very heart of the mystery, even from the depths rose a thrill of joy. It was morning; I had slept and eaten; the fatigue and dust of the long journey no longer oppressed me; my courage rose to meet the greatness of the world. The benevolent landlady told of a trail which led to Point Lookout, a mile and a half away, beneath whose cliffs the old deserted inn lay in a hollow. I set out with two companions of the stage, who were armed with cameras and possessed of modern ideas. They pleaded for improvements: built [sic] a railroad from Flagstaff to the rim, a summer hotel on one of those frowning cliffs; yes, even a funicular railway down to the hidden river, and pumping works which should entice its waters up the steep slope to the thirsty beasts and travelers whose drink must now be hauled from the halfway house, forty miles away. But I rose up and defended the wilderness; rejoiced in the dusty stage ride, in the rough cabin that rose so fitly from the clearing, in the vast unviolated solitudes,—in all these proofs that one of the glories of earth was still undesecrated by the chatter of facile tourists; that here we must still propitiate nature with sacrifices, pay her with toil, prove the temper of our souls before assailing her immensities. And when my companions accused me of selfishness, opened the hidden wonder to all the world, and made it the common property of literature and art, the theme of all men's praise, even like Mont Blanc and the Colosseum and Niagara, my tongue had no words of defense to utter, but my heart rejoiced the more that I had arrived before all these.

We wandered along the quietest sylvan path, which led us up and down little ravines and dales, always under the shade of tall pines, always over the brown carpet of their needles. Now and then a sudden chasm would lift a corner of the veil, and we would wonder how we dared go on. Yet on and on we went,—a mile and a half, two miles, three, and still no deserted cabin under slanting cliffs. My companions recalled the landlady's words, were sure that we had missed the road, and resolved to go back and find it; so I urged them to the search, and promised to rest and follow. But when I had rested the trail allured me; surely it was too clear to lead me wrong. I would explore it yet a little. I walked on,—five minutes, ten,—and there below me lay the hollow and the cabin. I passed it, the little silent lodge, with rough hewn seats under the broad eaves of its porch, its doors hospitably unlatched, its rooms still rudely furnished; but all dusty, voiceless, forsaken. I climbed the steep slope to the rocks, crawled half prostrate to the barest and highest, and lay there on the edge of the void, the only living thing in some unvisited world.

For surely it was not our world, this stupendous, adorable vision. Not for human needs was it fashioned, but for the abode of gods. It made a coward of me; I shrank and shut my eyes, and felt crushed and beaten under the intolerable burden of the flesh. For humanity intruded here; in these warm and glowing purple spaces disembodied spirits must range and soar, souls purged and purified and infinitely daring. I felt keenly sure of mighty presences among the edifices vast in scope and perfect in design that rose from the first foundations of the earth to the lofty level of my jagged rock. Prophets and poets had wandered here before they were born to tell their mighty tales,—Isaiah and Aeschylus and Dante, the giants who dared the utmost. Here at last the souls of great architects must find their dreams fulfilled; must recognize the primal inspiration which, after long ages, had achieved Assyrian palaces, the temples and pyramids of Egypt, the fortresses and towered cathedrals of medieval Europe. For the inscrutable Prince of builders had reared these imperishable monuments, evenly terraced upward from the remote abyss; had so cunningly planned them that mortal foot could never climb and enter, to disturb the everlasting hush. Of all richest elements they were fashioned,—jasper and chalcedony, topaz, beryl, and amethyst, firehearted opal and pearl; for they caught and held the most delicate colors of a dream, and flashed full recognition to the sun. Never on earth could such glory be unveiled,—not on level spaces of sea, not on the cold bare peaks of mountains. This was not earth; for was not heaven itself across there, rising above yonder alabaster marge in opalescent ranks for the principalities and powers? This was not earth,—I intruded here. Everywhere the proof of my unfitness abased and dazed my will: this vast unviolated silence, as void of life and death as some newborn world; this mystery of omnipotence revealed, laid bare, but incomprehensible to my weak imagining; this inaccessible remoteness of depths and heights, from the sinuous river which showed afar one or two tawny crescents curving out of impenetrable shadows, to the mighty temple of Vishnu which gilded its vast tower loftily in the sun. Not for me, not for human souls, not for any form of earthly life, was the secret of this unveiling. Who that breathed could compass it?

The strain of existence became too tense against these infinities of beauty and terror. My narrow ledge of rock was a prison. I fought against the desperate temptation to fling myself down into that soft abyss, and thus redeem the affront which the eager beating of my heart offered to its inviolable solitude. Death itself would not be too rash an apology for my invasion,—death in those happy spaces, pillowed on purple immensities of air. So keen was the impulse, so slight at that moment became the fleshly tie, that I might almost have yielded but for a sudden word in my ear,—the trill of an oriole from the pine close above me. The brave little song was a message personal and intimate, a miracle of sympathy or prophecy. And I cast myself on that tiny speck of life as on the heart of a friend,—a friend who would save me from intolerable loneliness, from utter extinction and despair. He seemed to welcome me to the infinite; to bid me go forth and range therein, and know the lords of heaven and earth who there had drunk the deep waters and taken the measure of their souls. I made him the confidant of my unworthiness; asked him for the secret, since, being winged, he was at home even here. He gave me healing and solace; restored me to the gentle amenities of our little world; enabled me to retreat through the woods, as I came, instead of taking the swift dramatic road to liberty.

I do not know how one could live long on the rim of that abyss of glory, on the brink of sensations too violent for the heart of man. I looked with wonder at the guides and innkeepers, the miners and carriers, for whom the utmost magnificence of earth is the mere background of daily living. Does it crush or inspire? Do they cease to feel it, or does it become so close a need that all earth's fields and brooks and hills are afterward a petty prison for hearts heavy with longing? When they go down to the black Inferno where that awful river still cuts its way through the first primeval shapeless rocks, where the midday darkness reveals night's stars in a cleft of sky, while the brown torrent roars and laughs at its frowning walls,—when they, mere men of the upper air, descend to that nether world, do they recognize the spirits of darkness who shout and strain and labor there? And when they emerge, and step by step ascend the shining cliffs, do they feel like Dante when he was led by his celestial love to paradise?

The days of my wanderings along the edge of the chasm were too few to reconcile my littleness with its immensity. To the end it effaced me. I found comfort in the forests, whose gentle and comprehensible beauty restored me to our human life. It was only the high priest who could enter the Holy of Holies, and he only once a year; so here, in nature's innermost sanctuary, man must be of the elect, must purify his soul with fasting and prayer and clothe it in fine raiment, if he would worthily tread the sacred ground. It is not for nothing that the secret is hidden in the wilderness, and that the innermost depths of it are inaccessible to our wingless race. At this point one or two breakneck trails lead down to the Styx-like river, but he who descends to the dark waters must return by the same road; he may not follow the torrent through the bowels of the earth except to be its sport or prey. Even though he embarks upon that fearsome journey, and even though, like Major Powell and his handful of adventurers, he escapes death by a thousand miracles, yet he may not emerge from the depths of hell through all the days and nights of the journey; he may not set foot on the purple slopes and climb to the pearly mansions,—nay, nor even behold them, overshadowed as he is by frowning walls that seem to cut the sky. For a few miles along the rim and down a trail or two to the abyss, human feet and human eyes may risk body and soul for an exceeding great reward; but for an hundred miles beyond, both to right and left, the mystery is still inviolate. He who attempts it dies of thirst in the desert, or of violence in the chasm.

Tragic stories are told of men who have lost their lives in the search for precious metals which may lie hidden or uncovered here. The great primeval flood cut its broad V through all the strata of rock, with all their veins of metallic ore, down to the earliest shapeless mass, leaving in its wake the terraced temples and towers which seem to have been planned by some architect of divinest genius to guard their treasures inviolate till the end of time. And the river, rising far to the north among mountains rich in mineral, has been washing away the sand for ages, and depositing its gold and silver and lead in the still crevices of the impenetrable chasm. Here the earth laughs at her human master, and bids him find her wealth if he dare, and bear it away if he can. A young Californian who accepted the challenge, and set forth upon the turgid water to sift its sands for gold, never emerged with his hapless men to tell the story of his search. Only near the brink of the cleft are a few miners burrowing for copper, and sending their ore up to the rim on the backs of hardy burros; as who should prick the mountain with a pin, or measure the ocean with a cup.

As I grew familiar with the vision, I could not quite explain its stupendous quality. From mountain tops one looks across greater distances, and sees range after range lifting snowy peaks into the blue. The ocean reaches out into boundless space, and the ebb and flow of its waters have the beauty of rhythmic motion and exquisitely varied color. And in the rush of mighty cataracts are power and splendor and majestic peace. Yet for grandeur appalling and unearthly, for ineffable, impossible beauty, the cañon transcends all these. It is as though to the glory of nature were added the glory of art; as though, to achieve her utmost, the proud young world had commanded architecture to build for her and color to grace the building. The irregular masses of mountain, cast up out of the molten earth in some primeval war of elements, bear no relation to these prodigious symmetrical edifices, mounted on abysmal terraces and grouped into spacious harmonies which give form to one's dreams of heaven. The sweetness of green does not last forever, but these mightily varied purples are eternal. All that grows and moves must perish, while these silent immensities endure. Lovely and majestic beyond the cunning of human thought, the mighty monuments rise to the sun as lightly as clouds that pass. And forever glorious and forever immutable, they must rebuke man's pride with the vision of ultimate beauty, and fulfill earth's dream of rest after her work is done.

THE RIVER

THE SONG OF THE COLORADO

Sharlot Hall

Sharlot Hall's family moved to the Arizona Territory from Kansas in 1882 and established a homestead, Orchard Ranch, where they raised horses and panned for gold. Hall left home for schooling in Prescott and Los Angeles, and she soon began publishing articles, essays, and poems in territorial newspapers and in the important regional magazine *Land of Sunshine*. Her writing earned her an appointment as territorial historian from 1909 to 1912, the first time a woman held public office in Arizona. In 1911, she explored the Arizona Strip north of Grand Canyon and then published a series of influential articles that convinced the territorial government to defend its claim to the area against attempted annexation by Utah. Her first book of poems, *Cactus and Pine: Songs of the Southwest* (1911), was dedicated "to the land that mothered my soul." Hall's poetry, like that of many of her contemporaries, can sound overly theatrical to modern readers, but in the case of this poetic tribute to the power and permanence of the Colorado River, her grandiose style fits well with her imposing subject.

. . .

From the heart of the mighty mountains strong-souled for my fate I came,
My far-drawn track to a nameless sea through a land without a name;
And the earth rose up to hold me, to bid me linger and stay;
And the brawn and bone of my mother's race were set to bar my way.

Yet I stayed not, I could not linger; my soul was tense to the call
The wet winds sing when the long waves leap and beat on the far sea wall.

I stayed not, I could not linger; patient, resistless, alone,
I hewed the trail of my destiny deep in the hindering stone.

How narrow that first dim pathway—yet deepening hour by hour!
Years, ages, eons, spent and forgot, while I gathered me might and power
To answer the call that led me, to carve my road to the sea,
Till my flood swept out with that greater tide as tireless and tameless and free.

From the far, wild land that bore me, I drew my blood as wild—
I, born of the glacier's glory, born of the uplands piled
Like stairs to the door of heaven, that the Maker of All might go
Down from His place with honor, to look on the world and know

That the sun and the wind and the waters, and the white ice cold and still,
Were moving aright in the plan He had made, shaping His wish and will.
When the spirit of worship was on me, turning alone, apart,
I stayed and carved me temples deep in the mountain's heart,

Wide-domed and vast and silent, meet for the God I knew,
With shrines that were shadowed and solemn and altars of richest hue;
And out of my ceaseless striving I wrought a victor's hymn,
Flung up to the stars in greeting from my far track deep and dim.

For the earth was put behind me; I reckoned no more with them
That come or go at her bidding, and cling to her garment's hem.
Apart in my rock-hewn pathway, where the great cliffs shut me in,
The storm-swept clouds were my brethren, and the stars were my kind and kin.

Tireless, alone, unstaying, I went as one who goes
On some high and strong adventure that only his own heart knows.
Tireless, alone, unstaying, I went in my chosen road—
I trafficked with no man's burden—I bent me to no man's load.

On my tawny, sinuous shoulders no salt-gray ships swung in;
I washed no feet of cities, like a slave whipped out and in;
My will was the law of my moving in the land that my strife had made—
As a man in the house he has builded, master and unafraid.

O ye that would hedge and bind me—remembering whence I came!
I, that was, and was mighty, ere your race had breath or name!
Play with your dreams in the sunshine—delve and toil and plot—
Yet I keep the way of my will to the sea, when ye and your race are not!

CANYON SOLITUDE

Patricia McCairen

When Patricia McCairen was growing up in New York City, her mother expected her to follow tradition by getting married and becoming a housewife. While rafting down the Colorado as a passenger on a commercial river trip, McCairen found the courage to strike out on her own path. Life on the river was irresistible, so she defied the opinions of family and friends, left her home in New York, and moved west to start a new life as a whitewater raft guide. At the time, the late 1970s, the river business was a man's world, and McCairen struggled unsuccessfully to find a job in the canyon. But she did work on other western rivers for five years, before turning to full-time writing and photography. Her 1998 memoir, *Canyon Solitude,* describes her journey to complete independence during a solo river trip through Grand Canyon. Rowing alone for twenty-five days in the Colorado's towering rapids and swirling eddies, she tested the depths of her own self-reliance, disproving the doubts of those who said a woman should not go down the river alone.

. . .

Solitude has a sound all its own, a feeling, a special vision. With each stroke on the oars, I draw myself deeper into its realm. This solitude differs distinctly from the times I've spent alone in my home or walking through the woods by myself. Hesitantly, I sample it. Otherworldly, risky, fascinating. Intimidating, serene, vulnerable. Yes, I'm terribly small and vulnerable, minuscule compared to this deep, green river and the walls growing up around me.

The canyon is familiar, yet strange, like an old friend under new circumstances. An imperceptible inner excitement pulsates through my veins, compelling me to absorb every impression I feel, hear, see. My senses sharpen, taking me beyond myself, beyond my fears, into another world. Within two miles of Lees Ferry, the well-known walls have risen quickly on either side of a river that has wedged itself between solid rock. The vermillion cliffs are gone, hidden behind Kaibab Limestone that sits on top of the Toroweap Formation. The rest of the world has disappeared. It is just the canyon, the river and me. To be here, that is all there is. Nothing more is necessary. Nothing more exists.

Complex designs created by the walls cracking and breaking under great pressure form filigree patterns; a cactus growing out of a crevice in bare rock illustrates survival under sparse conditions; a rock balanced on the edge of a precipice waits for the right moment to fall. Not if, but when. Sometime in the next million years, or a moment after I pass.

I hold still and listen. The river gurgles as it plays around a rock; a birdsong penetrates the silence with sharp, sweet notes, then stops. Silence upon silence.

Abruptly, the quiet is terminated by a sudden movement. Startled, I look around and see a pair of ducks take off, squandering energy in their haste to flee. Then, with a quack that undoubtedly says, "Wait for me," a third duck follows. They land within sight downstream, and as I approach, take off again in the same formation: first the couple, then the lone duck. This is repeated three or four times, until I begin to hope they'll accompany me on my voyage. But the next time I draw near, they circle overhead and fly back upstream.

I sweep my oars through the water, pushing on one while pulling on the other—a Double-Oar Pivot, in rafter's language. The stern, or rear of the raft, now faces downstream, and I look upstream. I glance over my shoulder, line up the boat in the direction I want to go and pull evenly on both oars.

Rowing is a clean action, unadulterated in its purpose or movement. In flowing, flat water with no upstream wind, the relaxing, repetitive rhythm has a meditative quality to it. Lean forward, dip blades in water, lean back, pull; lean forward, dip blades in water, lean back, pull. Over and over and over.

I glance over my shoulder again. Navajo Bridge is in sight. The "what color is the river" bridge. The only motorized crossing of Grand Canyon. It looks farther away from down below than the river looked from above. I pivot the raft and face downstream toward the bridge. . . .

I study the bridge carefully. Have our times coincided? My heart leaps and I smile. A small yellow truck creeps slowly across the steel structure. Midway, Dee leans out the window, arm raised high, waving back and forth. I return the wave, eagerly trying to close the gap between us. In a minute he is gone. A few minutes later the bridge is behind me, and solitude closes in once again.

Now I am truly alone. It is the aloneness of the wilderness, starkly real and present—I can no longer even look forward to a glimpse of my friend. The next place I can expect to see anyone is Phantom Ranch, eighty-three miles and seven days downriver.

"This is it," I say out loud. "Another Grand trip, another few weeks between the walls." Elation takes shape deep inside me and rises like a bubble seeking the surface of the river, bursting forth in laughter that evolves to love as I stare at the river. *The* river. A green, brown, chocolate, red, clear, silty, raging, tranquil ribbon of energy. The river is everything: nothing more, nothing less. A power that courses through the artery of the canyon, transforming, converting, quietly and slowly, steadily and persistently. Powerful even in tranquility. Powerful even when tamed by humans. A power that is there by its very existence. Not a greedy, controlling power, but one to be respected, a power of an entity so complete, so self-contained, it has no need of another.

She is a power that teaches those who open themselves to her. Her lessons may be subtle, or frightening. She cares not if we learn: It is up to us to seek her out. I have chosen to join her here in her home. The pupil coming to the mentor, the lover to the beloved, the searching soul to the guru. The child returning home to her mother.

Changing, changing, constantly changing, she casts a rhythmic, sensuous spell. A sleek, beautiful goddess, alluringly seductive, forgiving to those who love her, dispassionately indifferent to those who do not. Lovingly she folds herself around a rock, teasingly she laps at the shore, stroking and caressing it, forming and molding it to her desires. Playfully she gurgles, laughing and talking to whoever will listen. As late afternoon arrives, her surface sparkles. Bedecked in a million diamonds, she dances a sunlit dream lost in ecstasy. In the flash of an instant she is capable of creating a bubbling, intoxicating happiness or a frustrating helplessness, the highest exhilaration or the deepest, darkest fear.

She vacillates in these first few miles. Slowly she swirls around, swinging one way, then another, crossing from shore to shore, ambling upstream, then down, losing the thread of her current so that I must dig deep with my oars to keep from aimlessly strolling with her. In this languid state she entices the uninitiated into a false sense of confidence, beguiling them with the belief that they are more powerful than she and nothing she does will affect them. I know better, for I have seen her in her fury, or just simply playing in her own mysterious way. Without a moment's notice her mood changes, and suddenly she leaps high into the air, crashing over and around boulders, flinging herself on them with wild abandon and an ebullience that can be unsettling. She dances with excitement, enjoying her display of potency, enticing me to join in her play. Then just as abruptly, she settles down, heaving and churning as if breathing deeply after her great exertion. Once again she flows with a gentle nonchalance, encouraging me to forget the display she put on only moments before.

I surrender myself to her and, in so doing, gain strength. Now, drifting alone in my little boat, I pray to her and the canyon gods to be kind and allow me to pass unharmed.

I grab the oars and pull in earnest. I need to make miles and chase away the October chill that steals energy from my bones. Even without a watch, I know it's late afternoon, and the place I want to camp is still four miles away.

Dark green water slips under my boat. Soon I hear the rumbling of Badger Rapid. As the noise grows louder, my skin tingles in familiar anticipation. I look over my shoulder. The river disappears over the rapid's steep drop, leaving me viewing a straight, horizontal line. Occasionally a spray of white jumps high above the line, inviting me to play.

In the 277-mile length of Grand Canyon there are approximately seventy-five named rapids, plus numerous riffles. Sometime in the past, someone rated the rapids on a scale of one to ten, ten being the most difficult. An accomplished boatman I know claims that a rapid is nothing more than water running downhill over rocks. Zen or denial? I'm not sure. I do know that too much fear or not enough can create confusion, so that anything can happen and often does.

I glance quickly at the guidebook lying on top of the load. At this water level Badger is rated a six. I tuck everything away and, to gain height, stand up on the boxes tied directly in front of my seat. Meticulously, I study the rapid, gauging the nuances of the current. I float closer, still standing, until I'm near the brink. A touch of adrenaline adds a keen edge to my senses. Then in one motion I hit the seat, grab my oars and align *Sunshine Lady* between two breaking waves. Four- and five-foot standing waves follow. She rises just enough to keep from taking on water, feeling solid and steady with the weight of the load in the bow. In less than a minute I am at the bottom of the rapid. I pull over to a white sand beach.

A sandbar estate waits to be settled. It's large enough for a party of twenty-five or thirty, so I have ample space to furnish it as I wish. I decide upon a place for the kitchen and bedroom, change my mind and decide upon another. The novelty of being in my first camp alone adds an element of excitement to an otherwise mundane chore. I find a level place and set up my tent. When it is erect, I unpack my Therm-A-Rest mattress, releasing the valve so it will inflate itself. Next I unroll my sleeping bag and arrange the cotton sheet liner inside it. With everything ready for the night, I open a waterproof bag and pull out dry clothes. Cotton and wool hug my chilled skin.

I walk back to *Sunshine Lady*. It's time to set up the kitchen. I grab a plywood board that serves as a rear deck and screw four two-foot lengths of pipe into the deck's flanges. A moment later I have a table. I then place two twenty-millimeter ammo boxes next to the table. The heavier one contains my entire kitchen commissary—pots, pans and utensils—while the lighter box holds staple items—flour, honey, tea, oil, powdered milk, matches, and so on. I rout around a box or two still tied on the raft and take out a quick and easy meal.

With dinner started, I level out a place in the sand upwind of the table for a firepan and go in search of fuel. The beach is strewn with driftwood, and within half an hour I have more than enough wood for the night and following morning. I start a fire and sit next to it while I fill the empty cavern in my midsection. The late afternoon sun burns the canyon walls crimson.

A fire, hot food, a cozy tent and a warm bed—this is my home for the night. River runners, backpackers, adventurers of all types know how to create an instant home, as snug and restful as any permanent structure. All true wanderers can quickly set up lodging that reflects both their personality and their familiarity with a wilderness setting. Though we may have a dwelling elsewhere to contain our everyday life, this is the home of our soul. . . .

The Colorado is a typical desert river with a negligible gradient that drops eight feet per mile throughout the length of Grand Canyon, yet it contains some of the biggest rapids in North America. Unlike mountain rivers with their steep gradients, where water crashes through a narrow passageway over and around rocks creating a technical obstacle course, the Colorado heaves itself into towering waves or powerful hydraulics that form holes, reversals, boils, whirlpools and turbulent eddy fences. Voluminous amounts of water course through the bottom of the canyon. While mountain streams often flow at one or two thousand cubic feet per second, the Colorado River is considered low at levels below ten thousand cfs. As volume grows so does velocity and power.

Between each big drop, the Colorado River pools out, sometimes for less than a mile, more frequently for a distance of two to five miles and occasionally for more than twenty miles. The topography of the canyon determines where rapids occur. Adjacent to every drop on the Colorado lies the inevitable side canyon. A build-up of cumulus clouds over a particular drainage sends a heavy rainfall down a dry wash, turning it into a raging turmoil. As a flash flood gains momentum, rocks and boulders are spewed into the river, forcing it into a narrower space. If the flash flood is small, an inconsequential riffle is formed. But when a major storm drives huge boulders and tons of mud down a side drainage into the river, a rapid is born.

For many years, whitewater was considered unrunnable. During his trips of 1869 and 1872, Major [John Wesley] Powell portaged or lined his boats around most of the canyon's big drops. He was an explorer and a scientist, not a whitewater boatman. But as time passed and interest grew, river runners developed techniques for navigating rapids, and a new sport was born.

A myth existed for many years, and lingers still, that maintains it takes a large, powerful man to row a boat through whitewater. The truth is, it takes brains to run a rapid—not brawn. The key to a flawless run is understanding the dynamics of a river. The direction and velocity of the current, the power of a hydraulic and the force of a cresting wave deliver specific messages to be read and examined closely, like important documents. I take it seriously. This chronicle could save my life.

Learning to maneuver a boat was a challenge, full of mistakes and triumphs. But when my heavy oars finally felt light, when my awkward strokes evolved into fluid motion and when I learned to read the complex language of a rapid, I gave myself a gift of exhilaration and vitality that transcended ordinary experience. And for every year I row, the joy of running rivers increases.

I walk along the narrow pathways that meander between the tamarisks to scout Granite Rapid. At the mouth of Monument Creek the jungle of feathery branches ends, cut off as abruptly as a sharp knife cuts off the head of a fish. The massive boulder garden that once barreled down the side canyon wiped out the trees. I step carefully over the boulders looking for a good vantage point.

A boulder garden on the left pushes most of the current to the right against a sheer wall, resulting in ten-foot curling waves that rebound off the wall at a forty-five-degree angle to the main current. Meanwhile, other curlers angle off the first, creating an upside down V. It's an ugly hydraulic, for it's often difficult, if not impossible, to keep a boat from turning sideways to one or another of the waves. As a result, runs through Granite are often wildly out of control. And there's no easy way to avoid the right run, for the left passage is blocked by two unrunnable holes, one at the top of the rapid and the other in the center.

I like holes as much as a cat likes a bath. They're dangerous and unpredictable. From exploding monsters that curl back upstream to quiet "keepers" filled with white, foaming, aerated water, holes always pose a problem. When water pours over a rock that is fairly close to the surface, it dives to the bottom of the river leaving a "hole" that must be filled in. The filling takes place when the surface of the river reverses itself into a backflow. Rowing a raft into a hole is akin to riding a bicycle at high speed into a pothole.

If a rock is very close to the surface or partially exposed, the hole behind it appears flat as water rushes back upstream toward the rock. The hole is called a "keeper" when it stops a raft cold and holds it in the bubbling froth where the backwash meets the downstream rush of water. I've had intimate rendezvous with keeper holes, and they've all been terrifying.

When a raft slips over the brink into one of these killers, it is pounded, spun around and shaken. Gear can be ripped off the raft, a frame bent, a seat snapped in two. During frantic seconds that seem like hours, as you try to keep the raft from flipping and from falling in the hole yourself, you search for a downstream current to grab with an oar in order to pull the boat out of the hole's grasp. If the hole is large enough, the downstream current is far out of reach and you remain stuck, looking into the face of death while recirculating around the hole until it decides to release you—usually after the raft is full of water.

It's easy enough to keep away from Granite's holes. The challenge lies in staying upright in the V-waves and missing a large swirling eddy at the bottom right of the rapid. The force of the water going downstream against the surge of the water traveling upstream forms the eddy fence, a fluvial barrier sometimes strong enough to flip a raft. Many, such as the one at the bottom of Granite Rapid, are powerful enough to make it extremely difficult, if not impossible, to cross in order to rejoin the main current.

I scout large rapids, reading them from the bottom up. I note each obstacle, its location and relationship to the main current. I have to: Once I start my run I'm committed, and if a hole or rock is in my path, I might need to take strokes away from it long before I actually reach it.

I push off from shore and pull hard on the oars, using my entire body to row the boat across the width of the river. My race with the current is a close one, and at the last moment I slip to the right of the hole and drop over the lip into the rapid. I point *Sunshine Lady*'s bow into the apex of a curling V and begin a wild ride up the side of one wave and down another. At the end of the rapid the boat is brimming with water. I turn and look upstream. The rapid graces the brown river with a beautiful white bodice of froth. Seconds later the river carries me around a bend, and Granite is out of sight. As I float in the calm stretch between Granite and Hermit Rapids I bail gallons of water out of the raft. . . .

In the distance, against a black wall darkened by its own shadow, a fine, almost imperceptible mist ascends out of the river. Far above the mist and the occasional splash of water leaping high into the air, far above the sound that resembles the roar of fans in a stadium, I pull *Sunshine Lady* over to the right shore. Involuntarily my stomach muscles tighten.

The rapid that causes the mist to hang heavy in the air is a legend. A Sagittarius with a reputation. Before December 7, 1966, she contained burbles and bubbles and not much more. Then a heavy storm moved over the North Rim and dropped fourteen inches of rain within a thirty-six-hour period, turning the side canyon into a raging monster. The flood wiped out pueblo sites that had existed for nine hundred years and washed a fan of boulders into the river, giving birth to a wild child known as Crystal Rapid.

Crystal's fame grew, and for more than sixteen years she terrified boaters with a nightmarish hole and a rock garden. The hole snuggled against the left wall just below the mouth of Slate Creek, randomly mushrooming twenty feet above its trough before crashing in upon itself like an explosion gone awry. The rock garden, downstream from the hole, loomed in the center of the river with naked fangs of granite and schist.

As if dissatisfied with her notoriety, in 1983 she expanded to awesome proportions. That summer the Colorado River peaked at ninety-two thousand cfs [cubic feet per second]. Giant boulders rumbled beneath the raging waters, and a new hole, rising to heights of forty feet, formed a barrier across the gateway of the rapid. Within a week Crystal demolished seven thirty-three-foot pontoon motor rigs and killed one person. More than one hundred people had to be evacuated from the canyon by helicopter.

Boatmen and women prayed for the flood to transform Crystal. Their prayers were answered. When the high water subsided, the old hole was gone, replaced by a solid wall of water at her entrance that can lead straight to hell. . . .

I'm more alone than I have ever been before. On previous trips I had someone else with whom to confer and share the excitement and apprehension. Which leaves me in a unique situation: I'm alone and I'm not going to wait for someone else to show up.

Fear erupts like the exploding waves in a rapid; rowing Crystal is suddenly unthinkable. My shoes are lead weights, affixed to this rock I'm standing on. Stuck once again. What difference does it make where it happens or what causes it? Fear is a prison door waiting to confine me when I give in to it. All my fears congregate, each one clamoring for attention. Fear of being confined and losing my freedom. Fear of loving, fear of being intimate and exposing myself to another. Fear of rejection. Fear of being dependent on another. Fear of leaving a job I hate because it provides security. Fears that cause me to create excuses for my contradictory behavior, to spend months searching for an ideal, then run from it as soon as it is within my grasp.

I've tried burying my fears in the sand and writing them on a piece of paper to be thrown into a fire. These symbolic acts struck me as a beautiful way to rid myself of my fears so I could be free. But my fears returned, stronger than they were before. All the running and burying and denying and excuses have not worked. Once again I'm plagued with fear and self-doubt as I stand above Crystal.

A sensible side of myself provides an excuse. A certain amount of fear can serve a purpose, honing me to a razor's edge so that I am keen and sharp and able to make fast, decisive moves. The secret is knowing whether I have crossed the thin line between having just enough apprehension to see danger clearly and being so overwhelmed by fear that I'm paralyzed. I think back to the first time I rowed Lava Falls. I was overcome with fear, until a friend told me to turn my negative energy positive by putting my fear into the river and not allowing it to disarm me of my power. My run through Lava that day was excellent.

"Your fear has very little to do with my ferocity," Crystal declares. "The hole is no larger than it was when you went through it years ago. It's your emotions you're afraid of, not me."

I nod. Her truth is too penetrating to ignore.

My emotional fears may not be as tangible as her rocks or holes, and they may be easier to deny, but by not dealing with them I'm running the same rapid over and over, going into the same holes that continually tear me apart. I'm repeating mistakes by not looking at myself and accepting the fears that are part of me.

They need to be acknowledged in the same way that the river's obstacles require attention. Fears must be embraced, treated like friends instead of enemies, acknowledged in the same way I respond to whitewater—with reverence and respect.

I watch the river roll by, and as I study Crystal, my perspective changes. I've stopped coming apart. She is steadying me, bringing me back to reality and away from the illusory world of fear.

When I first met Mother River, I realized immediately that she was a source of knowledge for me. As a beginner, I'd sit in an eddy behind a boulder in the middle of a rapid, fascinated by the water's motion. I wanted to learn to row well, and as I learned, I gained a sense that if I managed my life the same way I guided a raft through a rapid, I would be very successful. When I rowed too hard and fought the current, I usually didn't get where I wanted to go. Or worse, I might be thrown out of the boat into the river, where I was truly helpless. If I let the boat go without guidance, I was no better off. As my rowing improved, I came to understand that using the river's strength, direction and flow helped me more than absolute control or total passivity.

I uproot my feet and walk along the edge of the river, studying the rapid, picking out a particular curl of a wave, a pillow of water as it flows up on a rock. I examine each subtlety until it is established firmly in my memory, and there is no chance I will get lost when I begin my run.

Back at *Sunshine Lady*, I tuck things away, untie and gently shove off. I float slowly downstream, holding the raft just outside the eddy that hugs the right shoreline. As I near the head of the rapid, I pivot the raft, turning the stern downstream at a forty-five-degree angle to the current, which gives me additional power when I pull on the oars. It is at this moment, on the edge of the rapid, that everything else disappears. I am totally focused—nothing else matters, nothing else exists. Everything blends together: Even *Sunshine Lady* no longer exists of her own entirety, but instead becomes part of me, and the two of us together become part of the rapid.

I hug the right shoreline, skirting smooth stones and small holes, neither pushing the river nor allowing her to sweep me away. I pass by Crystal Hole with more than a boat length to spare, awed by her power and majesty. Maybe I have finally learned to acknowledge and accept my fears, learned that they are more like a collection of rapids than the monsters I make them out to be. If I can deal with them as I do rapids, I may even learn something about my own vulnerability.

At the bottom of the rapid I catch an eddy and look back upstream. This river is my mother and she loves me. I'm certain of that.

STONE CREEK WOMAN

Terry Tempest Williams

Six generations ago, in 1847, Terry Tempest Williams's ancestors marched to Utah with Brigham Young. For five generations since, her family has both lived in and made its living from the desert, for they are avid outdoorspeople and hardworking owners of a business that lays the long-distance pipes and cables that connect the modern West. Her classic memoir, *Refuge: An Unnatural History of Family and Place* (1992), exposes the sometimes painful ironies of the region's environmental history; the book tells how, during her mother Diane's struggle with cancer that may have been caused by exposure to atomic bomb tests, the two women found spiritual strength in their shared bond with the Bear River Migratory Bird Refuge on the Great Salt Lake. For two decades, Williams has been one of the most principled and passionate voices for environmental justice and wilderness preservation in the West, a spokesperson for what she calls the "Coyote Clan," those "hundreds, maybe even thousands, of individuals who are quietly subversive on behalf of the land." In this essay, she describes one of the places, Stone Creek in Grand Canyon, where she finds both the inspiration and the determination to speak out for nature.

. . .

Few know her, but she is always there—Stone Creek Woman—watching over the Colorado River.

Over the years, I have made pilgrimages to her, descending into the Grand Canyon, passing through geologic layers with names like Kayenta, Moenave, Chinle, Shinarump, Toroweap, Coconino, and Supai to guide me down the stone staircase of time. It is always a pleasant journey downriver to Mile 132—Stone

Creek, a small tributary that flows into the Colorado. We secure our boats and meander up the side canyon where the heat of the day seeps into our skin, threatens to boil our blood, and we can imagine ourselves as lizards pushing up and down on the hot, coral sand. They watch us step from stone to stone along the streambed. The lizards vanish and then we see her. Stone Creek Woman: guardian of the desert with her redrock face, maidenhair ferns, and waterfall of expression. Moss, the color of emeralds, drapes across her breasts.

I discovered her by accident. My husband, Brooke, and I were with a group on a river trip. It was high noon in June. Twice that morning the boatman had mentioned Stone Creek and what a refuge it would be: the waterfall, the shade-filled canyon; the constant breeze; the deep green pool. Searing heat inspired many of us to jump off the boats before they had been tied down. The group ran up Stone Creek in search of the enchanted pool at the base of the waterfall, leaving me behind.

I sauntered up Stone Creek. Sweat poured off my forehead and I savored the salt on my lips. The dry heat reverberated off the canyon's narrow walls. I relished the sensation of being baked. I walked even more slowly, aware of the cicadas, their drone that held the pulse of the desert. An evening primrose bloomed. I knelt down and peeked inside yellow petals. The pistil and stamens resembled stars. My index finger brushed them, gently, and I inhaled pollen. No act seemed too extravagant in these extreme temperatures. Even the canyon wren's joyous anthem, each falling note, was slow, full, and luxurious. In this heat, nothing was rushed.

Except humans.

Up ahead, I heard laughter, splashing, and the raucous play of friends. I turned the corner and found them bathing, swimming, and sunning. It was a kalcidoscope of color. Lycra bodies, some fat, some thin, sunburned, forgetting all manner of self-consciousness. They were drunk with pleasure.

I sat on a slab of sandstone near the edge of the pool with my knees pulled into my chest and watched, mesmerized by the throbbing waterfall at Stone Creek, its sudden surges of energy, how the moss anchored on the redrock cliff became neon in sunlight, how the long green strands resembled hair, how the fine spray rising from the water nurtured rainbows.

I eventually outwaited everyone. As Brooke led them back to the boats, the glance we exchanged told me I had a few precious moments I could steal for myself. And in that time, I shed my clothing like snakeskin. I swam beneath the waterfall, felt its pelting massage on my back, stood up behind it, turned and touched the moss, the ferns, the slippery rock wall. No place else to be.

I sank into the pool and floated momentarily on my back. The waterfall became my focus once again. Suddenly, I began to see a face emerging from behind the veil of water. Stone Creek Woman. I stood. I listened to her voice.

Since that hot June day, I have made a commitment to visit Stone Creek Woman as often as I can. I believe she monitors the floods and droughts of the Colorado Plateau, and I believe she can remind us that water in the West is never to be taken for granted. When the water flows over the sandstone wall, through the moss and the ferns, she reveals herself. When there is no water, she disappears.

For more than five million years, the Colorado River has been sculpting the Grand Canyon. Stone Creek, as a small tributary to the Colorado, plays its own role in this geologic scheme. The formation I know as Stone Creek Woman has witnessed these changes. The Colorado River, once in the soul-service of cutting through rocks, is now truncated by ten major dams generating twelve million kilowatts of electricity each year. Red water once blessed with sediments from Glen Canyon is now sterile and blue. Cows drink it. We drink it. And crops must be watered. By the time twenty million people in seven western states quench their individual thirsts and hose down two million acres of farmland for their food, the Colorado River barely trickles into the Gulf of California.

If at all.

Water in the American West is blood. Rivers, streams, creeks, become arteries, veins, capillaries. Dam, dike, or drain any of them and somewhere, silence prevails. No water: no fish. No water: no plants. No water: no life. Nothing breathes. The land-body becomes a corpse. Stone Creek Woman crumbles and blows away.

Deserts are defined by their dryness, heat, and austerity of form. It is a landscape best described not by what it is, but by what it is not.

It is not green.

It is not lush.

It is not habitable.

Stone Creek Woman knows otherwise. Where there is water, the desert is verdant. Hanging gardens on slickrock walls weep generously with columbines, monkey flowers, and mertensia. A thunderstorm begins to drum. Lightning dances above the mesa. Clouds split. Surging rain scours canyons in a flash of flood. An hour later, there is a clearing. Potholes in the sandstone become basins to drink from. Creatures—coyote, kit fox, rattlesnake, mule deer—adapted to the call of aridity, drink freely, filling themselves from this temporary abundance. Stone Creek Woman begins to dance.

I want to join them.

Wallace Stegner, in his book *The Sound of Mountain Water,* says, "In this country you cannot raise your eyes without looking a hundred miles. You can hear coyotes who have somehow escaped the air-dropped poison baits designed to exterminate them. You can see in every sandy pocket the pug tracks of wildcats, and every water pocket in the rock will give you a look backward into geologic time, for every such hole swarms with triangular crablike creatures locally called tadpoles but actually first cousins to the trilobites who left their fossil skeletons in the Paleozoic."

And here stands Stone Creek Woman, guardian and gauge of the desert, overlooking the Colorado River, with her redrock face, her maidenhair ferns, and waterfall of expression. I have found a handful of people who have seen her. There may be more. Some say she cannot speak. Others will tell you she is only to be imagined. But in the solitude of that side canyon where I swam at her feet, she reminds me we must stand vigilant.

GONE BACK INTO THE EARTH

Barry Lopez

Winner of the National Book Award and many other honors, Barry Lopez explores the way that spiritual connections to the natural world can help people imagine and live what he calls "lives of resistance." In a world where people are pressured to conform and consume, a world where most people can identify hundreds of corporate logos but only a few wild plants or animals, Lopez believes that immersing oneself in nature can be a radical act. In our amnesiac world, nature writing is an "act of defiance" that "works against our tendency to forget" that our lives depend on the health of the planet that is our only home. In his essay "Gone Back into the Earth," Lopez tells the story of a river trip with a group of artists who set out to create new kinds of music in collaboration with the intimate spaces of the inner gorge's side canyons. After a week and a half on the river, Lopez finds that he has been changed in fundamental ways, and he asks whether the power of wilderness to bring forth new and empowering forms of awareness is not its highest value.

· · ·

I am up to my waist in a basin of cool, acid-clear water, at the head of a box canyon some 600 feet above the Colorado River. I place my outstretched hands flat against a terminal wall of dark limestone, which rises more than a hundred feet above me, and down which a sheet of water falls—the thin creek in whose pooled waters I now stand. The water splits at my fingertips into wild threads; higher up, a warm canyon wind lifts water off the limestone in a fine spray; these droplets intercept and shatter sunlight. Down, down another four waterfalls and fern-shrouded pools below, the water spills into an eddy of the Colorado River, in the shadow of a huge boulder. Our boat is tied there.

This lush crease in the surface of the earth is a cleft in the precipitous desert walls of Arizona's Grand Canyon. Its smooth outcrops of purple-tinged travertine stone, its heavy air rolled in the languid perfume of columbine, struck by the sharp notes of a water ouzel, the trill of a disturbed black phoebe—all this has a name: Elves Chasm.

A few feet to my right, a preacher from Maryland is staring straight up at a blue sky, straining to see what flowers those are that nod at the top of the falls. To my left a freelance automobile mechanic from Colorado sits with an impish smile by helleborine orchids. Behind, another man, a builder and sometime record producer from New York, who comes as often as he can to camp and hike in the Southwest, stands immobile at the pool's edge.

Sprawled shirtless on a rock is our boatman. He has led twelve or fifteen of us on the climb up from the river. The Colorado entrances him. He has a well-honed sense of the ridiculous, brought on, one believes, by so much time in the extreme remove of this canyon.

In our descent we meet others in our group who stopped climbing at one of the lower pools. At the second to the last waterfall, a young woman with short hair and dazzling blue eyes walks with me back into the canyon's narrowing V. We wade into a still pool, swim a few strokes to its head, climb over a boulder, swim across a second pool, and then stand together, giddy, in the press of limestone, beneath the deafening cascade—filled with euphoria.

One at a time we bolt and glide, fishlike, back across the pool, grounding in fine white gravel. We wade the second pool and continue our descent, stopping to marvel at the strategy of a barrel cactus and at the pale shading of color in the ledges to which we cling. We share few words. We know hardly anything of each other. We share the country.

The group of us who have made this morning climb are in the middle of a ten-day trip down the Colorado River. Each day we are upended, if not by some element of the landscape itself then by what the landscape does, visibly, to each of us. It has snapped us like fresh-laundered sheets.

After lunch, we reboard three large rubber rafts and enter the Colorado's quick, high flow. The river has not been this high or fast since Glen Canyon Dam—135 miles above Elves Chasm, 17 miles above our starting point at Lees Ferry—was closed in 1963. Jumping out ahead of us, with its single oarsman and three passengers, is our fourth craft, a twelve-foot rubber boat, like a water strider with a steel frame. In Sockdolager Rapid the day before, one of its welds burst and the steel pieces were bent apart. (Sockdolager: a nineteenth-century colloquialism for knockout punch.)

Such groups as ours, the members all but unknown to each other on the first day, almost always grow close, solicitous of each other, during their time together. They develop a humor that informs similar journeys everywhere, a humor founded in tomfoolery, in punning, in a continuous parody of the life-in-civilization all have so recently (and gleefully) left. Such humor depends on context, on an accretion of small, shared events; it seems silly to those who are not there. It is not, of course. Any more than that moment of fumbling awe one feels on seeing the Brahma schist at the dead bottom of the canyon's Inner Gorge. Your fingertips graze the 1.9-billion-year-old stone as the boat drifts slowly past.

With the loss of self-consciousness, the landscape opens.

There are forty-one of us, counting a crew of six. An actor from Florida, now living in Los Angeles. A medical student and his wife. A supervisor from Virginia's Department of Motor Vehicles. A health-store owner from Chicago. An editor from New York and his young son.

That kind of diversity seems normal in groups that seek such vacations—to trek in the Himalaya, to dive in the Sea of Cortez, to go birding in the Arctic. We are together for two reasons: to run the Colorado River, and to participate with jazz musician Paul Winter, who initiated the trip, in a music workshop.

Winter is an innovator and a listener. He had thought for years about coming to the Grand Canyon, about creating music here in response to this particular landscape—collared lizards and prickly pear cactus, Anasazi Indian ruins and stifling heat. But most especially he wanted music evoked by the river and the walls that flew up from its banks—Coconino sandstone on top of Hermit shale on top of the Supai formations, stone exposed to sunlight, a bloom of photons that lifted colors—saffron and ochre, apricot, madder orange, pearl and gray green, copper reds, umber and terra-cotta browns—and left them floating in the air.

Winter was searching for a reintegration of music, landscape, and people. For resonance. Three or four times during the trip he would find it for sustained periods: drifting on a quiet stretch of water below Bass Rapids with oboist Nancy Rumbel and cellist David Darling; in a natural amphitheater high in the Muav limestone of Matkatameba Canyon; on the night of a full June moon with euphonium player Larry Roark in Blacktail Canyon.

Winter's energy and passion, and the strains of solo and ensemble music, were sewn into the trip like prevailing winds, like the canyon wren's clear, whistled, descending notes, his glissando—seemingly present, close by, or at a distance, whenever someone stopped to listen.

But we came and went, too, like the swallows and swifts that flicked over the water ahead of the boats, intent on private thoughts.

On the second day of the trip we stopped at Redwall Cavern, an undercut recess that spans a beach of fine sand, perhaps 500 feet wide by 150 feet deep. Winter intends to record here, but the sand absorbs too much sound. Unfazed, the others toss a Frisbee, practice Tai-chi, jog, meditate, play recorders, and read novels.

No other animal but the human would bring to bear so many activities, from so many different cultures and levels of society, with so much energy, so suddenly in a new place. And no other animal, the individuals so entirely unknown to each other, would chance together something so unknown as this river journey. In this frenetic activity and difference seems a suggestion of human evolution and genuine adventure. We are not the first down this river, but in the slooshing of human hands at the water's edge, the swanlike notes of an oboe, the occasional hugs among those most afraid of the rapids, there is exploration.

Each day we see or hear something that astounds us. The thousand-year-old remains of an Anasazi footbridge, hanging in twilight shadow high in the canyon wall above Harding Rapid. Deer Creek Falls, where we stand knee-deep in turquoise water encircled by a rainbow. Havasu Canyon, wild with grapevines, cottonwoods and velvet ash, speckled dace and mule deer, wild grasses and crimson monkey flowers. Each evening we enjoy a vespers: cicadas and crickets, mourning doves, vermilion flycatchers. And the wind, for which chimes are hung in a salt cedar. These notes leap above the splash and rattle, the grinding of water and the roar of rapids.

The narrow, damp, hidden worlds of the side canyons, with their scattered shards of Indian pottery and ghost imprints of 400-million-year-old nautiloids, open onto the larger world of the Colorado River itself; but nothing conveys to us how far into the earth's surface we have come. Occasionally we glimpse the South Rim, four or five thousand feet above. From the rims the canyon seems oceanic; at the surface of the river the feeling is intimate. To someone up there with binoculars, we seem utterly remote down here. It is this known dimension of distance and time and the perplexing question posed by the canyon itself—What is consequential? (in one's life, in the life of human beings, in the life of a planet)—that reverberate constantly, and make the human inclination to judge (another person, another kind of thought) seem so eerie.

Two kinds of time pass here: sitting at the edge of a sun-warmed pool watching blue dragonflies and black tadpoles. And the rapids: down the glassy-smooth tongue into a yawing trench, climb a ten-foot wall of standing water and fall into boiling, ferocious hydraulics, sucking whirlpools, drowned voices, stopped hearts. Rapids can fold and shatter boats and take lives if the boatman enters at the wrong point or at the wrong angle.

Some rapids, like one called Hermit, seem more dangerous than they are and give us great roller-coaster rides. Others—Hance, Crystal, Upset—seem less spectacular, but are technically difficult. At Crystal, our boat screeches and twists against its frame. Its nose crumples like cardboard in the trough; our boatman makes the critical move to the right with split-second timing, and we are over a standing wave and into the haystacks of white water, safely into the tail waves. The boatman's eyes cease to blaze.

The first few rapids—Badger Creek and Soap Creek—do not overwhelm us. When we hit the Inner Gorge—Granite Falls, Unkar Rapid, Horn Creek Rapid— some grip the boat, rigid and silent. (On the ninth day, when we are about to run perhaps the most formidable rapid, Lava Falls, the one among us who has had the greatest fear is calm, almost serene. In the last days, it is hard to overestimate what the river and the music and the unvoiced concern for each other have washed out.)

There are threats to this separate world of the Inner Gorge. Down inside it, one struggles to maintain a sense of what they are, how they impinge.

In 1963, Glen Canyon Dam cut off the canyon's natural flow of water. Spring runoffs of more than two hundred thousand cubic feet per second ceased to roar through the gorge, clearing the main channel of rock and stones washed down from the side canyons. Fed now from the bottom of Lake Powell backed up behind the dam, the river is no longer a warm, silt-laden habitat for Colorado squawfish, razorback sucker, and several kinds of chub, but a cold, clear habitat for trout. With no annual scouring and a subsequent deposition of fresh sand, the beaches show the evidence of continuous human use: they are eroding. The postflood eddies where squawfish bred have disappeared. Tamarisk (salt cedar) and camel thorn, both exotic plants formerly washed out with the spring floods, have gained an apparently permanent foothold. At the old high-water mark, cat-claw acacia, mesquite and Apache plume are no longer watered and are dying out.

On the rim, far removed above, such evidence of human tampering seems, and perhaps is, pernicious. From the river, another change is more wrenching. It floods the system with a kind of panic that in other animals induces nausea and the sudden evacuation of the bowels: it is the descent of helicopters. Their sudden arrival in the canyon evokes not jeers but staring. The violence is brutal, an intrusion as criminal and as random as rape. When the helicopter departs, its rotor-wind walloping against the stone walls, I want to wash the sound off my skin.

The canyon finally absorbs the intrusion. I focus quietly each day on the stone, the breathing of time locked up here, back to the Proterozoic, before there were seashells. Look up to wisps of high cirrus overhead, the hint of a mare's tail sky. Close my eyes: tappet of water against the boat, sound of an Anasazi's six-hole flute. And I watch the bank for beaver tracks, for any movement.

The canyon seems like a grandfather.

One evening, Winter and perhaps half the group carry instruments and record-ing gear back into Blacktail Canyon to a spot sound engineer Mickey Houlihan says is good for recording.

Winter likes to quote from Thoreau: "The woods would be very silent if no birds sang except those that sing best." The remark seems not only to underscore the ephemeral nature of human evolution but the necessity in evaluating any phenomenon—a canyon, a life, a song—of providing for change.

After several improvisations dominated by a cappella voice and percussion, Winter asks Larry Roark to try something on the euphonium; he and Rumbel and Darling will then come up around him. Roark is silent. Moonlight glows on the canyon's lips. There is the sound of gurgling water. After a word of encouragement, feeling shrouded in anonymous darkness like the rest of us, Larry puts his mouth to the horn.

For a while he is alone. God knows what visions of waterfalls or wrens, of boats in the rapids, of Bach or Mozart, are in his head, in his fingers, to send forth notes. The whine of the soprano sax finds him. And the flutter of the oboe. And the rumbling of the choral cello. The exchange lasts perhaps twenty minutes. Furious and sweet, anxious, rolling, delicate and raw. The last six or eight hanging notes are Larry's. Then there is a long silence. Winter finally says, "My God."

I feel, sitting in the wet dark in bathing suit and sneakers and T-shirt, that my fingers have brushed one of life's deep, coursing threads. Like so much else in the canyon, it is left alone. Speak, even notice it, and it would disappear.

I had come to the canyon with expectations. I had wanted to see snowy egrets flying against the black schist at dusk; I saw blue-winged teal against the deep green waters at dawn. I had wanted to hear thunder rolling in the thousand-foot depths; I heard Winter's soprano sax resonating in Matkatameba Canyon, with the guttural caws of four ravens which circled above him. I had wanted to watch rattlesnakes; I saw in an abandoned copper mine, in the beam of my flashlight, a wall of copper sulphate that looked like a wall of turquoise. I rose each morning at dawn and washed in the cold river. I went to sleep each night listening to the cicadas, the pencil-ticking sound of some other insect, the soughing of river waves in tamarisk roots, and watching bats plunge and turn, looking like leaves blown around against the sky. What any of us had come to see or do fell away. We found ourselves at each turn with what we had not imagined.

The last evening it rained. We had left the canyon and been carried far out onto Lake Mead by the river's current. But we stood staring backward, at the point where the canyon had so obviously and abruptly ended. A thought that stayed with me was that I had entered a private place in the earth. I had seen exposed nearly its oldest part. I had lost my sense of urgency, rekindled a sense of what people were, clambering to gain access to high waterfalls where we washed our hair together; and a sense of our endless struggle as a species to understand time and to estimate the consequences of our acts.

It rained the last evening. But before it did, Nancy Rumbel moved to the highest point on Scorpion Island in Lake Mead and played her oboe before a storm we could see hanging over Nevada. Sterling Smyth, who would return to programming computers in twenty-four hours, created a twelve-string imitation of the canyon wren, a long guitar solo. David Darling, revealed suddenly stark, again and then again, against a white-lightning sky, bowed furious homage to the now overhanging cumulonimbus.

In the morning we touched the far shore of Lake Mead, boarded a bus and headed for the Las Vegas airport. We were still wrapped in the journey, as though it were a Navajo blanket. We departed on various planes and arrived home in various cities and towns and at some point the world entered again, and the hardest thing, the translation of what we had touched, began.

I sat in the airport in San Francisco, waiting for a connecting flight to Oregon, dwelling on one image. At the mouth of Nankoweap Canyon, the river makes a broad turn, and it is possible to see high in the orange rock what seem to be four small windows. They are entrances to granaries, built by the Anasazi who dwelled in the canyon a thousand years ago. This was provision against famine, to ensure people would survive.

I do not know, really, how we will survive without places like the Inner Gorge of the Grand Canyon to visit. Once in a lifetime, even, is enough. To feel the stripping down, an ebb of the press of conventional time, a radical change of proportion, an unspoken respect for others that elicits keen emotional pleasure, a quick, intimate pounding of the heart.

Some parts of the trip will emerge one day on an album. Others will be found in a gesture of friendship to some stranger in an airport, in a letter of outrage to a planner of dams, in a note of gratitude to nameless faces in the Park Service, in wondering at the relatives of the ubiquitous wren, in the belief, passed on in whatever fashion—a photograph, a chord, a sketch—that nature can heal.

The living of life, any life, involves great and private pain, much of which we share with no one. In such places as the Inner Gorge the pain trails away from us. It is not so quiet there or so removed that you can hear yourself think, that you would even wish to; that comes later. You can hear your heart beat. That comes first.

A RIVER

John McPhee

During his long career, Pulitzer Prize–winning journalist John McPhee has written about an amazingly wide range of subjects, from birch bark canoes to wingless airplanes to basketball stars to farmers' markets. His many best-selling books have one thing in common: they capture strong characters in action, including inventors, geologists, winemakers, athletes, anglers, hermits, and more. In *Encounters with the Archdruid* (1971), McPhee profiles legendary Sierra Club president David Brower, hoping to understand the new environmentalist ideas that came into full bloom on the first Earth Day, just a year before the book's publication. McPhee invited Brower on a Grand Canyon river trip with Floyd Dominy, head of the Bureau of Reclamation, the federal agency that built Boulder and Glen Canyon dams, and that planned to build additional dams between them. The on-river debates between Brower and Dominy exemplify the sometimes bitter national argument between proponents of economic development and advocates of environmental protection.

. . .

Mile 141. We are in a long, placid reach of the river. The Upset Rapid is eight miles downstream, but its name, all morning, has been a refrain on the raft. People say it as if they were being wheeled toward it on a hospital cart. We have other rapids to go through first—the Kanab Rapid, the Matkatamiba Rapid—but everyone has been thinking beyond them to Upset.

"According to the *River Guide*, there hasn't been a death in the Upset Rapid for a little over two years," someone joked.

"The map says Upset is very bad when the water is low."

"How is the water, Jerry?"

"Low."

"Under today's controlled river, we're riding at the moment on last Sunday's releases," Dominy explained. "This is as low as the river will get under controlled conditions. Tomorrow, Monday's conditions will catch up with us, so things will improve."

"Thank you very much, Commissioner, but what good will Monday's releases do us today?"

"Let's camp here," someone put in.

"It's ten-thirty in the morning."

"I don't care."

"The river has its hands tied, but it's still running," said Brower. "If the Commissioner gets very wet today, it's his own fault."

Jerry Sanderson has cut the engine—a small, cocky outboard that gives the raft a little more speed than the river and is supposed to add some control in rapids. We drift silently.

Brower notices a driftwood log, bleached and dry, on a ledge forty feet above us. "See where the river was before you turned it off, Floyd?"

"I didn't turn it off, God damn it, I turned it on. Ten months of the year, there wasn't enough water in here to boil an egg. My dam put this river in business."

Dominy begins to talk dams. To him, the world is a tessellation of watersheds. When he looks at a globe, he does not see nations so much as he sees rivers, and his imagination runs down the rivers building dams. Of all the rivers in the world, the one that makes him salivate most is the Mekong. There are chances in the Mekong for freshwater Mediterraneans—huge bowls of topography that are pinched off by gunsight passages just crying to be plugged. "Fantastic. Fantastic river," he says, and he contrasts it with the Murrumbidgee River, in New South Wales, where the Australians have spent twenty-two years developing something called the Snowy Mountains Hydroelectric Scheme—"a whole lot of effort for a cup of water." Brower reminds Dominy that dams can break, and mentions the disaster that occurred in Italy in 1963. "That dam didn't break," Dominy tells him. "That dam did *not* break. It was nine hundred feet high. Above it was a granite mountain with crud on top. The crud fell into the reservoir, and water splashed *four hundred feet* over the top of the dam and rushed down the river and killed two thousand people. The dam is still there. It held. Four hundred feet of water over it and it held. Of course, it's useless now. The reservoir is full of crud."

"Just as all your reservoirs will be. Just as Lake Powell will be full of silt."

"Oh, for Christ's sake, Dave, be rational."

"Oh, for Christ's sake, Floyd, *you* be rational."

"Have you ever been *for* a dam, Dave? Once? Ever?"

"Yes. I testified in favor of Knowles Dam, on the Clark Fork River, in Montana. I saw it as a way to save Glacier National Park from an even greater threat. Tell me this, Floyd. Have you ever built a dam that didn't work?"

"Yes, if you want to know the truth. I'm not afraid to tell you the truth, Dave. On Owl Creek, near Thermopolis, Wyoming. Geologic tests were done at one point in the creek and they were O.K., and then the dam was built some distance upstream. We learned a lesson. Never build a dam except exactly where tests are conducted. Cavities developed under the dam, also under the reservoir. Every time we plug one hole, two more show up. Plugs keep coming out. The reservoir just won't fill. Someday I'll tell you another story, Dave. I'll tell you about the day one of our men opened the wrong valve and flooded the *inside* of Grand Coulee Dam."

"I've heard enough."

Dominy and Brower call for [beers], open them, and dutifully drop the tongues inside. Brower now attacks Dominy because a dam project near Ventura, California, is threatening the existence of thirty-nine of the forty-five remaining condors in North America. "We've got to get upset about the condor," Brower tells him. "No one likes to see something get extinct."

"The condor was alive in the days of the mastodons," Dominy says. "He is left over from prehistoric times. He can't fly without dropping off something first. He is so huge a kid with a BB gun can hit him. He's in trouble, dam or no dam. If you give him forty thousand acres, he's still in trouble. He *is* in trouble. His chances of survival are slim. I think it would be nice if he survived, but I don't think this God-damned project would have any real bearing on it."

Dominy draws deeply on his beer. He takes off his Lake Powell hat, smooths his hair back, and replaces the hat. I wonder if he is thinking of the scale-model bulldozer in his office in Washington. The bulldozer happens to have a condor in it—a rubber scale-model condor, sitting in the operator's seat.

Dominy's thoughts have been elsewhere, though. "Who was that old man who tried to read poetry at Kennedy's Inaugural? With the white hair blowing all over the place."

"Robert Frost."

"Right. He and I went to Russia together. I was going to visit Russian dams, and he was on some cultural exchange, and we sat beside each other on the plane all the way to Moscow. He talked and talked, and I smoked cigars. He said eventually, 'So you're the dam man. You're the creator of the great concrete monoliths—turbines, generators, stored water.' And then he started to talk poetically about me, right there in the plane. He said, 'Turning, turning, turning . . . creating, creating . . . creating energy for the people . . . for the people. . . .'

"Most of the day, Frost reminisced about his childhood, and he asked about mine, and I told him I'd been born in a town so small that the entrance and exit signs were on the same post. Land as dry and rough as a cob. You'll never see any land better than that for irrigating. God damn, she lays pretty. And he asked about my own family, and I told him about our farm in Virginia, and how my son and I put up nine hundred and sixty feet of fence in one day. I told my son, 'I'll teach you how to work. You teach yourself how to play.'"

We have been through the Kanab Rapid—standing waves six feet high, lots of splash—and we are still wet. It is cold in the canyon. A cloud—a phenomenon in this sky—covers the sun. We are shivering. The temperature plunges if the sun is obscured. The oven is off. Clothes do not quickly dry. Fortunately, the cloud seems to be alone up there.

Mile 144.8. "Here we are," Brower says. He has the map in his hand. Nothing in the Muav Limestone walls around us suggests that we are anywhere in particular, except in the middle of the Grand Canyon. "We are entering the reservoir," Brower announces. "We are now floating on Lake Dominy."

"Jesus," mutters Dominy.

"What reservoir?" someone asks. Brower explains. A dam that Dominy would like to build, ninety-three miles downstream, would back still water to this exact point in the river.

"Is that right, Commissioner?"

"That's right."

The cloud has left the sun, and almost at once we feel warm again. The other passengers are silent, absorbed by what Brower has told them.

"Do you mean the reservoir would cover the Upset Rapid? Havasu Creek? Lava Falls? All the places we are coming to?" one man asks Dominy.

Dominy reaches for the visor of his Lake Powell hat and pulls it down more firmly on his head. "Yes," he says.

"I'd have to think about that."

"So would I."

"I would, too."

Our fellow-passengers have become a somewhat bewildered—perhaps a somewhat divided—chorus. Dominy assures them that the lake would be beautiful, like Powell, and, moreover, that the Hualapai Indians, whose reservation is beside the damsite, would have a million-dollar windfall, comparable to the good deal that has come to the Navajos of Glen Canyon. The new dam would be called Hualapai Dam, and the reservoir—Brower's humor notwithstanding—would be called Hualapai Lake.

"I'm prepared to say, here and now, that we should touch nothing more in the lower forty-eight," Brower comments. "Whether it's an island, a river, a mountain wilderness—nothing more. What has been left alone until now should be left alone permanently. It's an extreme statement, but it should be said."

"That, my friend, is debatable."

The others look from Brower to Dominy without apparent decision. For the most part, their reactions do not seem to be automatic, either way. This might seem surprising among people who would be attracted, in the first place, to going down this river on a raft, but nearly all of them live in communities whose power and water come from the Colorado. They are, like everyone, caught in the middle, and so they say they'll have to think about it. At home, in New Jersey, I go to my children's schoolrooms and ask, for example, a group of fourth graders to consider a large color photograph of a pristine beach in Georgia. "Do you think there should be houses by this beach, or that it should be left as it is?" Hands go up, waving madly. "Houses," some of the schoolchildren say. Others vote against the houses. The breakdown is fifty-fifty. "How about this? Here is a picture of a glorious mountain in a deep wilderness in the State of Washington. There is copper under the mountain." I list the uses of copper. The vote is close. A black child, who was for houses on the beach, says, "Take the copper." I hold up the Sierra Club's Exhibit-Format book *Time and the River Flowing* and show them pictures of the Colorado River in the Grand Canyon. Someone wants to build a dam in this river. A dam gives electricity and water—light and food. The vote is roughly fifty-fifty.

After Brower ran his ad about the flooding of the Sistine Chapel, Dominy counterattacked by flying down the Colorado in a helicopter, hanging by a strap from an open door with a camera in his hand. He had the pilot set the helicopter down on a sandbar at Mile 144.8, and he took a picture straight down the river. The elevation of the sandbar was eighteen hundred and seventy-five feet above sea level. Taking pictures all the way, Dominy had the pilot fly at that exact altitude down the river from the sandbar to the site of Hualapai Dam. ("That pilot had the God-damned props churning right around the edge of that inner-gorge wall, and he was *noivous,* but I made him stay there.") At the dam site, the helicopter was six hundred feet in the air. Dominy took his collection of pictures to Congress. "Brower says we want to ruin the canyon. Let's see whether we're going to ruin it," he said, and he demonstrated that Hualapai Lake, for all its length, would be a slender puddle hidden away in a segment of the Grand Canyon that was seven miles wide and four thousand feet deep. No part of the lake would be visible from any public observation point in Grand Canyon National Park, he told the congressmen. "Hell, I know more about this river than the Park Service, the Sierra Club, and everyone else," he says, finishing the story. "I took my pictures to Congress because I thought that this would put the ball in their court, and if they wanted to field it, all right, and if they wanted to drop it, that was all right, too."

We have gone through Matkatamiba and around a bend. Jerry Sanderson has cut the motor again, and we are resting in the long corridor of flat water that ends in the Upset Rapid. There is a lot of talk about "the last mile," the low water, "the end of the rainbow," and so on, but this is just fear chatter, dramatization of the unseen.

"Oh, come on, now. One of these rafts could go over Niagara Falls."

"Yes. With no survivors."

Brower hands Dominy a beer. "Here's your last beer," he says. It is 11 A.M., and cool in the canyon. Another cloud is over the sun, and the temperature is seventy-seven degrees. The cloud will be gone in moments, and the temperature will go back into the nineties.

"Here's to Upset," Brower says, lifting his beer. "May the best man win."

The dropoff is so precipitous where Upset begins that all we can see of it, from two hundred yards upstream, is what appears to be an agglomeration of snapping jaws—the leaping peaks of white water. Jerry cannot get the motor started. "It won't run on this gas," he explains. "I've tried river water, and it won't run on that, either." As we drift downstream, he works on the motor. A hundred and fifty yards. He pulls the cord. No sound. There is no sound in the raft, either, except for the *psss* of a can being opened. Dominy is having one more beer. A hundred yards. Jerry starts the motor. He directs the raft to shore. Upset, by rule, must be inspected before the running.

We all got off the raft and walked to the edge of the rapid with Sanderson. What we saw there tended to erase the thought that men in shirtsleeves were control-ling the Colorado inside a dam that was a hundred and sixty-five river miles away. They were there, and this rapid was here, thundering. The problem was elemental. On the near right was an enormous hole, fifteen feet deep and many yards wide, into which poured a scaled-down Canadian Niagara—tons upon tons of water per second. On the far left, just beyond the hole, a very large boulder was fixed in the white torrent. High water would clearly fill up the hole and reduce the boulder, but that was not the situation today.

"What are you going to do about this one, Jerry?"

Sanderson spoke slowly and in a voice louder than usual, trying to pitch his words above the roar of the water. "You have to try to take ten per cent of the hole. If you take any more of the hole, you go in it, and if you take any less you hit the rock."

"What's at the bottom of the hole, Jerry?"

"A rubber raft," someone said.

Sanderson smiled.

"What happened two years ago, Jerry?"

"Well, the man went through in a neoprene pontoon boat, and it was cut in half by the rock. His life jacket got tangled in a boat line, and he drowned."

"What can happen to the raft, Jerry?"

"Oh, parts of them sometimes get knocked flat. Then we have to stop below the rapid and sew them up. We have a pump to reinflate them. We use Dacron thread, and sew them with a leather punch and a three-inch curved needle. We also use contact adhesive cement."

"Wallace Stegner thinks this river is dead, because of Glen Canyon Dam, but I disagree," Brower said. "Just look at it. You've got to have a river alive. You've just got to. There's no alternative."

"I prefer to run this rapid with more water," Sanderson said, as if for the first time.

"If you want to sit here twenty-four hours, I'll get you whatever you need," said Dominy.

Sanderson said, "Let's go."

We got back on the raft and moved out into the river. The raft turned slightly and began to move toward the rapid. "Hey," Dominy said. "Where's Dave? Hey! We left behind one of our party. We're separated now. Isn't he going to ride?" Brower had stayed on shore. We were now forty feet out. "Well, I swear, I swear, I swear," Dominy continued, slowly. "He isn't coming with us." The Upset Rapid drew us in.

With a deep shudder, we dropped into a percentage of the hole—God only knows if it was ten—and the raft folded almost in two. The bow and the stern became the high points of a deep V. Water smashed down on us. And down it smashed again, all in that other world of slow and disparate motion. It was not speed but weight that we were experiencing: the great, almost imponderable, weight of water, enough to crush a thousand people, but not hurting us at all because we were part of it—part of the weight, the raft, the river. Then, surfacing over the far edge of the hole, we bobbed past the incisor rock and through the foaming outwash.

"The great outdoorsman!" Dominy said, in a low voice. "The great outdoorsman!" He shook water out of his Lake Powell hat. "The great outdoorsman standing safely on dry land wearing a God-damned life jacket!"

The raft, in quiet water, now moved close to shore, where Brower, who had walked around the rapid, stood waiting.

"For heaven's sake, say nothing to him, Floyd."

"Christ, I wouldn't think of it. I wouldn't dream of it. What did he do during the war?"

The raft nudged the riverbank. Dominy said, "Dave, why didn't you ride through the rapid?"

Brower said, "Because I'm chicken."

A Climber's Guide to the High Sierra (Sierra Club, 1954) lists thirty-three peaks in the Sierra Nevada that were first ascended by David Brower. "*Arrowhead.* First ascent September 5, 1937, by David R. Brower and Richard M. Leonard. . . .

Glacier Point. First ascent May 28, 1939, by Raffi Bedayan, David R. Brower, and Richard M. Leonard. . . . *Lost Brother.* First ascent July 27, 1941, by David R. Brower. . . ." Brower has climbed all the Sierra peaks that are higher than fourteen thousand feet. He once started out at midnight, scaled the summit of Mount Tyndall (14,025) by 3 A.M., reached the summit of Mount Williamson (14,384) by 7 A.M., and was on top of Mount Barnard (14,003) at noon. He ate his lunch—nuts, raisins, dried apricots—and he went to sleep. He often went to sleep on the high peaks. Or he hunted around for ice, removing it in wedges from cracks in the granite, sucking it to slake his thirst. If it was a nice day, he would stay put for as much as an hour and a half. "The summit is the anticlimax," he says. "The way up is the thing. There is a moment when you know you have the mountain by the tail. You figure out how the various elements go together. You thread the route in your mind's eye, after hunting and selecting, and hitting dead ends. Finally, God is good enough. He built the mountain right, after all. A pleasant surprise. If you don't make it and have to go back, you play it over and over again in your mind. Maybe this would work, or that. Several months, a year, or two years later, you do it again." When Brower first tried to climb the Vazquez Monolith, in Pinnacles National Monument, he was stopped cold, as had been every other climber ever, for the face of the monolith was so smooth that Brower couldn't even get off the ground. Eventually, someone else figured out how to do that, but, as it happened, was stopped far shy of the summit. When Brower heard about this, he went to his typewriter, wrote a note identifying himself as the first man to ascend Vazquez Monolith, and slipped the note into a small brass tube. In his mind, he could see his route as if he were carrying a map. He went to Pinnacles National Monument, went up the Vazquez Monolith without an indecisive moment, and, on top, built a cairn around the brass tube. When Brower led a group to Shiprock in 1939, at least ten previous climbing parties had tried and failed there. Shiprock is a seven-thousand-foot monadnock that looks something like a schooner rising in isolation from the floor of the New Mexican desert. Brower studied photographs of Shiprock for many months, then planned an ornately complicated route— about three-quarters of the way up one side, then far down another side, then up a third and, he hoped, final side, to the top. That is how the climb went, without flaw, start to finish. Another brass tube. "I like mountains. I like granite. I particularly like the feel of the Sierra granite. When I climbed the Chamonix Aiguilles [France], the granite felt so much like the granite in the Yosemite that I felt right at home. Once, in the Sierra, when I was learning, I was going up the wall of a couloir and I put both hands and one knee on a rock. The rock moved, and fell. It crashed seventy-five feet below. One of my hands had shot upward, and with two fingers I caught a ledge. I pulled myself up, and I sat there on that ledge and thought for a long while. Why was I that stupid—to put that much faith in one rock? I have an urge to get up on top. I like to get up there and see around. A three-hundred-and-sixty-degree view is a nice thing to have. I like to recognize where I've been, and look for routes where I might go."

Mile 156. Already the talk is of Lava Falls, which lies twenty-four miles ahead but has acquired fresh prominence in the aftermath of Upset. On the table of rated rapids—copies of which nearly everyone is at the moment studying—categories run from "Riffle" through "Heavy" to "Not Recommended." Upset was a "Heavy" rapid, like Deubendorff. In the "Not Recommended" category there is only Lava Falls.

"Do you agree with that, Jerry?"

Sanderson grins with amusement, and speaks so slowly he seems wistful. "It's the granddaddy of them all," he says. "There's a big drop, and a lot of boulders, and several holes like the one at Upset. You have to look the rapid over carefully, because the holes move."

In the stillness of a big eddy, the raft pauses under an overhanging cliff. Lava Falls fades in the conversation. Twenty-four miles is a lot of country. Through a cleft that reaches all the way down through the overhanging cliff a clear green stream is flowing into the river. The cleft is so narrow that the stream appears to be coming straight out of the sandstone. Actually, it meanders within the cliff and is thus lost to view. The water is so clear that it sends a pale-green shaft into the darker Colorado. The big river may no longer be red with silt, but it carries enough to remain opaque. In the small stream, the pebbles on the bottom are visible, magnified, distinct. "Dive in," Brower suggests. "See where it goes."

Brower and I went into the stream and into the cliff. The current was not powerful, coming through the rock, and the water was only four feet deep. I swam, by choice—the water felt so good. It felt cool, but it must have been about seventy-five degrees. It was cooler than the air. Within the cliff was deep twilight, and the echoing sound of the moving water. A bend to the right, a bend to the left, right, left—this stone labyrinth with a crystal stream in it was moment enough, no matter where it ended, but there lay beyond it a world that humbled the mind's eye. The walls widened first into a cascaded gorge and then flared out to become the ovate sides of a deep valley, into which the stream rose in tiers of pools and waterfalls. Some of the falls were only two feet high, others four feet, six feet. There were hundreds of them. The pools were as much as fifteen feet deep, and the water in them was white where it plunged and foamed, then blue in a wide circle around the plunge point, and pale green in the outer peripheries. This was Havasu Canyon, the immemorial home of the Havasupai, whose tribal name means "the people of the blue-green waters." We climbed from one pool to another, and swam across the pools, and let the waterfalls beat down around our shoulders. Mile after mile, the pools and waterfalls continued. The high walls of the valley were bright red. Nothing grew on these dry and flaky slopes from the mesa rim down about two-thirds of the way; then life began to show in isolated barrel cactus and prickly pear. The cacti thickened farther down, and below them was riverine vegetation—green groves of oak and cottonwood, willows and tamarisk, stands of cattail, tall grasses, moss, watercress, and maidenhair fern. The Havasupai have lived in this place for hundreds, possibly thousands, of years, and their population has remained stable. There are something like two hundred of them. They gather nuts on the canyon rim in winter and grow vegetables in the canyon in summer. They live about twelve miles up Havasu Creek from the Colorado. Moss covered the rocks around the blue-and-green pools. The moss on dry rock was soft and dense, and felt like broadloom underfoot. Moss also grew below the water's surface, where it was coated with travertine, and resembled coral. The stream was loaded with calcium, and this was the physical explanation of the great beauty of Havasu Canyon, for it was the travertine—crystalline calcium carbonate—that had both fashioned and secured the all but unending stairway of falls and pools. At the downstream lip of each plunge pool, calcium deposits had built up into natural dams, and these travertine dams were what kept Havasu Creek from running freely downhill. The dams were whitish tan, and so smooth and symmetrical that they might have been finished by a mason. They were two or three feet high. They sloped. Their crests were flat and smooth and with astonishing uniformity were about four inches thick from bank to bank. Brower looked up at the red canyon walls. He was sitting on the travertine, with one foot in a waterfall, and I was treading the green water below him. He said, "If Hualapai Dam had been built, or were ever built, this place where you are swimming would be at the bottom of a hundred feet of water." It was time to go back to the Colorado. I swam to the travertine dam at the foot of the pool, climbed up on it and dived into the pool below it, and swam across and dived again, and swam and dived—and so on for nearly two miles. Dominy was waiting below. "It's fabulous," he said. "I know every river canyon in the country, and this is the prettiest in the West."

Mile 171. Beside the minor rapids at Gateway Canyon, we stop, unload the raft, and lay out our gear before settling down to drinks before dinner. Brower is just beyond earshot. Dominy asks me again, "What did Dave do during the war?"

I tell him all I happen to know—that Brower trained troops in climbing techniques in West Virginia and Colorado, and that he later went with the 10th Mountain Division to Italy, where he won the Bronze Star.

Dominy contemplates the river. Brower goes to the water's edge and dips his Sierra Club cup. He will add whiskey to the water. "Fast-moving water is a very satisfying sound," Dominy says to him. "There is nothing more soothing than the sound of running or falling water."

"The river talks to itself, Floyd. Those little whirls, the sucks and the boils—they say things."

"I love to see white water, Dave. In all my trips through the West over the years, I have found moving streams with steep drops to them the most scenic things of all."

Over the drinks, Brower tells him, "I will come out of this trip different from when I came in. I am not in favor of dams, but I am in favor of Dominy. I can see what you have meant to the Bureau, and I am worried about what is going to happen there someday without you."

"No one will ever say that Dominy did not tell anyone and everyone exactly what he thinks, Dave."

"I've never heard anything different, Floyd."

"And, I might say, I've never heard anything different about you."

"I needed this trip more than anyone else."

"You're God-damned right you did, with that white skin."

Dominy takes his next drink out of the Sierra Club cup. The bottle of whiskey is nearly empty. Dominy goes far down into his briefcase and brings out another. It is Jim Beam. Dominy is fantastically loyal to Jim Beam. At his farm in Virginia a few weeks ago, he revived a sick calf by shooting it with a hypodermic syringe full of penicillin, condensed milk, and Jim Beam. Brower says he does not believe in penicillin.

"As a matter of fact, Dave Brower, I'll make a trip with you any time, anywhere."

"Great," Brower mutters faintly.

"Up to this point, Dave, we've won a few and lost a few—each of us. Each of us. Each of us. God damn it, everything Dave Brower does is O.K.—tonight. Dave, now that we've buried the hatchet, you've got to come out to my farm in the Shenandoah."

"Great."

To have a look at the map of the river, Dominy puts on Brower's glasses. Brower's glasses are No. 22s off the counter of F. W. Woolworth in San Francisco. Dominy rolls the scroll back to the Upset Rapid.

"How come you didn't go through there, Dave?"

"I'm chicken."

"Are you going to go through Lava Falls?"

"No."

"No?"

"No, thank you. I'll walk."

Upstream from where we sit, we can see about a mile of straight river between the high walls of the inner gorge, and downstream this corridor leads on to a bold stone portal. Dominy contemplates the scene. He says, "With Hualapai Dam, you'd really have a lake of water down this far."

"Yes. A hundred and sixty feet deep," notes Brower.

"It would be beautiful, and, like Lake Powell, it would be better for *all* elements of society."

"There's another view, and I have it, and I suppose I'll die with it, Floyd. Lake Powell is a drag strip for power boats. It's for people who won't do things except the easy way. The magic of Glen Canyon is dead. It has been vulgarized. Putting water in the Cathedral in the Desert was like urinating in the crypt of St. Peter's. I hope it never happens here."

"Look, Dave. I don't live in a God-damned apartment. I didn't grow up in a God-damned city. Don't give me the crap that you're the only man that understands these things. I'm a greater conservationist than you are, by far. I do things. I make things available to man. Unregulated, the Colorado River wouldn't be worth a good God damn to anybody. You conservationists are phony outdoorsmen. I'm sick and tired of a democracy that's run by a noisy minority. I'm fed up clear to my God-damned gullet. I had the guts to come out and fight you bastards. You're just a bunch of phonies and you'll stoop to any kind of God-damned argument. That's why I took my pictures. You were misleading the public about what would happen here. You gave the impression that the whole canyon was going to be inundated by the reservoir. Your weapon is emotion. You guys are just not very God-damned honorable in your fights."

"I had hoped things would not take this turn, Floyd, but you're wrong."

"Do you want to keep this country the way it is for a handful of people?"

"Yes, I do. Hualapai Dam is not a necessity. You don't even want the water."

"We mainly want the power head, but the dam would be part of the over-all storage project under the Colorado Compact."

"The Colorado Compact was not found on a tablet written on Mount Sinai. Hualapai Dam is not necessary, and neither was Glen Canyon. Glen Canyon Dam was built for the greater good of Los Angeles."

"You're too intelligent to believe that."

"You're too intelligent not to believe that."

"For Christ's sake, be objective, Dave. Be reasonable."

"Some of my colleagues make the error of trying to be reasonable, Floyd. Objectivity is the greatest threat to the United States today."

Mile 177, 9:45 A.M. The water is quite deep and serene here, backed up from the rapid. Lava Falls is two miles downstream, but we have long since entered its chamber of quiet.

"The calm before the storm," Brower says.

The walls of the canyon are black with lava—flows, cascades, and dikes of lava. Lava once poured into the canyon in this segment of the river. The river was here, much in its present form. It had long since excavated the canyon, for the volcanism occurred in relatively recent time. Lava came up through the riverbed, out from the canyon walls, and even down over the rims. It sent the Colorado up in clouds. It hardened, and it formed a dam and backed water two hundred miles.

"If a lava flow were to occur in the Grand Canyon today, Brower and the nature lovers would shout to high heaven that a great thing had happened," Dominy said, addressing everyone in the raft. "But if a man builds a dam to bring water and power to other men, it is called desecration. Am I right or wrong, Dave? Be honest."

"The lava dam of Quaternary time was eventually broken down by the river. This is what the Colorado will do to the Dominy dams that are in it now or are ever built. It will wipe them out, recover its grade, and go on about its business. But by then our civilization and several others will be long gone."

We drift past an enormous black megalith standing in the river. For eighty years, it was called the Niggerhead. It is the neck of a volcano, and it is now called Vulcan's Forge. We have a mile to go. Brower talks about the amazing size of the crystals on the canyon walls, the morning light in the canyon, the high palisades of columnar basalt. No one else says much of anything. All jokes have been cracked twice. We are just waiting, and the first thing we hear is the sound. It is a big, tympanic sound that increasingly fills the canyon. The water around us is dark-green glass. Five hundred yards. There it is. Lava Falls. It is, of course, a rapid, not a waterfall. There is no smooth lip. What we now see ahead of us at this distance appears to be a low whitewashed wall.

The raft touches the riverbank. Sanderson gets out to inspect the rapid, and we go, too. We stand on a black ledge, in the roar of the torrent, and look at the water. It goes everywhere. From bank to bank, the river is filled with boulders, and the water smashes into them, sends up auroras of spray, curls thickly, and pounds straight down into bomb-crater holes. It eddies into pockets of lethal calm and it doubles back to hit itself. Its valleys are deeper and its hills are higher than in any other rapid in North America. The drop is prodigious—twenty-six feet in a hundred yards—but that is only half the story. Prospect Creek, rising black-walled like a coal chute across the river, has shoved enough rock in here to stop six rivers, and this has produced the preëminent rapid of the Colorado.

When Dominy stepped up on the ledge and into the immediacy of Lava Falls, he shouted above the thunder, "Boy, that's a son of a bitch! Look at those *rocks!* See that hole over there? Jesus! Look at that one!"

Brower said, "Look at the way the water swirls. It's alive!"

The phys.-ed. teacher said, "Boy, that could tear the hell out of your bod."

Brower said, "Few come, but thousands drown."

Dominy said, "If I were Jerry, I'd go to the left and then try to move to the right."

Lava protruded from the banks in jagged masses, particularly on the right, and there was a boulder there that looked like an axe blade. Brower said, "I'd go in on the right and out on the left."

My own view was that the river would make all the decisions. I asked Sanderson how he planned to approach what we saw there.

"There's only one way to do it," he said. "We go to the right."

The raft moved into the river slowly, and turned, and moved toward the low white wall. A hundred yards. Seventy-five yards. Fifty yards. It seems odd, but I did not notice until just then that Brower was on the raft. He was, in fact, beside me. His legs were braced, his hands were tight on a safety rope, and his Sierra Club cup was hooked in his belt. The tendons in his neck were taut. His chin was up. His eyes looked straight down the river. From a shirt pocket Dominy withdrew a cigar. He lighted it and took a voluminous drag. We had remaining about fifteen seconds of calm water. He said, "I might bite an inch off the end, but I doubt it." Then we went into Lava Falls.

Water welled up like a cushion against the big boulder on the right, and the raft went straight into it, but the pillow of crashing water was so thick that it acted on the raft like a great rubber fender between a wharf and a ship. We slid off the rock and to the left—into the craterscape. The raft bent like a V, flipped open, and shuddered forward. The little outboard—it represented all the choice we had—cavitated, and screamed in the air. Water rose up in tons through the bottom of the raft. It came in from the left, the right, and above. It felt great. It covered us, pounded us, lifted us, and heaved us scudding to the base of the rapid.

For a moment, we sat quietly in the calm, looking back. Then Brower said, "The foot of Lava Falls would be two hundred and twenty-five feet beneath the surface of Lake Dominy."

Dominy said nothing. He just sat there, drawing on a wet, dead cigar. Ten minutes later, however, in the dry and baking Arizona air, he struck a match and lighted the cigar again.

LAVA FALLS

Bill Beer

In 1955, two young thrill-seekers from Los Angeles, Bill Beer and John Daggett, decided that, since they could not afford a boat, they would swim the Colorado River through Grand Canyon. The legendary Georgie Clark had swum parts of the lower Canyon before, but Beer and Daggett were the first to go all the way from Lees Ferry to Lake Mead, and no one has matched their feat since. They wore life jackets over leaky rubber shirts, and they carried their equipment and supplies in army surplus dry bags that doubled as water wings. As the river dragged them downstream, it smashed them into rocks, tore their clothes, destroyed their gear and food, and nearly killed Daggett in President Harding Rapid. Anticipating generations of extreme outdoor adventurers after them, they brought along a camera and filmed their exploits. The story became a national media sensation, especially when one paper reported falsely that they had drowned. In this selection from Beer's memoir, *We Swam the Grand Canyon: The True Story of a Cheap Vacation That Got a Little Out of Hand* (1988), he describes their nearly disastrous run of the biggest rapid in the canyon, Lava Falls.

. . .

The next morning was our nineteenth day since leaving Lees Ferry, and a splendid day it was. After breakfast it was a delight to go swimming in warm water for a change. The warmth lasted only two or three minutes and then we were shoved out of the glowing blue tunnel of Havasu into the cold, brown Colorado and whisked down Havasu Rapid.

We took only short breaks—just enough to drive the cold out of our bones—by rolling back and forth in the hot sand. No fires for us this day. We were relaxed and confident, swimming a rapid about every mile—none of them offering any real challenge, just fun. John even took a nap on one break.

This was the narrowest part of the Grand Canyon, the only place where you can shout from rim to rim—that is, if your voice will carry two to three miles. The North Rim appeared to be almost straight up over our heads, 5,000 feet above us.

Camping time was again signaled to us by one of nature's clocks. With thousands of limestone caves to choose from, it's not surprising that tens of millions of bats live in the Grand Canyon. As soon as we saw what we called the "bourgeois" bats, we knew it was time to stop. These were the ordinary bats that came out in great hordes just before dark. We gave pet names to two other classes of bats: the "misfits" and the "gluttons." The gluttons stayed out gorging themselves until well after everybody else had gone home. But our favorites were the poor misfits, who just couldn't adjust themselves to the routines of bat society. They stayed out all day wandering around in the blinding light, scavenging what bugs they could.

We camped that night opposite Lava Pinnacle, one of the landmarks of the river. It's a chunk of black lava as big as a three-story building and looks like the end of a large Tootsie Roll jutting out of the water. Our map showed us that we had made 21 miles that day—our best so far—and we had swum through 18 rapids, none of which were of any consequence on the Colorado though they would have been major rapids on many other rivers.

We were again in high spirits. Lava Falls would be tomorrow, but tonight we were undaunted by any upcoming problems. We were both unable to walk much and mostly crawled around camp, but even that seemed trivial. After all, we could still swim. In the event of a broken leg or other injury, we knew there was no climbing out of the canyons in our condition so there would be no choice but to splint the leg, make a raft of our rubber boxes and driftwood, and carry on down river.

We had a little celebration that night for another reason. It was my 26th birthday. John dug out a beautiful canned ham he had hidden for the occasion; I made biscuits and we gorged ourselves on the best goodies from each store of supplies. John even had a present for me: a jackknife he had been keeping as a birthday present. When he was buying it in L.A. he said he knew that it would be a great celebration when he gave it to me. If for no other reason than that we would both still be alive.

The next morning we were up and down at the river early. We were eager to tackle Lava Falls, to take on the worst the Colorado River had to offer. But, the cold water again dampened our enthusiasm and we discovered an immediate need to make some more movies. The banks were nice and muddy here and it seemed a great place to do a "quicksand" sequence. John, of course, was chosen for the role of the hapless victim of the slimy mud while I got to be the clean, dry cameraman. This took a good couple of hours, at the end of which time we were heated up enough to go swimming.

It was a short drift down to Lava Falls. Even when we first heard it from a mile upstream, we knew we were facing something different. The voice of Lava Falls was deeper and seemed more ominous than that of other rapids. It chewed and growled in an angry basso and from a half mile upstream we could look down toward this uproar and see jets of water spitting into the air.

A little apprehensive, we pulled into the right bank a quarter mile above the brink, a good deal farther upstream than was our custom. Taking the movie camera we began a painful and slow climb along the hot black lava and sharp rocks. We couldn't see more than a corner of Lava Falls until we were almost on top of it. When we finally climbed up the last forty-foot chunk of lava and stood looking down on the rapid, we were dumbfounded. At first sight, Lava Falls seemed to deserve its ugly reputation.

On second sight, it still deserved it. We had never seen such an angry, snarling maelstrom. Half-way through the tumult, a black rock jutted out toward the center of the rapid. I climbed down to it while John made movies of me surveying the rapid. Then he joined me and we stood together on the rock in the rapid while the water leaped up trying to wash us off. We were near the middle of the clamor and had to shout in each other's ear to be heard.

"How does it look to you from here?"

"Worse!"

"Think there's a chance, Bill?"

"What?"

"I say, do you think there's a chance we can swim it?"

"No."

Talking was difficult; we silently stared at the rapid. Then I took the camera and shot some footage of the boiling water. Through the tiny hole of the viewfinder there was room only for brown waves and spray, and I wondered if I weren't wasting film.

What a place! Four thousand feet above the rapid the volcano Vulcan's Throne poises on the North Rim. Not long ago in geologic terms this volcano poured liquid streams of lava into the Colorado, damming up the river for miles in a boiling, fuming lake. A few eons later, the Colorado had cut its way back down through the lava, leaving little sign of its great dam except Lava Falls. Prospect Canyon, coming in here from the south, had shoved its boulders into the river, nearly joining the lava that had poured down the north wall, damming up the Colorado and resulting in a vicious frothing rapid. The water whips and churns violently and the rocks all seem to have been whetted sharp—just for us.

From the north side where we stood, fingers of lava pointed out toward midstream. The one we stood on lifted a knuckle above the tormented surface like the crooked finger of a giant's hand. The others lay beneath the water, revealed from time to time by the great curling waves and holes they created. Each of these lava ridges was guarded by a wave that constantly rolled upstream, ready to pound any bit of flotsam that came its way. From the other bank, well out toward the middle of the stream, rocks broke to the surface like hobnails on a boot.

The currents were a maze obscured by the spray. Standing on the giant's finger near the center of Lava Falls, I tried to watch hunks of driftwood tumbling through, but the water was so frothy that the only ones I saw were those that were hurled onto the rock at our feet. The water rushed by at nearly 30 miles per hour. The whole thing looked hopeless.

There was almost no tongue to this rapid. Instead there was a brink. Like water pouring over a wall, Lava Falls started with an abrupt drop; the rest of the way was just pure confusion. In all, the rapid dropped 37 feet. There appeared to be one narrow break in the wall but it was too close to the north side. If we came that way we were sure to be slammed against one of the fingers of lava. The only normal thing about this rapid was that it did stream out into a long tail, flanked by the usual whirlpools. No wonder it was regarded as the worst rapid on the river, the standard by which all others were measured.

The only possible course was to come through that break, but since no swimmer had enough power to avoid the lava, somehow or other we'd have to bounce off it. Or maybe we would be dragged across one or two or three ridges of lava before being bashed into the last. It would be something like Bedrock, where we'd needed to catch the wave just right. Except that here there were several waves in succession that needed to be caught. There were about 14,000 cubic feet of water *per second* pouring over that lava very fast and we were both thinking how helpless we would be once we ventured into this rapid.

John didn't like the rocks. He was willing to let me take the lead here and would do whatever I did. I was not at all sure I was going to swim through *this* rapid. I worked my way back toward our first vantage point. I wished that I had taken the trouble to open a box and get out my sneakers—the lava was very sharp and very hot and there were thorny cacti about. I also wished I had a pair of gloves.

I reached a little knot of driftwood just above one of the big breaking waves and tossed a chunk of wood into the spume.

Lost.

I threw in a bigger piece.

Gone.

I found a log I could barely lift and slung it out. I caught one or two glimpses of it as it swirled through the waves and passed John. Well, at least it didn't get jammed up against a rock. I tried another log, but barely saw it after it hit the water.

No sense standing here throwing wood in the river all day.

I climbed higher for a different perspective.

Down by the water with the camera, John was thinking all the while that I would give it up, but the more I watched the rapid, the less dangerous it seemed. Familiarity breeding contempt? I chose what looked like the best course for a swimmer and then compared it with a couple of alternatives. I imagined myself in the water and mentally followed myself through the rapids.

It was horrible.

But after I swam it 10 or 15 times in my mind the whole process began to seem more like a dream than reality. Oh, why not?

A little hypnotized, I saw myself signaling John that I was going to swim through, and started working my way upstream. All the while I kept my mind busy with little details of the course, estimates of current speeds and direction. I looked for a guidepost so I would enter at the optimum spot. Of course from six inches off the water it would all look different, and a few feet one way or another were important—vital actually.

Down at the river's edge, where I couldn't see any of the rapid, I caught sight of a persistent little spout of water that kept shooting higher than the brink in the same spot every few seconds. I felt sure it would guide me.

Fear began to take hold of me. It was the strangest feeling; I was so scared there wasn't room for any other emotion, and hardly room for any thoughts. At this point I had swum through some hundred plus rapids. This was just one more, I tried to tell myself. But I wasn't convincing; I really had found no safe way through the rapid; it was going to be a matter of trusting to luck. Not my nature.

Much sooner than I wanted to, I found myself back at my boxes. It seemed so much quieter here; the river slid by me smooth and oily, the roar of Lava Falls now somewhat muted. I stood hesitating for long moments, like a kid about to jump off a high wall. "Ready? Here I come. One . . . two . . . three . . . "

Couldn't jump. Bladder too full.

That taken care of, my body demanded further attention.

"You can't go swimming now," it said. "I'm hungry."

So the condemned man sat down to lunch.

Down on the lava by the Falls, John was alone with the camera and his thoughts as I had been way back at Soap Creek Rapid. He cautioned himself to keep on filming as long as there was nothing else he could do to help me and then to be sure not to drop the camera in the water if he had to go after me, but to lay it down carefully so he could return for it if possible. From his rock downstream the rapid posed little threat; he could even dive in the water from where he stood. It seemed like I had been away for a week. It was probably about an hour. He got bored waiting for me. And hungry.

Back upstream I finished my lunch and strapped my boxes up tightly. With no further diversions available I waded toward deep water and the current. As I lowered my chest into the water between my boxes I tried to give our customary howl at the cold, but my tightened throat only permitted a peep.

As I drifted toward the brink and the unseen rapid I tried to prepare somehow, swim around or something, like a fighter shadow boxing and dancing around the ring before a bout. And I played a little game, estimating every few moments whether I could still chicken out and reach shore. When I passed the point where nothing was possible but to swim Lava Falls, I relaxed. There were no more decisions to make. In peace I studied the cliffs, the water, a piece of driftwood or two floating along with me and chuckled at myself for being there. The roar came closer. Thirty or forty feet from the brink I sought my little water spout.

It wasn't to be seen.

I rushed toward the rapid without any idea of whether I was where I was supposed to be. Way downstream I could see the big rock and little John sitting on top taking movies. I levered myself higher on the boxes to see the rapid—to get oriented.

It was too late. I was 20 feet too far left and was going to drop over the worst brink of the rapid. I slipped backwards from my boxes stretching them out in front of me as far as I could, clinging to the straps with a madman's clutch. The current grabbed my boxes and sucked them downward with a yank that nearly pulled my arms out of their sockets. I plummeted down after them, and when they reached bottom and stopped momentarily, my face was jammed into them and my feet were flung over my head in an unwilling somersault.

The river grabbed my boxes and jerked them downstream again and I spun after them like the tail of a kite. We, my heavy boxes and I, were rolled and whipped somewhere in the mad mass of spray and rocks between the bottom and the roiled surface. It was dark underwater in that muddy river and I couldn't see where I was, where I was going or even which way was up. All I could do was hang on to my gyrating equipment in a violent crack-the-whip game. The river I thought I knew so well, that I thought I had mastered, was suddenly an angry giant pummeling and twisting me. It was trying to drown me in dark violence.

For a quick moment I was flung to the surface. It was a surprise to see daylight. I grabbed a lucky lung full of air and was plunged into the blackness again. I was rolled sideways, I was rolled end for end, my arms were jerked out then in, my legs were pumping frantically but for no good reason. I hit a couple of things, the bottom, maybe—scary enough, but trivial in light of what I knew was coming.

I wondered how I would hit the lava. With an arm, a leg, my back? Hopefully my boxes, still thrust out at arm's length when possible, would hit first.

I popped to the surface a second time. I was three feet from the lava knuckle and there was John sitting on top winding the camera!

"Why isn't he taking pictures? Here I am, nearly dead, about to be hurled at his feet and he's sitting on his duff."

Then a lucky surge threw me sideways, submerging me again, and I flew past the lava barely flicking it with my foot. Back on the surface, and on it to stay, I bounded on into the tail of the rapid. Wild with exuberance, I screamed triumph to the cliffs and swam for shore as hard as I could. When I reached shore the reaction set in; I was weak and motionless as the fear and excitement drained away with most of my strength.

I had, in understandable confusion, landed on the opposite shore. There was no way to communicate to John except by signals. I wanted to give him some idea of the safest channel. But I only confused him. One garbled set of signals included a slitting of the throat motion, and he understandably thought I was telling him it was too dangerous to try.

So John was confused, too. He had seen me swim Lava Falls. Or at least he had seen the beginning and the end since I was underwater for about three quarters of the run. And I was obviously safe and sound, so how could I be telling him to give it up? That wasn't our custom; if there was a decent chance we would take it, and if I'd gotten through, there was obviously a good chance John would too. So regardless of what nonsense I was trying to communicate from the other bank, John was going to go ahead and swim Lava Falls. But my little pantomime had him worried.

I watched John go through the same process I had. He stopped and looked at the water from every vantage point and threw in chunks of driftwood and paused for long spells just looking. Then he passed out of sight upstream.

I took my cheap little 35mm camera and hopped from boulder to boulder out into the rapid as far as I could, stationed myself on a slippery rock and waited while the dancing spray tried to soak my camera.

He wasn't long in coming.

I first saw John as a little yellow life jacket drifting downstream between two black rubber boxes. As he gathered speed I began clicking off pictures, the first one above the brink, then another as he plunged down through the break I had planned to follow. He was lost in the spray in the next picture, then he came to the surface too close to the right bank just upstream from that last block of lava. I took another picture. He was surely going to hit.

Then John showed he had learned his lessons—Harding and Bedrock, and the others—he rode the curling wave guarding the lava knuckle up into the wave and back down again, catching the edge and surfing neatly away from danger. He could have been at the beach. I took one more picture as he bounced through the tail.

He had run the rapid perfectly! I had goofed and was punished for my mistake, but John had been flawless. I was sure his confidence would be totally restored.

When I got back downstream to him he was indeed happy and smug, even suggesting we go back and swim Lava Falls again to get more movies. I offered to be cameraman.

He reconsidered and ate his lunch.

We agreed there was no doubt Lava Falls was the most difficult rapid of them all, but we weren't really sure we had done anything like "risk our lives." There was no doubt we'd do it again if the occasion arose, the next time with far less hesitation.

We jumped back into the water and swam downstream another three miles and called it quits for the day. We had only swum four miles that day; our worst mileage of the trip. But we had swum Lava Falls!

THREE BOYS AND AN OLD MAN

Bert Loper

In his journal, Bert Loper wrote, "I was born in 1869 just two months and one week after Major [John Wesley] Powell started his trip, and on my birthday he was at the mouth of the San Juan Canyon, which happens to be the first canyon that I ever ran." Loper struggled through life as a backcountry miner, rancher, river guide, and laborer, and he amassed years of experience running the rapids of the Green and Colorado rivers. Despite a decades-long obsession with Grand Canyon, he never found a way to get below Lees Ferry until 1939, when a group of young men met him in a hospital room and asked him to run the river with them. Loper's previously unpublished journal of the trip captures his joy and pride at finally living his dream at the age of seventy. Ten years later, Loper made his second trip through Grand Canyon, hoping to celebrate his eightieth birthday on the river. He died at the oars in 24½ Mile Rapid, probably of heart failure. His body was lost to the river, but his companions found his hand-built boat about twenty miles downstream, where they pulled it onshore to serve as a monument. A year later, another pioneering river runner, Norm Nevills, painted an epitaph on the boat's bow, memorializing Loper as "The Grand Old Man of the Canyon."

. . .

This is to be—in a way—an introduction to a trip through Grand Canyon which was made during the year of 1939. The trip was made by Bert Loper and Don Harris, and at the time that the plans were made, I (Bert Loper) was an inmate of the Veterans Hospital, where I was confined to my bed for 5 months during the winter of late '38 and early '39. And it was there that Mr. Harris and I became acquainted, for he had heard of me as a boatman and came up to see me, and it was there that the plans were made. I will say here and now that if it had not been for Mr. Harris, I would not have made the trip. And just a word in passing—I had been planning this trip long before Don was born, but there seemed to be a jinx that would head me off at Lee's Ferry every time that I tried to go through. All he knew of me was what he had heard, and I knew nothing of him; but in the laying plans for the trip, he would brook no interference. It was always: we ARE GOING THROUGH, so that is the reason for this introduction. On my discharge from the hospital, I started to make my boat the very next day, and then I received an engagement with the USGS to take them through the Glen Canyon. We layed our plans to meet at Lee's Ferry, where the USGS [trip] ended, so July 6th at 12:30 P.M., we pushed off on our journey through the greatest wonder of all of the seven wonders of the world.

July 6, 1939

As I just said, we were on our way, and in about 6 miles we ran under the Navajo bridge. As I passed under it I recalled the many times I had stood on that very same bridge and wondered if the time would ever come when I would get to go under it. So I finally got to go under it, but just going under it was a very mild starter, for we still had 240 miles before we could say HURRAH. In about 3 miles, below the bridge, we came to Badger Creek Rapid, and it is a rather bad rapid. As I said before, Don only knew me from what he had heard, so he wanted to know what I was going to do. I said I was going to run it so I did, and after I was through he followed. The next one was much worse, so he seemed very dubious about running it; but I told him that it was made to order. I will always believe that the foundation for the successful completion of the trip was laid right there.

In describing the personnel of the trip, I will say first the members of the expedition are Don Harris, Boatman—Bill Gibson, Photographer—Chet Klevin, which we might call a cook, but on top of that he is a good-fellow, but as for that so are the others too—and last as well as least, myself (Bert Loper). It might be interesting to give the approximate ages of each, but suffice it to say that the combined ages of the first 3 adds up to 77 years, and my age is 70, so it is to be seen that there is 3 Boys and an old Man. In many instances it would be an impossible combination, but there will be more to say along that line after we reach Mead Lake. Mr. Gibson was the photographer for [Norm] Nevills's party for his 1938 trip, so we are having the benefit of the education he received from a picture stand-point on that trip, so perhaps I may have something more to say at the Lake.

The Boats are what is called a canyon-type boat—that is, along the lines of the Galloway type but they differ somewhat. Suffice it to say that they were decked over both fore and aft and had an open cock-pit of about 3½ feet. Don's boat is 16 feet long and has a wider beam than mine, but is much more shallow than mine. His boat also has more rake than mine, and that makes it handle or turn more easy than mine, or in other words he can load more in his front compartment than I can. My boat is 18 feet long and is made along the same lines. There is much to a river education, and while I have been on and off the river for more than 50 years, I still am adding to my education as I go along.

After running Soap Creek Rapid we continued on and ran several small sheer wall rapids and then House Rock Rapid. When we approach a major rapid it is our custom to land above and inspect the rapid, and we did that to both of Badger and Soap Creek. So we landed and inspected this major [rapid] and decided on the way to run it. In running this rapid which was very rough, we each shipped some water—but just a little word of praise for our boats, for they sure do wonderful work, and if things continue on as they have started, I think I will have something to say about my partner-boat-man later. After running this rapid we landed on the left bank and made our No. 1 camp at mile 18. We made 18 miles and ran 10 rapids, and considering that I put in all winter in the hospital, I am doing fine. I do not like to pass snap judgment on any one or thing, so I will try to keep from doing that, until we reach Mead Lake anyway.

July 7, Friday, 1939

After a very nice breakfast prepared by our most able cook, we proceeded on our way. We had much rough water but nothing serious so far, and even [in] Soap Creek Rapid, which has a rather noted reputation, there is nothing so far that has Cataract tied. I notice that the most of those that have made Grand Canyon, they seem to discredit Cataract, but if the rapids below are much worse than Gypsum or Dark Canyon, in Cataract Canyon we will be in for some hard work. There is sure a thrill in running rough water, and I hope that the sense of elation never leaves me, but there is much more to a trip of this kind than the rapids or the wonders of the majestic walls. The grandeur and stupendousness of the mighty chasms through which the Colorado wends its way is sure an awe-inspiring sight, and I would sure feel sorry for the one that fails to appreciate it—but I think I had better record the day's work instead of going off on my elation of the grandeurs of the canyon proper. The rapids have all been charted by the Birdseye expedition of 1923, so on this day we ran 16 of those charted and many little ones. Bill had a little mishap about mile 24½ when a big side swiper washed him off, but he had hold of the hand rope and it is safe to say that he did not relinquish that hold. He managed to climb back on, and it summed up to a little more experience—we had our cockpits filled too when we ran on to a pour over. About 2:30 P.M. we reached Vasey's Paradise, which is most appropriately named. The walls at this place are perfectly perpendicular, and 100 feet up there is an opening in the solid wall and the coldest purest and clearest water in the world comes gushing out, and that causes much beautiful vegetation to grow at the foot of the cliff. It was here that we took about ¾ of an hour's rest before pushing on—and after reaching mile

39, we made camp on the right bank, making 39 miles in 1&½ days travel and running 26 major rapids besides many small ones. After a very nice supper we call it a day. . . .

Saturday, July 15, 1939

We got a fine start, and the first was Gateway canyon rapid, which was so unimportant that we never stopped to look it over. But as we dropped in I told Chet that we were going to miss a picture, and as we dove down—nearly straight and came up like-wise—we were caught by a side twister and went up-side down. We climbed on the overturned boat and caught hold of the edge and gave a pull, and she righted beautifully. All oars was in place, but we lost our bucket and the grate that we had for to cook on, but other-wise everything was fine. While I have been doing this—off and on—for more than 50 years, that is my first capsize, so I should not feel bad. It makes me feel a little proud of the old boat for it was so easy to right, besides giving me some new ideas how to build my next boat. While Don was following me, he never knew—until I told him—that I had been up-side-down. We landed on the left bank and Don followed. And, while there, Bill came near stepping on a rather large rattlesnake. To size Bill up, I would never have taken him to be a champion jumper, but when he saw how close he was to the snake I really believe he made the championship jump—I think about 18 feet. So after taking a movie of Mr. Snake, I killed him and we continued on our way. It was not long after that we reached the noted Lava Falls. There was never anyone that claimed to have run it but Buzz Holmstrom. After looking it over from both sides we decided that we could run it, and did so from the right side; and while I think we both lightly touched a rock, we came through in fine shape. . . .

Wednesday, July 19, 1939

Up and away before 6 A.M., and what a beautiful body of water. The surround-ings are also beautiful, but I cannot say so much for the motive power we are destined to endure as long as we are supposed to go places on this lake, for there is no current to help us out a bit. It seems rather dull after having those roaring rapids for company all the time and now everything is peaceful and quiet. After watching Chet do a little rowing I became rather wormy, so I took the oars and did the rest of the rowing for the day. About noon we were out of sight of Don, so we hunted a little shade on the right bank and waited, and in the course of time they made their appearance. We had lunch in the shade of some rocks and stayed there until the shade began to make its appearance on the left bank. We rowed over in the shade, and I—very lazily—rowed along until we made the turn to the left. When we were out of the shade we witnessed a big fight between two burros—it seemed that they fought for at least an hour. We were soon in sight of Pierce's Ferry, and then we picked up on our rowing and soon made our landing. After a rather long wait Don and Bill came along and we made camp. We met some C-C-C-Boys and there were some other Gov't men there, and they were very nice to us. We got 3 loaves of bread, which was very nice, and after our evening meal we declared the trip ended.

It was then that I expressed—to the boys—my appreciation of the most wonderful trip and their kind consideration shown me. I always tried to remember that I was the old man of the expedition, and the only way that I was reminded of the difference was their kindness to me. I will say that I was waited on more on this trip than about all the rest of my life, and when I speak of a wonderful trip there was never a more successful one. As I have mentioned before, [we were] three boys and an old man, and for all this trip there was never a cross or a harsh word spoken. And me being the leader of the trip, I often wonder if there was ever a leader that had the whole hearted support that I had. When we started out I did not know Don (from a boating standpoint), and all he knew of me was what he had heard; and I will always think the foundation for this wonderful trip was laid at Badger and Soap Creek Rapids, for it was there that Don and I became acquainted. From there on we never had any other idea than that of running every rapid as we came to them. Incidentally, that is another dream of mine that came true. To think of the many years that I have wended my lonely way along some part of the Colorado water shed; with my blankets unrolled on some sand bar, with the starry canopy of heaven over me, have I dreamed not only of making this trip but of making it as we did make it, with every one of these ferocious rapids conquered. To think I had to wait until I had rounded out my three score and ten before the dream came true.

THE LOG OF THE *PANTHON*

George Flavell

In the late summer of 1896, George Flavell, a professional hunter and sailor, rowed from Green River, Wyoming, to Yuma, Arizona, along with a companion, Ramon Montéz. Flavell and Montéz were only the third party to complete a traverse of Grand Canyon by boat, and they ran all but one of the rapids in a homemade fifteen-foot skiff that was framed with two-by-fours and sheathed with tongue-and-groove planks. Unlike the boatmen on previous expeditions, who had portaged most of the rapids, Flavell pioneered the modern technique of facing downstream, using the oars to slow the boat in fast current. Speaking to a reporter for the *Arizona Sentinel,* Flavell listed his reasons for running the river: "First, for the adventure; second, to see what so few people have seen; third, to hunt and trap; fourth, to examine the perpendicular walls of rock for gold." Despite this nod to sensible economic motives, Flavell said almost nothing about trapping and mining in his trip log (first published in 1987); instead, he wrote excitedly about the sheer pleasure of running rapids and exploring wild country.

．．．

October 17. Ha ha! We are here! I don't know exactly where, but somewhere on top of a rapid [in Marble Canyon]. It is the second heavy rapid—Badger or Soap Creek. I don't know which is last and which is first, but the first came very near being our last. We started out this morning singing, with two pairs of oars (having up to this time only had one) and the *Panthon* soon put 10 miles behind, when we came to a rapid that seemed to make considerable noise. After an investigation, we dove in, and came very near going a little too deep for our health. The bottom of the boat found a rock just in time to throw her sideways in the combing sea below. The shock was so hard, I had to drop the oars to catch myself from going overboard. I cast my eye to the lee gunwale—it was at the edge. I thought we were gone, but she raised and then I grabbed for the oars again. One had gone overboard, but with the remaining one I got her stem to the sea (it was not any too soon) and in a second we were winding and twisting around in the whirlpools below. It was all done in a flash. I don't suppose it was more than 20 seconds from the time we entered till we were out, so a person don't have much time to think. But after one is safe and thinks of it, they wonder how it was that the waves gave up when they had the power. It cannot be that water has mercy.

But we did not have long to meditate over our past danger. We found a pumpkin and that healed our wounds. It was not long till we heard the river groaning ahead which told of more work ahead, and soon we were tied up at the head of another rapid, crawling down over the boulders where we could get a good view. We viewed something to impress us for some time to come. It was some four or five hundred yards in length, the first 50 yards having about 12 feet of fall. It was rocky and seemed to be lashed into one mass of lather. We sat and gazed on it for two or three hours before our eyes had got their fill. The spray bounced 10 or 12 feet high, and as I was looking I noticed some 20 feet high, a dim mist of spray which puffed up like smoke. And it flashed across my mind, "If you have any doubt where that smoke comes from, just try to run it!" Still, I could of run it with an empty boat, but it would have been too far to carry the stuff and it was decided best to make a portage. Everything was taken out of the boat, the tackles hooked on, and the boat was soon 10 feet above water. And though it was only 50 yards from the place of exit to entrance, it took half a day.

After sliding her in the water again, we lowered her away 50 yards farther, behind a big boulder so as to break the waves, and got her sparred off and fixed up just in time to go to bed, which was pretty early. We were pretty tired, having a little more exercise than we were used to, such as carrying boxes, trunk, sacks of flour, beans, bacon, skinning our shins slipping over rocks, and other such little amusements. The inswell of the waves is making the *Panthon* dance, and we will be more than rocked to sleep tonight. The roar is so great it has made us dizzy. One side of the river seems to be running one way, and the other, the other. Progress made: 12 miles.

October 18. It was 11:30 before we were ready to start, but once on the way lost time was made up for. During the afternoon 26 rapids were passed, seven very heavy ones. One place Ramon was almost knocked overboard. The sea struck the boat so hard that the load was knocked from side to side. The river in one place was almost blocked with boulders. Tonight we have marble slabs to sit on. Some of it is beautiful and there were brown, red, blue, yellow, and white in the same piece.

Thought it seemed to be float, for there is no marble ledge visible above. Progress made: 18 miles.

October 19. After going ahead for a short time, a ledge of white marble gradually rose up from the river and kept raising till both walls were one shining, glittering mass, probably 1,000 feet high. Then they ran back some distance, then up two or three thousand feet more. Several springs of clear water were passed, something new to us. Several caves were seen in the cliffs, but as the walls are too steep to climb, we only got to one. It ran in 100 feet and the top was covered with soot which showed someone had been there, but they were a more modern race than the Cliff Dwellers for a piece of rope was found there, something not used in those days, at least not grass rope.

This part of the canyon is very abrupt and a shipwrecked sailor's eyes would water a long time before he could find a place to climb to the top of these walls. To stand on the summit and look down at the river (I doubt if it could be seen) must be an awful sight. It is far different looking up. After a thousand feet or so the top looks kind of dim, and if it was ten times as high it looks the same. There is marble enough here to build houses for the whole world to live in, and plenty to give them all a block to mark the spot where they take their last sleep. That little amount would not be missed from such a vast quantity.

This has been one of the most pleasant days we have passed. The rapids, probably feeling a little ashamed of treating us so rough, have been smoother than usual, and when we camped things were dry in the boat, something that had not happened for several days. We are down to dried beef and beans again, and the first animal that heaves in sight will be in immediate danger of being destroyed. Progress made: 25 miles.

October 20. When we started out we noticed the marble was raising and another formation was coming up underneath. It kept raising till it capped the highest peaks and later disappeared altogether. At 1 P.M. we reached the mouth of the Little Colorado River where we stopped and had dinner. This point is the terminus of Marble Canyon, and now the last, if not the least, is at hand, and when we pushed off with a rapid some ½ mile long to give us a good start, the *Panthon* shot into the great Grand Canyon at a lively rate and we camped with the Little Colorado far behind.

Marble Canyon was wonderful in its make up. It was a sight that made the heart shrink. To look up, it was truly awe inspiring! It made a man feel small. It showed him how small and insignificant he was. It made him not wonder, but *fear* and shrink before such mighty work! We saw nothing which gave us any reason to think that ever any such people as Cliff Dwellers had ever lived in the canyon.

We saw a good many caves but nearly all were in perpendicular walls, and I have a doubt as to the Cliff Dweller story. Progress made: 20 miles.

October 21. After going some 10 miles we came to a very bad rapid. Tying up the boat, we went down to investigate. It was one mass of boulders. The water entered by two channels at the head. It was perhaps as bad or worse (as for rocks) than any we had struck, and the show for running it was very slim, but to lower away would take at least a whole day.

While we were sitting there trying to decide what to do, we happened to look toward a little canyon that came in from the east side, and to our surprise three mounted men came up, dismounted, and tied their horses. We were not over 50 yards apart. There was a hotel on top of the summit, a kind of summer resort, and they had come down from there. They were much interested in the *Panthon*. One of these gentlemen was the Reverend Mr. George W. White, president of the University of Southern California at Los Angeles. He had preached at the Methodist church at San Fernando and if I had attended church a little more regular, I might of known him. They were anxious to see us get over the rapid, and after having a long talk he gave me his card and requested me to write to him when we got through.

I decided to run the rapid (though I would not if they had not been there) and pushed off. We took the east entrance which was only a small portion of the river. We had to make exact points to get through, which we failed to do, and in the flash of an eye an oar was broke, a rowlock tore out, and the *Panthon* was piled up in the boulders. We were not yet in the main part. We took off our shoes and pants, and with the big end of the broken oar, I pried her off. Twenty feet more and we came up again. Again we pried her loose. This time we whirled out in the main rapid. I took the head oars (the only ones left). She got across the current. Another rowlock busted—the oar went overboard—leaving no rowlocks on one side of the boat. There was only one narrow channel (crooked at that) where I thought it possible for a boat to pass, and we were hurled far from it. We went down sideways, endways, and every way, the three spectators standing on the rocks. I guess they would not of bid very high on what would be left of the *Panthon* and her crew when that rapid got through with them.

Well! Luck changes! Good follows bad. If we had bad luck in breaking the oar and rowlocks, we had good in getting through the rapid and we came out at the bottom never striking a rock. We picked up the oar that had followed up, and made shore just in time to keep from going over another rapid. Now, as I write these lines, I can look at the rapid that we came down not over 150 yards away. The rocks are as thick as seats in a theatre, and many are out of the water four feet. It seems impossible to think for a moment a boat could ever come through there in one piece. We made camp for the rest of the day and repaired the row locks and oars. Progress made: 10 miles.

October 22. This morning we were all ready again, but there was heavy water before us and before ten minutes had passed, we were again tied up to a rock, changing clothes, and bailing out the boat. We thought we had struck a rock slightly, but on investigation it was found that the bottom of the stem was cut off as clean as if with an ax, including a piece of iron which was also cut clean. Still, it did not damage the boat for the lost part was put there for a fender. In striking, it did not change the course of the boat in the least. At the time we were going about 15 miles an hour.

In a few moments we were off again, and in a few moments more we were again wet from head to foot, the boat about a third full of water, going down at 20 miles an hour. So much water had waterlogged her, she got sideways, but with will and strength I got head-on. This [rapid] was very long, some five or six hundred yards, and with a fall of at least 25 feet. Again the bailing began. Everything got wet again—the water in the boat was quite a way above shoe top. At the head of the rapid we ran over a sunken boulder, and as her bow went down between the next wave, some suction seemed to hold it down, some undercurrent, and the wave broke clear over. I never saw the like before.

It was no use to try to keep dry clothes, for any minute we were liable to be doused from head to foot (and were). There was no use to stop, so we pushed ahead. The rapids were thick! It seemed as though the boat was heavy—she would not raise quick and acted different than usual. She seemed stubborn and would not mind the oars.

It was 2 P.M. before we could find wood enough to make coffee. We, shortly after starting in the morning, had entered a box canyon. The walls came out of the water and were so straight that driftwood could not lodge. But at last, sighting a large stick that had jammed in a crevice, we had coffee and warmed ourselves for we were cold. It was cloudy and a fresh breeze coming down the canyon did not make wet clothes feel very comfortable.

After an hour we felt quite fresh again and off we went into another rapid. The spray flew—again we were bathed from head to foot, and so it was till we camped. It was nothing but bail and shiver all day. We ran somewhere in the vicinity of 40 rapids, and I think we had at least half that many barrels of water in the boat. Over half the time was spent in bailing, for it took ½ hour to bail out what came in in ½ second.

One place the rapid filled from wall to wall and there was not the least footing anywhere. It was about ½ mile long and straight and I think had a 30 foot fall. At the lower end the spray was flying high—it looked hazy! It was very risky to run it, knowing not what was at the bottom. To try to lower away would probably take two or three days. To avoid that much work by one single minute's risk was tempting (though that one minute is enough to smash the boat into a thousand pieces and put ourselves in a destitute condition if not in eternity). We were tempted; and a minute later we were past and once more the gauntlet was run. But this kind of water cannot last long. We are taking up too much fall and, to make a rough guess, I should think we are between three and four hundred feet lower than when we started this morning.

We dried ourselves out and after supper we talked over the day's proceedings. It was decided by the majority as being the most dangerous, as well as the luckiest, day of the whole trip. Lucky to think we are afloat tonight. If we had lowered over all the bad places it would have taken a month, and by risk it was run in a day. Still, I feel confident we will get through. We must expect some accidents and expect to hit some rocks. There is only one stone we must not hit, that we must miss at all hazard—our tombstone! Progress made: 17 miles.

October 23. After breakfast the cargo was all hung out to dry for the third time, and for the fourth time the *Panthon* was hauled up for repairs. The few scattering pieces left on her bow were torn off and in a short time she had a new bow. As it needed a piece of iron, it was necessary to procure it from some source, so a steel trap fell victim. It was heated in the fire to bend it in the right shape (a pair of scissors were used as tongs). It fit to a tee. She was once more pushed back into the river (and later on loaded up) where she swung to the pointer like a gentle horse, scarcely drawing the line tight and ready to dare the water tomorrow. Let them be smooth or rough, but rough though they be, they will only get a chance to dash against her side as she passes, for the great, like the small, are all the same—they are seen at hand, and at last left far behind. Rocks once passed are harmless. Those that are far ahead can harm us not. We only watch those close under the bow, that lay low in the water to stick, like a murderer, in the back.

October 24. Today was not without its accidents. We had not gone far before we were wet to the skin and, as usual, bailing occupied most of the time. We got in a whirlpool that took complete charge of everything. It spun us around for several minutes and then hurled us against the rocks. Taking us back again, whirling us around for another small eternity, it threw us in a little cove about 30 feet square. Every time we tried to get out we were sent back. After trying this a few times to no avail, we stopped to figure out some way of escape. We watched the whirlpool and noticed it was not always the same. It boiled with a great force, then it calmed a little for a new start. We got everything all ready and when it lulled we shot out. It was too quick for us and back we went against the rocks again. After four or five trials we got out.

After 5 P.M. we ran a heavy rapid. Though smooth in the middle, it was very rough at both top and bottom. It did not look very bad so in we went. The first dash filled the boat half full. I thought we were going to fill, for the next dash was as bad if not worse. I kept her head-on and as level as possible. She went through. As usual, when we have bad luck with a rapid there is always another just at its foot, but our luck was in and we made the shore about 20 feet above it.

Needless to say things in the boat were somewhat damp. Camp was soon made. We had collided with several rocks during the day and we find, for the first time, the boat to be leaking a little. The country is changing somewhat. For the last 25 miles the canyon has been very narrow. The walls, though not very high (1,000 feet) were stood on their edge, the strata stood straight up and down, and all kinds of formations mixed together till they resembled a bookcase with all kinds of different colored books standing side by side. But in the afternoon the hills broke down and showed a little verdure in places. The high mountains have receded so far back they are shut out from view by the smaller ones that still hem the river.

We find the water the most pleasant in deep box canyons. When we get into broken country where the sun can get in, it seems to make the water playful and it tries to see how high it can jump. But so far the *Panthon* has been equal to the occasion. When we get knocked around so that we can't manage her, she hunts her own way through, tapping a rock now and then just to see if it is solid. Progress made: 20 miles.

October 25. This morning the sun came in to see us at 9:30. The rapids took a change—instead of trying to swamp us (as was their usual habit) they shot us ahead at a lively rate, now and then playfully sprinkling us a little.

At 1 P.M. we stopped to have lunch. While eating, a large buck ibex came down the mountain to see what the smoke meant. After coming to within 300 yards, he stopped. I expected to see him go back a-flying. We needed meat, and a random shot was better than none. Taking a rest against a rock, the ball passed over his back, but the next broke a leg. Then there was a race up the mountain till the foot of the main wall was reached, then along the wall, over canyons, gulches, ravines. But he refused to give us his hide and I was forced to come back without meat.

We traveled on. At 4 P.M. heavy rapids were encountered again, but they were soon passed. In one I think the boat dropped 10 feet in a hole made by a sunken boulder, but she raised on the next wave which lifted us high in the air and we came out dry.

At 5 P.M. we came to a very bad rapid, full of rocks. To try to run the main channel was sure destruction, but it was possible to run the inside of the curve. It was also full of rocks and shallow, but we thought we would run it anyway. If we hung up we would pry off, and going through that way was better than lowering. In we went. We missed the exact place to enter. She struck once, turned clear around, and came out flying, but that blow was harder than we had expected.

We made a landing on the bar below and found the side was mashed in, including the piece of iron. This was the first time the boat had been actually damaged—it called for a sudden discharge of cargo. The bow was pulled up on the rocks so the damaged part was above water. The splinters were cut away, and pieces fitted on the inside, nailed and caulked. Progress made: 16 miles.

October 26. At 10 A.M. this morning she was ready to proceed. We passed through a dark, or rather black, formation that shone like coal, though it was not. It was about 60 feet high and about two miles long, and it lacked about one degree of being perpendicular. The channel for the river was narrowed to 60 feet in the narrowest place and not over 80 in the widest, this being the narrowest cut so far on the river. As we drifted along we noticed the lower walls were sinking and the second bench was closing in; and at 1 P.M. we were encased in walls thousands of feet high, perhaps a mile or more, lacking only a degree or so of being perpendicular. The east side had three benches, the first 600 to 1,000 feet being mostly of marble of a dark soapstone color. From the top of the first bench it was two or three hundred yards back at the angle of 45° to the foot of the second, then an abrupt wall of 2,000 feet more, the third bench being the same way. It was wonderful to look up (being necessary to look twice to see the top). The tops looked dim. The few scattering pines on their summit looked like small blades of grass. The river being so crooked, it could only be seen for a few hundred yards each way, and made it appear as though we were in a great deep pit.

This had been another fine day and we shot along at five miles an hour. Only six bad rapids were encountered, but these were run without getting wet. A falls was passed about noon that fell from the west wall. It was small, being a stream four feet wide and a foot thick. It had a fall of about 400 feet.

Later in the day an old doe and fawn ibex were seen on the first bench. A landing was made and after hunting along the wall for ½ mile, I found a crevice and, with a few minutes of hard climbing, I gained the bench, but no ibex in sight. I climbed to the foot of the second bench and followed around the rim for a mile or so, but was forced to go back to camp and eat *carne seca* for supper. The foot of the second bench gave an extensive view of the river. It looked very small from a perch of nearly 3,000 feet, and the cliff above seemed to be just as high above as when I was at the water's edge 3,000 feet lower. The wind, toward dark, began to come up the canyon with a vengeance which seemed to indicate a storm. Progress made: 25 miles.

October 27. This morning it was very dark (not being any too light at the best of times). The weather looked bad. Preparations were made to start, but a few large drops of rain warned us to keep covered up. The drops kept increasing till they fell in torrents, and I fear there will be a raise of the river. If such be the case we will have to lay up till it goes down. I am not much stuck on storms in such a place as this, for every rain loosens rocks above which come plunging down to the river as though they wanted to knock it out of existence. No thanks! I don't wish any 10 or 20 thousand ton boulders flying around my ears!

At 2 P.M. it cleared up a little. Camp was broke and though it sprinkled some again, we kept going and did not stop till the shadows of night had drawn their curtain over the canyon. Progress made: 15 miles.

October 28. This morning it was cold. At 9 A.M. the *Panthon* was moving. A bad rapid was run which put about eight inches of water in the boat. It was pretty fresh, but we had to stand it. The north wall (for the river runs west the entire length of this canyon) commenced to show indications of having been warmer some day than it is at present. It had been boiled up, the lava had run down the side in streams, in some places it had run down canyons, cooling before it reached the bottom, making quite a contrast between the light colored sandstone and the black lava. And though it lasted for many miles, it seemed as though the great river had even dared to face a burning volcano and did not allow it to cross, for only now and then a small knob or bed could be seen on the south side and seemed to be thrown across. The appearance of the rock shows the volcano was not in action long, for the rock was not burnt to any great extent, and in my estimation it was just an upheaval.

Early in the morning we saw some little streams coming down from a bench about 20 feet above the river, and on investigation we found there was a *cienega* of five or six acres. On the edge we saw what seemed to be the skeleton of some beast, but on closer examination it was found to be petrified tules, reeds, rushes, and other kinds of grass. The ground seemed to have been heated up from underneath, heating everything to what seemed to be a melting heat, and then cooling, turning everything to stone. The earth seemed to be consumed and in many places there were cavities three or four feet deep, the roots hanging there like icicles, all hard as stone. In walking around it was like walking on clay pipes as they cracked and snapped underfoot. Picking up a few pieces, we moved on.

Seeing a shack on a bar, we landed again and found eight teepees or wigwams which showed the red man had been there (but was gone then). We saw moccasin tracks at another place and other evidence of the red man.

It was 12 P.M. before the sun got down to see us. The river running west as it does, and the sun so far south, it cannot get down over such barricades as these walls and we have not had, on an average, one hour a day of sunshine since we left Lee's Ferry. But after 1 P.M. the walls on the south broke down and continued to do so all the afternoon. The river took a turn south and tonight the sun set on the west side for the first time in many days. At 4 P.M. the river, seeming (like ourselves) tired of being hemmed in, shot ahead, anxious to get out of the canyon (for the end is now near) and carried us along at seven miles an hour. Progress made: 40 miles.

October 29. This morning the sun came in at 8 o'clock, the east walls having broken down completely, leaving only a rugged, broken, chopped up country. But before many miles were passed, a new set of walls (granite) slowly arose out of the river and again we were walled in. But the river now commenced to run in all directions, giving the sun a chance every now and then to glance up-and-down the canyon.

After our 2½ days of pleasant sailing, bad water was encountered. The rapids were numerous, crooked, and rocky. We were getting reckless, so much so we drew no line. We ran 13 heavy and very dangerous ones. After running everything so far in Grand Canyon, we will now take very desperate chances for, if our calculations are right, this is our last night in the Canyon.

The next to the last rapid we ran this afternoon was as dangerous as any on the whole river. There was a large boulder in the middle of the river the size of a small house where most of the water piled up and broke off on both sides. To the right it was filled with smaller rocks—it was impossible to pass that side. There was a pass of 30 feet between the rock and the left side, which was a high perpendicular wall that curved around behind the rock, so the water, after breaking off the rock, went to the wall. Where the water runs to the wall is a very bad place, for if the boat once touches she is gone. But we thought by cutting close to the rock we could shoot around behind. We went in, and having to pull quite a little to clear the rock (which was just as dangerous as the wall if struck), we pulled too far. I thought we were gone. I threw her around, head-on, to let her strike bow first. But just as her bow was within four or five feet of the wall, there was a boil-up—it stopped the headway of the boat, or rather gave her a kind of a push out (though we still were going 20 miles an hour) and in a second we were past, missing the point by less than two feet. That was the nearest call we have had and we consider ourselves under many obligations to that little boil-up, it being the only thing in the world that could have helped us.

The walls being so abrupt, we went till dark before we could find wood enough to make a fire. Well! Twenty-five miles more and the great Buckskin Mountains will be lost to view. Only 25 short miles. That is only a very short distance compared with the hundreds already passed, but still it is 25 miles and it must be passed before we can say our life is our own. But tomorrow night we will be safe on the lower Colorado, wrecked, or dead. Which will it be? Progress made: 35 miles.

October 30. Having an early start and desiring to have it over, the oars were bent, stopping only a few minutes for dinner. The rapids came regular, but one by one their waves were mashed down by the *Panthon*'s bow. The walls kept raising up and breaking down, only to raise again. Still, the same steady stroke was kept, and at 3:20 P.M. the walls stopped to raise no more. We looked ahead at the low, rolling hills and the river which spread wide, with groves of willows on both banks. We looked back at the high and rugged peaks now left behind. We were safe, a feeling no one could feel while in that terrible place! But now the Great, Grand, Beautiful, Wonderful, Fearful, Desolate Canyon is like yesterday—passed!

It is an awful place, and destitute to the extreme. In all its barren walls there is not a single bat's nest—not even they would live in such a desolate place. Language can convey only a faint idea of such a place, for the literature put before the public is so different in its description from the real canyon, it would not be recognized. I have a handy manual which says the walls are 7,000 feet perpendicular. There is no place on the Colorado River where there is a perpendicular wall raising out of the river that will exceed 3,000 feet. It appears more as though the river ran between two ranges instead of one. The highest peaks are seldom seen from the river, for they are far back (as a general thing) and the inner walls shut them out from view. And ofttimes when the walls are only a few hundred feet high, nothing can be seen beyond their tops, the higher peaks being so far back. Still, there are times when high peaks come close, but always in benches—four, five, or six, sometimes more. At the top of each bench it takes a slant back from a few feet to ½ mile which sets the summits far back. The most extensive formations are sandstone, granite, and marble. Streaks of marble can be found at the canyon's mouth.

I don't think there is another such barren country in the world as the one we have passed through (unless it is the Sahara). Over a thousand miles [from Green River], it is (properly speaking) one entire canyon from beginning to end. In all that long distance there is not one foot that can be called level land with the exception of 2,000 acres at Blake. There are in Utah a good many little bottoms and bars containing a few acres each, but it is a poor foundation to build on, for they were made by the river and are subject to transportation at any high water. In all that distance only fourteen deer, seven sheep, seven ibex, two jackrabbits, and two flocks of quail were seen. For the last 700 miles there are not enough beaver to count. Where we expected to find many we found none, and all we made from such a long and dangerous trip was our escape! Still it is worth half of a life (such as I lead) to see such a place.

THE GRAND CAÑON OF
THE COLORADO

John Wesley Powell

After losing an arm fighting for the Union Army at the Civil War battle of Shiloh, John Wesley Powell led the first expedition by boat down the Green and Colorado rivers from Wyoming to California. Together with his brother Walter and eight recruits, Powell covered almost a thousand river miles in three months during the summer of 1869. Powell made daily geological and astronomical observations; meanwhile, his crew carried their heavy oak boats around most of the rapids, clambering along the rocky shore in the heat of summer. Three men decided to separate from the expedition near the lower end of Grand Canyon, and they were never seen again. In the post–Civil War era of disunity and recrimination, Powell's stirring *Report on the Exploration of the Colorado River of the West and Its Tributaries* rekindled the national romance of westward expansion and put Grand Canyon on the map. His fame earned him an appointment as director of the U.S. Geological Survey, where he argued that intensive irrigation would be the key to settlement of the arid West. Lake Powell, upstream of Grand Canyon, was named in his honor. Written in the form of journal, Powell's story is rich with suspense and adventure, and has remained the most widely read piece of Grand Canyon literature since it was published in 1875.

. . .

August 13.—We are now ready to start on our way down the Great Unknown. Our boats, tied to a common stake, are chafing each other, as they are tossed by the fretful river. They ride high and buoyant, for their loads are lighter than we could desire. We have but a month's rations remaining. The flour has been resifted through the mosquito net sieve; the spoiled bacon has been dried, and the worst of it boiled; the few pounds of dried apples have been spread in the sun, and reshrunken to their normal bulk; the sugar has all melted, and gone on its way down the river; but we have a large sack of coffee. The lighting of the boats has this advantage: they will ride the waves better, and we shall have but little to carry when we make a portage.

We are three quarters of a mile in the depths of the earth, and the great river shrinks into insignificance, as it dashes its angry waves against the walls and cliffs, that rise to the world above; they are but puny ripples, and we but pigmies, running up and down the sands, or lost among the boulders.

We have an unknown distance yet to run; an unknown river yet to explore. What falls there are, we know not; what rocks beset the channel, we know not; what walls rise over the river, we know not. Ah, well! we may conjecture many things. The men talk as cheerfully as ever; jests are bandied about freely this morning; but to me the cheer is somber and the jests are ghastly.

With some eagerness, and some anxiety, and some misgiving, we enter the cañon below, and are carried along by the swift water through walls which rise from its very edge. They have the same structure as we noticed yesterday—tiers of irregular shelves below, and, above these, steep slopes to the foot of marble cliffs. We run six miles in a little more than half an hour, and emerge into a more open portion of the cañon, where high hills and ledges of rock intervene between the river and the distant walls. Just at the head of this open place the river runs across a dike: that is, a fissure in the rocks, open to depths below, has been filled with eruptive matter, and this, on cooling, was harder than the rocks through which the crevice was made, and, when these were washed away, the harder volcanic matter remained as a wall, and the river has cut a gate-way through it several hundred feet high, and as many wide. As it crosses the wall, there is a fall below, and a bad rapid, filled with boulders of trap; so we stop to make a portage. Then on we go, gliding by hills and ledges, with distant walls in view; sweeping past sharp angles of rock; stopping at a few points to examine rapids, which we find can be run, until we have made another five miles, when we land for dinner.

Then we let down with lines, over a long rapid, and start again. Once more the walls close in, and we find ourselves in a narrow gorge, the water again filling the channel, and very swift. With great care, and constant watchfulness, we proceed, making about four miles this afternoon, and camp in a cave.

August 14.—At daybreak we walk down the bank of the river, on a little sandy beach, to take a view of a new feature in the cañon. Heretofore, hard rocks have given us bad river; soft rocks, smooth water; and a series of rocks harder than any we have experienced sets in. The river enters the granite!

We can see but a little way into the granite gorge, but it looks threatening.

After breakfast we enter on the waves. At the very introduction, it inspires awe. The cañon is narrower than we have ever before seen it; the water is swifter; there are but few broken rocks in the channel; but the walls are set, on either side, with pinnacles and crags; and sharp, angular buttresses, bristling with wind and wave polished spires, extend far out into the river.

Ledges of rocks jut into the stream, their tops sometimes just below the surface, sometimes rising few or many feet above; and island ledges, and island pinnacles, and island towers break the swift course of the stream into chutes, and eddies, and whirlpools. We soon reach a place where a creek comes in from the left, and just below, the channel is choked with boulders, which have washed down this lateral cañon and formed a dam, over which there is a fall of thirty or forty feet; but on the boulders we can get foothold, and we make a portage.

Three more such dams are found. Over one we make a portage; at the other two we find chutes, through which we can run.

As we proceed, the granite rises higher, until nearly a thousand feet of the lower part of the walls are composed of this rock.

About eleven o'clock we hear a great roar ahead, and approach it very cautiously. The sound grows louder and louder as we run, and at last we find ourselves above a long, broken fall, with ledges and pinnacles of rock obstructing the river. There is a descent of, perhaps, seventy five or eighty feet in a third of a mile, and the rushing waters break into great waves on the rocks, and lash themselves into a mad, white foam. We can land just above, but there is no foot-hold on either side by which we can make a portage. It is nearly a thousand feet to the top of the granite, so it will be impossible to carry our boats around, though we can climb to the summit up a side gulch, and, passing along a mile or two, can descend to the river. This we find on examination; but such a portage would be impracticable for us, and we must run the rapid, or abandon the river. There is no hesitation. We step into our boats, push off and away we go, first on smooth but swift water, then we strike a glassy wave, and ride to its top, down again into the trough, up again on a higher wave, and down and up on waves higher and still higher, until we strike one just as it curls back, and a breaker rolls over our little boat. Still, on we speed, shooting past projecting rocks, till the little boat is caught in a whirlpool, and spun around several times. At last we pull out again into the stream, and now the other boats have passed us. The open compartment of the "Emma Dean" is filled with water, and every breaker rolls over us. Hurled back from a rock, now on this side, now on that, we are carried into an eddy, in which we struggle for a few minutes, and are then out again, the breakers still rolling over us. Our boat is unmanageable, but she cannot sink, and we drift down another hundred yards, through breakers; how, we scarcely know. We find the other boats have turned into an eddy at the foot of the fall, and are waiting to catch us as we come, for the men have seen that our boat is swamped. They push out as we come near, and pull us in against the wall. We bail our boat, and on we go again.

The walls, now, are more than a mile in height—a vertical distance difficult to appreciate. Stand on the south steps of the Treasury building, in Washington, and look down Pennsylvania Avenue to the Capitol Park, and measure this distance overhead, and imagine cliffs to extend to that altitude, and you will understand what I mean; or, stand at Canal street, in New York, and look up Broadway to Grace Church, and you have about the distance; or, stand at Lake street bridge, in Chicago, and look down to the Central Depot, and you have it again.

A thousand feet of this is up through granite crags, then steep slopes and perpendicular cliffs rise, one above another, to the summit. The gorge is black and narrow below, red and gray and flaring above, with crags and angular projections on the walls, which, cut in many places by side cañons, seem to be a vast wilderness of rocks. Down in these grand, gloomy depths we glide, ever listening, for the mad waters keep up their roar; ever watching, ever peering ahead, for the narrow cañon is winding, and the river is closed in so that we can see but a few hundred yards, and what there may be below we know not; but we listen for falls, and watch for rocks, or stop now and then, in the bay of a recess, to admire the gigantic scenery. And ever, as we go, there is some new pinnacle or tower, some crag or peak, some distant view of the upper plateau, some strange shaped rock, or some deep, narrow side cañon. Then we come to another broken fall, which appears more difficult than the one we ran this morning.

A small creek comes in on the right, and the first fall of the water is over boulders, which have been carried down by this lateral stream. We land at its mouth, and stop for an hour or two to examine the fall. It seems possible to let down with lines, at least a part of the way, from point to point, along the right hand wall. So we make a portage over the first rocks, and find footing on some boulders below. Then we let down one of the boats to the end of her line, when she reaches a corner of the projecting rock, to which one of the men clings, and steadies her, while I examine an eddy below. I think we can pass the other boats down by us, and catch them in the eddy. This is soon done and the men in the boats in the eddy pull us to their side. On the shore of this little eddy there is about two feet of gravel beach above the water. Standing on this beach, some of the men take the line of the little boat and let it drift down against another projecting angle. Here is a little shelf, on which a man from my boat climbs, and a shorter line is passed to him, and he fastens the boat to the side of the cliff. Then the second one is let down, bringing the line of the third. When the second boat is tied up, the two men standing on the beach above spring into the last boat, which is pulled up alongside of ours. Then we let down the boats, for twenty five or thirty yards, by walking along the shelf, landing them again in the mouth of a side cañon. Just below this there is another pile of boulders, over which we make another portage. From the foot of these rocks we can climb to another shelf, forty or fifty feet above the water.

On this bench we camp for the night. We find a few sticks, which have lodged in the rocks. It is raining hard, and we have no shelter, but kindle a fire and have our supper. We sit on the rocks all night, wrapped in our ponchos, getting what sleep we can.

August 15.—This morning we find we can let down for three or four hundred yards, and it is managed in this way: We pass along the wall, by climbing from projecting point to point, sometimes near the water's edge, at other places fifty or sixty feet above, and hold the boat with a line, while two men remain aboard, and prevent her from being dashed against the rocks, and keep the line from getting caught on the wall. In two hours we have brought them all down, as far as it is possible, in this way. A few yards below, the river strikes with great violence against a projecting rock, and our boats are pulled up in a little bay above. We must now manage to pull out of this, and clear the point below. The little boat is held by the bow obliquely up the stream. We jump in, and pull out only a few strokes, and sweep clear of the dangerous rock. The other boats follow in the same manner, and the rapid is passed.

It is not easy to describe the labor of such navigation. We must prevent the waves from dashing the boats against the cliffs. Sometimes, where the river is swift, we must put a bight of rope about a rock, to prevent her being snatched from us by a wave; but where the plunge is too great, or the chute too swift, we must let her leap, and catch her below, or the undertow will drag her under the falling water, and she sinks. Where we wish to run her out a little way from shore, through a channel between rocks, we first throw in little sticks of drift wood, and watch their course, to see where we must steer, so that she will pass the channel in safety. And so we hold, and let go, and pull, and lift, and ward, among rocks, around rocks, and over rocks.

And now we go on through this solemn, mysterious way. The river is very deep, the cañon very narrow, and still obstructed, so that there is no steady flow of the stream; but the waters wheel, and roll, and boil, and we are scarcely able to determine where we can go. Now, the boat is carried to the right, perhaps close to the wall; again, she is shot into the stream, and perhaps is dragged over to the other side, where, caught in a whirlpool, she spins about. We can neither land nor run as we please. The boats are entirely unmanageable; no order in their running can be preserved; now one, now another, is ahead, each crew laboring for its own preservation. In such a place we come to another rapid. Two of the boats run it perforce. One succeeds in landing, but there is no foot-hold by which to make a portage, and she is pushed out again into the stream. The next minute a great reflex wave fills the open compartment; she is water-logged, and drifts unmanageable. Breaker after breaker rolls over her, and one capsizes her. The men are thrown out; but they cling to the boat, and she drifts down some distance, alongside of us, and we are able to catch her. She is soon bailed out, and the men are aboard once more; but the oars are lost, so a pair from the "Emma Dean" is spared. Then for two miles we find smooth water.

Clouds are playing in the cañon to day. Sometimes they roll down in great masses, filling the gorge with gloom; sometimes they hang above, from wall to wall, and cover the cañon with a roof of impending storm; and we can peer long distances up and down this cañon corridor, with its cloud roof overhead, its walls of black granite, and its river bright with the sheen of broken waters. Then, a gust of wind sweeps down a side gulch, and, making a rift in the clouds, reveals the blue heavens, and a stream of sunlight pours in. Then, the clouds drift away into the distance, and hang around crags, and peaks, and pinnacles, and towers, and walls, and cover them with a mantle, that lifts from time to time, and sets them all in sharp relief. Then, baby clouds creep out of side cañons, glide around points, and creep back again, into more distant gorges. Then, clouds, set in strata, across the cañon, with intervening vista views, to cliffs and rocks beyond. The clouds are children of the heavens, and when they play among the rocks, they lift them to the region above.

It rains! Rapidly little rills are formed above, and these soon grow into brooks, and the brooks grow into creeks, and tumble over the walls in innumerable cascades, adding their wild music to the roar of the river. When the rain ceases, the rills, brooks, and creeks run dry. The waters that fall, during a rain, on these steep rocks, are gathered at once into the river; they could scarcely be poured in more suddenly, if some vast spout ran from the clouds to the stream itself. When a storm bursts over the cañon, a side gulch is dangerous, for a sudden flood may come, and the inpouring waters will raise the river, so as to hide the rocks before your eyes.

Early in the afternoon, we discover a stream, entering from the north, a clear, beautiful creek, coming down through a gorgeous red cañon. We land, and camp on a sand beach, above its mouth, under a great, overspreading tree, with willow shaped leaves.

August 16.—We must dry our rations again to day, and make oars.

The Colorado is never a clear stream, but for the past three or four days it has been raining much of the time, and the floods, which are poured over the walls, have brought down great quantities of mud, making it exceedingly turbid now. The little affluent, which we have discovered here, is a clear, beautiful creek, or river, as it would be termed in this western country, where streams are not abundant. We have named one stream, away above, in honor of the great chief of the "Bad Angels," and, as this is in beautiful contrast to that, we conclude to name it "Bright Angel."

Early in the morning, the whole party starts up to explore the Bright Angel

River, with the special purpose of seeking timber, from which to make oars. A couple of miles above, we find a large pine log, which has been floated down from the plateau, probably from an altitude of more than six thousand feet, but not many miles back. On its way, it must have passed over many cataracts and falls, for it bears scars in evidence of the rough usage which it has received. The men roll it on skids, and the work of sawing oars is commenced.

This stream heads away back, under a line of abrupt cliffs, that terminates the plateau, and tumbles down more than four thousand feet in the first mile or two of its course; then runs through a deep, narrow cañon, until it reaches the river.

Late in the afternoon I return, and go up a little gulch, just above this creek, about two hundred yards from camp, and discover the ruins of two or three old houses, which were originally of stone, laid in mortar. Only the foundations are left, but irregular blocks, of which the houses were constructed, lie scattered about. In one room I find an old mealing stone, deeply worn, as if it had been much used. A great deal of pottery is strewn around, and old trails, which in some places are deeply worn into the rocks, are seen.

It is ever a source of wonder to us why these ancient people sought such inaccessible places for their homes. They were, doubtless, an agricultural race, but there are no lands here, of any considerable extent, that they could have cultivated. To the west of Oraiby, one of the towns in the "Province of Tusayan," in Northern Arizona, the inhabitants have actually built little terraces along the face of the cliff, where a spring gushes out, and thus made their sites for gardens It is possible that the ancient inhabitants of this place made their agricultural lands in the same way. But why should they seek such spots? Surely, the country was not so crowded with population as to demand the utilization of so barren a region. The only solution of the problem suggested is this: We know that, for a century or two after the settlement of Mexico, many expeditions were sent into the country, now comprised in Arizona and New Mexico, for the purpose of bringing the town building people under the dominion of the Spanish government. Many of their villages were destroyed, and the inhabitants fled to regions at that time unknown; and there are traditions, among the people who inhabit the *pueblos* that still remain, that the cañons were these unknown lands. Maybe these buildings were erected at that time; sure it is that they have a much more modern appearance than the ruins scattered over Nevada, Utah, Colorado, Arizona, and New Mexico. Those old Spanish conquerors had a monstrous greed for gold, and a wonderful lust for saving souls. Treasures they must have; if not on earth, why, then, in heaven; and when they failed to find heathen temples, bedecked with silver, they propitiated Heaven by seizing the heathen themselves. There is yet extant a copy of a record, made by a heathen artist, to express his conception of the demands of the conquerors. In one part of the picture we have a lake, and near by stands a priest pouring water on the head of a native. On the other side, a poor Indian has a cord about his throat. Lines run from these two groups, to a central figure, a man with beard, and full Spanish panoply. The interpretation of the picture writing is this: "Be baptized, as this saved heathen; or be hanged, as that damned heathen." Doubtless, some of these people preferred a third alternative, and, rather than be baptized or hanged, they chose to be imprisoned within these cañon walls.

August 17.—Our rations are still spoiling; the bacon is so badly injured that we are compelled to throw it away. By an accident, this morning, the saleratus is lost overboard. We have now only musty flour sufficient for ten days, a few dried apples, but plenty of coffee. We must make all haste possible. If we meet with difficulties, as we have done in the cañon above, we may be compelled to give up the expedition, and try to reach the Mormon settlements to the north. Our hopes are that the worst places are passed, but our barometers are all so much injured as to be useless, so we have lost our reckoning in altitude, and know not how much descent the river has yet to make.

The stream is still wild and rapid, and rolls through a narrow channel. We make but slow progress, often landing against a wall, and climbing around some point, where we can see the river below. Although very anxious to advance, we are determined to run with great caution, lest, by another accident, we lose all our supplies. How precious that little flour has become! We divide it among the boats, and carefully store it away, so that it can be lost only by the loss of the boat itself.

We make ten miles and a half, and camp among the rocks, on the right. We have had rain, from time to time, all day, and have been thoroughly drenched and chilled; but between showers the sun shines with great power, and the mercury in our thermometers stands at 115°, so that we have rapid changes from great extremes, which are very disagreeable. It is especially cold in the rain to-night. The little canvas we have is rotten and useless; the rubber ponchos, with which we started from Green River City, have all been lost; more than half the party is without hats, and not one of us has an entire suit of clothes, and we have not a blanket apiece. So we gather drift wood, and build a fire; but after supper the rain, coming down in torrents, extinguishes it, and we sit up all night, on the rocks, shivering, and are more exhausted by the night's discomfort than by the day's toil.

August 18.—The day is employed in making portages, and we advance but two miles on our journey. Still it rains.

While the men are at work making portages, I climb up the granite to its summit, and go away back over the rust colored sandstones and greenish yellow shales, to the foot of the marble wall. I climb so high that the men and boats are lost in the black depths below, and the dashing river is a rippling brook; and still there is more cañon above than below. All about me are interesting geological records. The book is open, and I can read as I run. All about me are grand views, for the clouds are playing again in the gorges. But somehow I think of the nine days' rations, and the bad river, and the lesson of the rocks, and the glory of the scene is but half seen.

I push on to an angle, where I hope to get a view of the country beyond, to see, if possible, what the prospect may be of our soon running through this plateau, or, at least, of meeting with some geological change that will let us out of the granite; but, arriving at the point, I can see below only a labyrinth of deep gorges.

August 19.—Rain again this morning. Still we are in our granite prison, and the time is occupied until noon in making a long, bad portage.

After dinner, in running a rapid, the pioneer boat is upset by a wave. We are some distance in advance of the larger boats, the river is rough and swift, and we are unable to land, but cling to the boat, and are carried down stream, over another rapid. The men in the boats above see our trouble, but they are caught in whirlpools, and are spinning about in eddies, and it seems a long time before they come to our relief. At last they do come; our boat is turned right side up, bailed out; the oars, which fortunately have floated along in company with us, are gathered up, and on we go, without even landing.

Soon after the accident the clouds break away, and we have sunshine again.

Soon we find a little beach, with just room enough to land. Here we camp, but there is no wood. Across the river, and a little way above, we see some drift wood lodged in the rocks. So we bring two boat loads over, build a huge fire, and spread everything to dry. It is the first cheerful night we have had for a week; a warm, drying fire in the midst of the camp, and a few bright stars in our patch of heavens overhead.

August 20.—The characteristics of the cañon change this morning. The river is broader, the walls more sloping, and composed of black slates, that stand on edge. These nearly vertical slates are washed out in places—that is, the softer beds are washed out between the harder, which are left standing. In this way, curious little alcoves are formed, in which are quiet bays of water, but on a much smaller scale than the great bays and buttresses of Marble Cañon.

The river is still rapid, and we stop to let down with lines several times, but make greater progress as we run ten miles. We camp on the right bank. Here, on a terrace of trap, we discover another group of ruins. There was evidently quite a village on this rock. Again we find mealing stones, and much broken pottery, and up in a little natural shelf in the rock, back of the ruins, we find a globular basket, that would hold perhaps a third of a bushel. It is badly broken, and, as I attempt to take it up, it falls to pieces. There are many beautiful flint chips, as if this had been the home of an old arrow maker.

August 21.—We start early this morning, cheered by the prospect of a fine day, and encouraged, also, by the good run made yesterday. A quarter of a mile below camp the river turns abruptly to the left, and between camp and that point is very swift, running down in a long, broken chute, and piling up against the foot of the cliff, where it turns to the left. We try to pull across, so as to go down on the other side, but the waters are swift, and it seems impossible for us to escape the rock below; but, in pulling across, the bow of the boat is turned to the farther shore, so that we are swept broadside down, and are prevented, by the rebounding waters, from striking against the wall. There we toss about for a few seconds in these billows, and are carried past the danger. Below, the river turns again to the right, the cañon is very narrow, and we see in advance but a short distance. The water, too, is very swift, and there is no landing place. From around this curve there comes a mad roar, and down we are carried, with a dizzying velocity, to the head of another rapid. On either side, high over our heads, there are overhanging granite walls, and the sharp bends cut off our view, so that a few minutes will carry us into unknown waters. Away we go, on one long, winding chute. I stand on deck, supporting myself with a strap, fastened on either side to the gunwale, and the boat glides rapidly, where the water is smooth, or, striking a wave, she leaps and bounds like a thing of life, and we have a wild, exhilarating ride for ten miles, which we make in less than an hour. The excitement is so great that we forget the danger, until we hear the roar of a great fall below; then we back on our oars, and are carried slowly toward its head, and succeed in landing just above, and find that we have to make another portage. At this we are engaged until some time after dinner.

Just here we run out of the granite!

Ten miles in less than half a day, and limestone walls below. Good cheer returns; we forget the storms, and the gloom, and cloud covered cañons, and the black granite, and the raging river, and push our boats from shore in great glee.

Though we are out of the granite, the river is still swift, and we wheel about a point again to the right, and turn, so as to head back in the direction from which we come, and see the granite again, with its narrow gorge and black crags; but we meet with no more great falls, or rapids. Still, we run cautiously, and stop, from time to time, to examine some places which look bad. Yet, we make ten miles this afternoon; twenty miles, in all, to day.

August 22.—We come to rapids again, this morning, and are occupied several hours in passing them, letting the boats down, from rock to rock, with lines, for nearly half a mile, and then have to make a long portage. While the men are engaged in this, I climb the wall on the northeast, to a height of about two thousand five hundred feet, where I can obtain a good view of a long stretch of cañon below. Its course is to the southwest. The walls seem to rise very abruptly, for two thousand five hundred or three thousand feet, and then there is a gently sloping terrace, on each side, for two or three miles, and again we find cliffs, one thousand five hundred or two thousand feet high. From the brink of these the plateau stretches back to the north and south, for a long distance. Away down the cañon, on the right wall, I can see a group of mountains, some of which appear to stand on the brink of the cañon. The effect of the terrace is to give the appearance of a narrow winding valley, with high walls on either side, and a deep, dark, meandering gorge down its middle. It is impossible, from this point of view, to determine whether we have granite at the bottom, or not; but, from geological considerations, I conclude that we shall have marble walls below.

After my return to the boats, we run another mile, and camp for the night.

We have made but little over seven miles to day, and a part of our flour has been soaked in the river again.

August 23.—Our way to day is again through marble walls. Now and then we pass, for a short distance, through patches of granite, like hills thrust up into the limestone. At one of these places we have to make another portage, and, taking advantage of the delay, I go up a little stream, to the north, wading it all the way, sometimes having to plunge in to my neck; in other places being compelled to swim across little basins that have been excavated at the foot of the falls. Along its course are many cascades and springs gushing out from the rocks on either side. Sometimes a cottonwood tree grows over the water. I come to one beautiful fall, of more than a hundred and fifty feet, and climb around it to the right, on the broken rocks. Still going up, I find the cañon narrowing very much, being but fifteen or twenty feet wide; yet the walls rise on either side many hundreds of feet, perhaps thousands; I can hardly tell.

In some places the stream has not excavated its channel down vertically through the rocks, but has cut obliquely, so that one wall overhangs the other. In other places it is cut vertically above and obliquely below, or obliquely above and vertically below, so that it is impossible to see out overhead. But I can go no farther. The time which I estimated it would take to make the portage has almost expired, and I start back on a round trot, wading in the creek where I must, and plunging through basins, and find the men waiting for me, and away we go on the river.

Just after dinner we pass a stream on the right, which leaps into the Colorado by a direct fall of more than a hundred feet, forming a beautiful cascade. There is a bed of very hard rock above, thirty or forty feet in thickness, and there are much softer beds below. The hard beds above project many yards beyond the softer, which are washed out, forming a deep cave behind the fall, and the stream pours through a narrow crevice above into a deep pool below. Around on the rocks, in the cave like chamber, are set beautiful ferns, with delicate fronds and enameled stalks. The little frondlets have their points turned down, to form spore cases. It has very much the appearance of the Maiden's Hair fern, but is much larger. This delicate foliage covers the rocks all about the fountain, and gives the chamber great beauty. But we have little time to spend in admiration, so on we go.

We make fine progress this afternoon, carried along by a swift river, and shoot over the rapids, finding no serious obstructions.

The canyon walls, for two thousand five hundred or three thousand feet, are very regular, rising almost perpendicularly, but here and there set with narrow steps, and occasionally we can see away above the broad terrace, to distant cliffs.

We camp to night in a marble cave, and find, on looking at our reckoning, that we have run twenty two miles.

August 24.—The cañon is wider to day. The walls rise to a vertical height of nearly three thousand feet. In many places the river runs under a cliff, in great curves, forming amphitheaters, half dome shaped.

Though the river is rapid, we meet with no serious obstructions, and run twenty miles. It is curious how anxious we are to make up our reckoning every time we stop, now that our diet is confined to plenty of coffee, very little spoiled flour, and very few dried apples. It has come to be a race for a dinner. Still, we make such fine progress, all hands are in good cheer, but not a moment of daylight is lost.

August 25.—We make twelve miles this morning, when we come to monuments of lava standing in the river; low rocks mostly, but some of them shafts more than a hundred feet high. Going on down, three or four miles, we find them increasing in number. Great quantities of cooled lava and many cinder cones are seen on either side; and then we come to an abrupt cataract. Just over the fall, on the right wall, a cinder cone, or extinct volcano, with a well defined crater, stands on the very brink of the cañon. This, doubtless, is the one we saw two or three days ago. From this volcano vast floods of lava have been poured down into the river, and a stream of molten rock has run up the cañon, three or four miles, and down, we know not how far. Just where it poured over the cañon wall is the fall. The whole north side, as far as we can see, is lined with the black basalt, and high up on the opposite wall are patches of the same material, resting on the benches, and filling old alcoves and caves, giving to the wall a spotted appearance.

The rocks are broken in two, along a line which here crosses the river, and the beds, which we have seen while coming down the cañon for the last thirty miles, have dropped 800 feet, on the lower side of the line, forming what geologists call a fault. The volcanic cone stands directly over the fissure thus formed. On the side of the river opposite, mammoth springs burst out of this crevice, one or two hundred feet above the river, pouring in a stream quite equal in volume to the Colorado Chiquito.

This stream seems to be loaded with carbonate of lime, and the water, evaporating, leaves an incrustation on the rocks; and this process has been continued for a long time, for extensive deposits are noticed, in which are basins, with bubbling springs. The water is salty.

We have to make a portage here, which is completed in about three hours, and on we go.

We have no difficulty as we float along, and I am able to observe the wonderful phenomena connected with this flood of lava. The cañon was doubtless filled to a height of twelve or fifteen hundred feet, perhaps by more than one flood. This would dam the water back; and in cutting through this great lava bed, a new channel has been formed, sometimes on one side, sometimes on the other. The cooled lava, being of firmer texture than the rocks of which the walls are composed, remains in some places, in others a narrow channel has been cut, leaving a line of basalt on either side. It is possible that the lava cooled faster on the sides against the walls, and that the centre ran out; but of this we can only conjecture. There are other places, where almost the whole of the lava is gone, patches of it only being seen where it has caught on the walls. As we float down, we can see that it ran out into side cañons. In some places this basalt has a fine, columnar structure, often in concentric prisms, and masses of these concentric columns have coalesced. In some places, when the flow occurred, the cañon was probably at about the same depth as it is now, for we can see where the basalt has rolled out on the sands, and, what seems curious to me, the sands are not melted or metamorphosed to any appreciable extent. In places the bed of the river is of sandstone or limestone, in other places of lava, showing that it has all been cut out again where the sandstones and limestones appear; but there is a little yet left where the bed is of lava.

What a conflict of water and fire there must have been here! Just imagine a river of molten rock, running down into a river of melted snow. What a seething and boiling of the waters; what clouds of steam rolled into the heavens!

Thirty five miles to day. Hurrah!

August 26.—The cañon walls are steadily becoming higher as we advance. They are still bold, and nearly vertical up to the terrace. We still see evidence of the eruption discovered yesterday, but the thickness of the basalt is decreasing, as we go down the stream; yet it has been reinforced at points by streams that have come down from volcanoes standing on the terrace above, but which we cannot see from the river below.

Since we left the Colorado Chiquito, we have seen no evidences that the tribe of Indians inhabiting the plateaus on either side ever come down to the river; but about eleven o'clock to day we discover an Indian garden, at the foot of the wall on the right, just where a little stream, with a narrow flood plain, comes down through a side cañon. Along the valley, the Indians have planted corn, using the water which burst out in springs at the foot of the cliff, for irrigation. The corn is looking quite well, but is not sufficiently advanced to give us roasting ears; but there are some nice, green squashes. We carry ten or a dozen of these on board our boats, and hurriedly leave, not willing to be caught in the robbery, yet excusing ourselves by pleading our great want. We run down a short distance, to where we feel certain no Indians can follow; and what a kettle of squash sauce we make! True, we have no salt with which to season it, but it makes a fine addition to our unleavened bread and coffee. Never was fruit so sweet as these stolen squashes.

After dinner we push on again, making fine time, finding many rapids, but none so bad that we cannot run them with safety, and when we stop, just at dusk, and foot up our reckoning, we find we have run thirty five miles again.

What a supper we make; unleavened bread, green squash sauce, and strong coffee. We have been for a few days on half rations, but we have no stint of roast squash.

A few days like this, and we are out of prison.

August 27.—This morning the river takes a more southerly direction. The dip of the rocks is to the north, and we are rapidly running into lower formations. Unless our course changes, we shall very soon run again into the granite. This gives us some anxiety. Now and then the river turns to the west, and excites hopes that are soon destroyed by another turn to the south. About nine o'clock we come to the dreaded rock. It is with no little misgiving that we see the river enter these black, hard walls. At its very entrance we have to make a portage; then we have to let down with lines past some ugly rocks. Then we run a mile or two farther, and then the rapids below can be seen.

About eleven o'clock we come to a place in the river where it seems much worse than any we have yet met in all its course. A little creek comes down from the left. We land first on the right, and clamber up over the granite pinnacles for a mile or two, but can see no way by which we can let down, and to run it would be sure destruction. After dinner we cross to examine it on the left. High above the river we can walk along on the top of the granite, which is broken off at the edge, and set with crags and pinnacles, so that it is very difficult to get a view of the river at all. In my eagerness to reach a point where I can see the roaring fall below, I go too far on the wall, and can neither advance nor retreat. I stand with one foot on a little projecting rock, and cling with my hand fixed in a little crevice. Finding I am caught here, suspended 400 feet above the river, into which I should fall if my footing fails, I call for help. The men come, and pass me a line, but I cannot let go of the rock long enough to take hold of it. Then they bring two or three of the largest oars. All this takes time which seems very precious to me; but at last they arrive. The blade of one of the oars is pushed into a little crevice in the rock beyond me, in such a manner that they can hold me pressed against the wall. Then another is fixed in such a way that I can step on it, and thus I am extricated.

Still another hour is spent in examining the river from this side, but no good view of it is obtained, so now we return to the side that was first examined, and the afternoon is spent in clambering among the crags and pinnacles, and carefully scanning the river again. We find that the lateral streams have washed boulders into the river, so as to form a dam, over which the water makes a broken fall of eighteen or twenty feet; then there is a rapid, beset with rocks, for two or three hundred yards, while, on the other side, points of the wall project into the river. Then there is a second fall below; how great, we cannot tell. Then there is a rapid, filled with huge rocks, for one or two hundred yards. At the bottom of it, from the right wall, a great rock projects quite half way across the river. It has a sloping surface extending up stream, and the water, coming down with all the momentum gained in the falls and rapids above, rolls up this inclined plane many feet, and tumbles over to the left. I decide that it is possible to let down over the first fall, then run near the right cliff to a point just above the second, where we can pull out into a little chute, and, having run over that in safety, we must pull with all our power across the stream, to avoid the great rock below. On my return to the boat, I announce to the men that we are to run it in the morning. Then we cross the river, and go into camp for the night on some rocks, in the mouth of the little side cañon.

After supper Captain Howland asks to have a talk with me. We walk up the little creek a short distance, and I soon find that his object is to remonstrate against my determination to proceed. He thinks that we had better abandon the river here. Talking with him, I learn that his brother, William Dunn, and himself have determined to go no farther in the boats. So we return to camp. Nothing is said to the other men.

For the last two days, our course has not been plotted. I sit down and do this now, for the purpose of finding where we are by dead reckoning. It is a clear night, and I take out the sextant to make observation for latitude, and find that the astronomic determination agrees very nearly with that of the plot—quite as closely as might be expected, from a meridian observation on a planet. In a direct line, we must be about forty five miles from the mouth of the Rio Virgen. If we can reach that point, we know that there are settlements up that river about twenty miles. This forty five miles, in a direct line, will probably be eighty or ninety in the meandering line of the river. But then we know that there is comparatively open country for many miles above the mouth of the Virgen, which is our point of destination.

As soon as I determine all this, I spread my plot on the sand, and wake

Howland, who is sleeping down by the river, and show him where I suppose we are, and where several Mormon settlements are situated.

We have another short talk about the morrow, and he lies down again; but for me there is no sleep. All night long, I pace up and down a little path, on a few yards of sand beach, along by the river. Is it wise to go on? I go to the boats again, to look at our rations. I feel satisfied that we can get over the danger immediately before us; what there may be below I know not. From our outlook yesterday, on the cliffs, the cañon seemed to make another great bend to the south, and this, from our experience heretofore, means more and higher granite walls. I am not sure that we can climb out of the cañon here, and, when at the top of the wall, I know enough of the country to be certain that it is a desert of rock and sand, between this and the nearest Mormon town, which, on the most direct line, must be seventy five miles away. True, the late rains have been favorable to us, should we go out, for the probabilities are that we shall find water still standing in holes, and, at one time, I almost conclude to leave the river. But for years I have been contemplating this trip. To leave the exploration unfinished, to say that there is a part of the cañon which I cannot explore, having already almost accomplished it, is more than I am willing to acknowledge, and I determine to go on.

I wake my brother, and tell him of Howland's determination, and he promises to stay with me; then I call up Hawkins, the cook, and he makes a like promise; then Sumner, and Bradley, and Hall, and they all agree to go on.

August 28.—At last daylight comes, and we have breakfast, without a word being said about the future. The meal is as solemn as a funeral. After breakfast, I ask the three men if they still think it best to leave us. The elder Howland thinks it is, and Dunn agrees with him. The younger Howland tries to persuade them to go on with the party, failing in which, he decides to go with his brother.

Then we cross the river. The small boat is very much disabled, and unseaworthy. With the loss of hands, consequent on the departure of the three men, we shall not be able to run all of the boats, so I decide to leave my "Emma Dean."

Two rifles and a shot gun are given to the men who are going out. I ask them to help themselves to the rations, and take what they think to be a fair share. This they refuse to do, saying they have no fear but that they can get something to eat; but Billy, the cook, has a pan of biscuits prepared for dinner, and these he leaves on a rock.

Before starting, we take our barometers, fossils, the minerals, and some ammunition from the boat, and leave them on the rocks. We are going over this place as light as possible. The three men help us lift our boats over a rock twenty five or thirty feet high, and let them down again over the first fall, and now we are all ready to start. The last thing before leaving, I write a letter to my wife, and give it to Howland. Sumner gives him his watch, directing that it be sent to his sister, should he not be heard from again. The records of the expedition have been kept in duplicate. One set of these is given to Howland, and now we are ready. For the last time, they entreat us not to go on, and tell us that it is madness to set out in this place; that we can never get safely through it; and, further, that the river turns again to the south into the granite, and a few miles of such rapids and falls will exhaust our entire stock of rations, and then it will be too late to climb out. Some tears are shed; it is rather a solemn parting; each party thinks the other is taking the dangerous course.

My old boat left, I go on board of the "Maid of the Cañon." The three men climb a crag, that overhangs the river, to watch us off. The "Maid of the Cañon" pushes out. We glide rapidly along the foot of the wall, just grazing one great rock, then pull out a little into the chute of the second fall, and plunge over it. The open compartment is filled when we strike the first wave below, but we cut through it, and then the men pull with all their power toward the left wall, and swing clear of the dangerous rock below all right. We are scarcely a minute in running it, and find that, although it looked bad from above, we have passed many places that were worse.

The other boat follows without more difficulty. We land at the first practicable point below and fire our guns, as a signal to the men above that we have come over in safety. Here we remain a couple of hours, hoping that they will take the smaller boat and follow us. We are behind a curve in the cañon, and cannot see up to where we left them, and so we wait until their coming seems hopeless, and push on.

And now we have a succession of rapids and falls until noon, all of which we run in safety. Just after dinner we come to another bad place. A little stream comes in from the left, and below there is a fall, and still below another fall. Above, the river tumbles down, over and among the rocks, in whirlpools and great waves, and the waters are lashed into mad, white foam. We run along the left, above this, and soon see that we cannot get down on this side, but it seems possible to let down on the other. We pull up stream again, for two or three hundred yards, and cross. Now there is a bed of basalt on this northern side of the cañon, with a bold escarpment, that seems to be a hundred feet high. We can climb it, and walk along its summit to a point where we are just at the head of the fall. Here the basalt is broken down again, so it seems to us, and I direct the men to take a line to the top of the cliff, and let the boats down along the wall. One man remains in the boat, to keep her clear of the rocks, and prevent her line from being caught on the projecting angles. I climb the cliff, and pass along to a point just over the fall, and descend by broken rocks, and find that the break of the fall is above the break of the wall, so that we cannot land; and that still below the river is very bad, and that there is no possibility of a portage. Without waiting further to examine and determine what shall be done, I hasten back to the top of the cliff, to stop the boats from coming down. When I arrive, I find the men have let one of them down to the head of the fall. She is in swift water, and they are not able to pull her back; nor are they able to go on with the line, as it is not long enough to reach the higher part of the cliff, which is just before them; so they take a bight around a crag. I send two men back for the other line. The boat is in very swift water, and Bradley is standing in the open compartment, holding out his oar to prevent her from striking against the foot of the cliff. Now she shoots out into the stream, and up as far as the line will permit, and then, wheeling, drives headlong against the rock, then out and back again, now straining on the line, now striking against the rock. As soon as the second line is brought, we pass it down to him; but his attention is all taken up with his own situation, and he does not see that we are passing the line to him. I stand on a projecting rock, waving my hat to gain his attention, for my voice is drowned by the roaring of the falls. Just at this moment, I see him take his knife from its sheath, and step forward to cut the line. He has evidently decided that it is better to go over with the boat as it is, than to wait for her to be broken to pieces. As he leans over, the boat sheers again into the stream, the stem-post breaks away, and she is loose. With perfect composure Bradley seizes the great scull oar, places it in the stern rowlock, and pulls with all his power (and he is an athlete) to turn the bow of the boat downstream, for he wishes to go bow down, rather than to drift broadside on. One, two strokes he makes, and a third just as she goes over, and the boat is fairly turned, and she goes down almost beyond our sight, though we are more than a hundred feet above the river. Then she comes up again, on a great wave, and down and up, then around behind some great rocks, and is lost in the mad, white foam below. We stand frozen with fear, for we see no boat. Bradley is gone, so it seems. But now, away below, we see something coming out of the waves. It is evidently a boat. A moment more, and we see Bradley standing on deck, swinging his hat to show that he is all right. But he is in a whirlpool. We have the stem-post of his boat attached to the line. How badly she may be disabled we know not. I direct Sumner and Powell to pass along the cliff, and see if they can reach him from below. Rhodes, Hall, and myself run to the other boat, jump aboard, push out, and away we go over the falls. A wave rolls over us, and our boat is unmanageable. Another great wave strikes us, the boat rolls over, and tumbles and tosses, I know not how. All I know is that Bradley is picking us up. We soon have all right again, and row to the cliff, and wait until Sumner and Powell can come. After a difficult climb they reach us. We run two or three miles farther, and turn again to the northwest, continuing until night, when we have run out of the granite once more.

August 29.—We start very early this morning. The river still continues swift, but we have no serious difficulty, and at twelve o'clock emerge from the Grand Cañon of the Colorado.

We are in a valley now, and low mountains are seen in the distance, coming to the river below. We recognize this as the Grand Wash.

A few years ago, a party of Mormons set out from St. George, Utah, taking with them a boat, and came down to the mouth of the Grand Wash, where they divided, a portion of the party crossing the river to explore the San Francisco Mountains. Three men—Hamblin, Miller, and Crosby—taking the boat, went on down the river to Callville, landing a few miles below the mouth of the Rio Virgen. We have their manuscript journal with us, and so the stream is comparatively well known.

To night we camp on the left bank, in a *mesquite* thicket.

The relief from danger, and the joy of success, are great. When he who has been chained by wounds to a hospital cot, until his canvas tent seems like a dungeon cell, until the groans of those who lie about, tortured with probe and knife, are piled up, a weight of horror on his ears that he cannot throw off, cannot forget, and until the stench of festering wounds and anaesthetic drugs has filled the air with its loathsome burthen, at last goes out into the open field, what a world he sees! How beautiful the sky; how bright the sunshine; what "floods of delirious music" pour from the throats of birds; how sweet the fragrance of earth, and tree, and blossom! The first hour of convalescent freedom seems rich recompense for all—pain, gloom, terror.

Something like this are the feelings we experience to night. Ever before us has been an unknown danger, heavier than immediate peril. Every waking hour passed in the Grand Cañon has been one of toil. We have watched with deep solicitude the steady disappearance of our scant supply of rations, and from time to time have seen the river snatch a portion of the little left, while we were ahungered. And danger and toil were endured in those gloomy depths, where ofttimes the clouds hid the sky by day, and but a narrow zone of stars could be seen at night. Only during the few hours of deep sleep, consequent on hard labor, has the roar of the waters been hushed. Now the danger is over; now the toil has ceased; now the gloom has disappeared; now the firmament is bounded only by the horizon; and what a vast expanse of constellations can be seen!

The river rolls by us in silent majesty; the quiet of the camp is sweet; our joy is almost ecstacy. We sit till long after midnight, talking of the Grand Cañon, talking of home, but chiefly talking of the three men who left us. Are they wandering in those depths, unable to find a way out? are they searching over the desert lands above for water? or are they nearing the settlements?

THE PEOPLE

GRAND CANYON NATIONAL PARK

Michael Kabotie

Michael Kabotie grew up in a family of successful artists at Shungopavi, one of the villages in the Hopi homeland of Black Mesa. His father, Fred, painted the famous murals in Mary Colter's Desert View Watchtower and helped invent the modern Hopi style of silver jewelry, in which traditional designs are created with an overlay technique. Michael began painting professionally in the late 1960s and became a founding member of Artist Hopid, a group of painters dedicated to using the "artistic talents of the Hopi to instill pride and identity" in their people, as well as to testing "new ideas and techniques in art, using traditional Hopi designs and concepts." Kabotie's 1989 book of poems, *Migration Tears,* captures both the difficulty and the richness of life at the intersection of traditional and contemporary cultures. In this poem, he comments wryly on the transformation of his tribe's place of origin into a national shrine.

. . .

"Mike, look at how
pretty the canyon is!"
　　　Frances shouted

"I can't look, I'm driving;
besides I will make my
final journey
to the underworld
through the sipapuni,"
　　　I answered

A spiritual place
our symbolic womb-kiva
the place of emergence
through which we
enter our underworld
heaven

"The Grand Canyon
discovered in 1540
by Pedro de Cardenas"
        The National Parks pamphlet read

I smiled
knowing that my people
always knew
the Grand Canyon was there
and didn't need to be discovered

Cardenas came with
Hopi guides and
I learned how lies
are twisted to sound
        true

But on my final journey
I promise to stop at all
the sight-seeing points
to mingle with the tourists
        and
give them my last earthly
trinkets before I descend
into my
        eternal womb/kiva.

PLANT JOURNEY

Linda Hogan

Chickasaw poet and novelist Linda Hogan often writes about the colonization of North America, showing that genocidal displacement of native peoples and widespread destruction of the natural environment were two parts of the same violent process. Hogan sees the experiences of women, especially Native American women, as keys to changing our society's relationship with nature. In her early poem "Calling Myself Home," she writes: "This land is the house / we have always lived in. / The women, / their bones are holding up the earth." Hogan was invited by Kathleen Ryan to join a river trip on the Colorado and then write about the experience for the essay collection *Writing Down the River* (1998), which includes original work by sixteen women writers. In her contribution to the book, Hogan finds a metaphor for the modern history of the canyon and its native people in the sacred datura, a common but potentially deadly plant that can induce visions if used properly.

. . .

This canyon world where water yearns toward the ocean is a place so large I can't take it in. Instead, I am taken in, traveling a near dream as we journey by water, contained by rock walls. In order to see this shorn-away world, I narrow my vision to the small and nearly secret. Never mind the stone's illusion of permanence or the great strength of water. I look to the most fragile of things here, to the plant world of the canyon. The other river travelers seem taken in by stone, time, and water, and do not see the small things that tempt my attention, the minute fern between stones, the tiny black snails in a pond of water. I am drawn in by the growing life and not by the passing. It may be that I am simply a dreamer of the small and alive, or it may be that to see this world at our feet in the midst of the vast world above us requires a gaze shaped by another history than the ones recounted here by our river guides, a history that begins only with the journeys of white men.

This new history of the Colorado River, the one that began so recently, doesn't contain the vision of those who, for thousands of years, have known the land in all its sacred power and detail. This is a land so alive that the Havasupai address songs to it. And the Hopi people's place of origin is above the place where waters of the Little Colorado meet with larger waters, a place called Sipapu, opening, center. I know there is a wider way to see the canyon. I look for this wider way by looking down, at the plants. While I see plants as sacred, I am disturbed by the way in which they are unacknowledged by the others, treated with carelessness. It is hard for me to observe this, because I know that even something as small as a plant is not only alive and necessary, but that it can represent the known history and geography of a world.

Of all the plants we travel past, it is the short-lived blossom of the sacred datura that most strongly draws me in with its luminous white flower. Similar to a morning glory, even its trunk-stem glows with life, gold on deep green. I watch for these plants all along the way, and at each rest stop I walk about to find them, thinking of how their seed pods, which gave them the name "thornapple," have traveled along this water as we are traveling, how these plants have washed up and then staked a rooted claim in their place.

Perhaps its transience is what attracts me, because I, too, am only passing briefly through time and rock on the charge of water.

Or perhaps it is the datura's intimate beauty, shining with light and green intelligence. Or that datura has the sweetest of smells when I sit beside it trying to learn its secrets. But most probably what takes me in is its history, one that traveled from ancient worlds and times into the present.

For whatever reasons, in the canyon I find that this plant has a language that speaks of what's too large and immense for a mere human mind to grasp. You could say it holds the secrets of the world around it. It tells its story. Part of the story is in its relationships with other life forms. It opens its white evening flower, as if it is made of light, and the night-flying moths arrive, drawn to its sweetness. I see them enter the flower that is delicate as dusk, overpowering in its softness. By day, other pollinators arrive, insects, birds, some intoxicated by the plant's narcotic quality.

This plant is also kin to water. It has traveled many world rivers, not only the Colorado, on a mission unknown to us. Its use has been recorded in India, South America, Russia, and China. The Aztecs painted its likeness on murals. The priests of Apollo used it to treat such illnesses as epilepsy. Datura shines with a power as immense as the passage of water across the world, the movement of it as mysterious as the force that carries water upward through stem and leaf, as powerful as that which carries a river to the sea.

Like all plants, it has its relationship, as well, with light. But most significant is its long, ongoing relationship with humans. Every plant has been an offering to the human world and this relationship is what I wish to understand.

For the first peoples the plant world has always been an offering to humans, of richness, healing, and food. And to those who can read and understand the plants, knowledge resides in the body of the plant itself. For tribal peoples a plant is a living being, considered to be a person, as worthy of existence and survival as a human. To our ancestors, plant knowledge was both medical knowledge and a part of sacred history. In a relationship developed over many thousands of years, plants and people were allies in healing. This has not been the case in the more recent Western model of the world. Most humans in this time haven't been fortunate enough to learn the gifts of plants, have forgotten to regard the plants with their full measure of respect. These days, plants are likely to be overlooked, unseen, and unremembered in their subtle vitality. For this reason, I offer the plants my attention and affection. I know the subtle has power every bit as strong as the water we travel and the years of time shaped into canyon by this downward-rushing Colorado River. In the same way that the river never leaves anything unsaid, the plant expresses itself with every atom of its making.

Datura has been of great value as a medicine and as a spiritual ally for tribes on this continent. I love and admire this plant. I know that the story of this plant, how it was once worshipped and came to be considered a toxic weed, is the same as the story of the canyon itself, one of how the sacred loses its power. It is also the story of water, valuable only in its use to us.

This white-flowered medicine in use since nearly the beginning of all civilizations is now considered a poisonous weed, "rank and noxious" and hard to destroy. It is true that people have died from misusing it, even recently, but for those who know its ways, it is alive in its potence, and sacred. It is clear from the plant's history that it is a beautiful power, a flower of the dream, one used as a passageway to other dreams and places, the supernatural and the sacred. The plant that travels the water is esteemed for its offering of vision, of the spiritual journey to other worlds. In this, it is part of the same story of the luminous canyon that puts travelers in touch with the great beauty of a sacred world.

The world is not here just to be visited by humans. It has its own repose and turbulence, its own journey and destination. The sacred datura itself is one of many travelers. The whole world is a river through which its seed has journeyed. Unlike the Hopis who begin here, no one knows from where datura came. I say it came from here, this dream, this water and light.

But then, this is the land the tribal people sing to, with emotions deeply felt and love unsurpassed.

PACKHORSE PARADISE

Wallace Stegner

Wallace Stegner's boyhood in Montana, Utah, and Saskatchewan shaped his long career as a Pulitzer Prize–winning novelist, a historian of the West, and a powerful voice for the preservation of wilderness. Stegner edited and contributed an essay to *This Is Dinosaur*, the 1955 Sierra Club book that defeated federal plans to build a dam on the Green River in Dinosaur National Park. In his influential 1960 "Wilderness Letter," he argued that all the remaining wild nature in America should be preserved because it is "something that has helped form our character . . . as a people," because there we "see ourselves [as] part of the environment of trees and rocks and soil, brother to the other animals," and because, without wilderness, "we are committed wholly . . . to a headlong drive into our technological termite life, the Brave New World of a completely man-controlled environment." Stegner founded the creative writing program at Stanford University, where he mentored many of the next generation of western writers, including Ken Kesey, Wendell Berry, Larry McMurtry, Raymond Carver, and Edward Abbey. Stegner's meditative story about horse-packing in Havasu Canyon, and about the challenges facing the Havasupai, first appeared in the magazine the *Atlantic* in 1947.

. . .

One of the special pleasures about a back road in the West is that it sometimes ends dead against a wonderful and relatively unvisited wilderness. The road from Grand Canyon to Topacoba Hilltop ends dead against a ramshackle shed and a gate that closes the bottom of the gulch. The whole place looks less like a hilltop than anything we can imagine, but our Indian guide is there, along with a half-dozen other Indians, cooking beans over an open fire. He waves his hands, white with flour, and says we shall be ready to go in thirty minutes.

Eating a lunch of oranges and cookies and a thermos of milk, we look out from the end of the gulch to the outer rim of a larger and much deeper canyon— possibly the Grand Canyon itself, possibly some tributary or bay. The heat is intense, and light glares from the rock faces and talus slopes. Ahead of us is a fourteen-mile ride into Havasu Canyon, the deep-sunk, cliff-walled sanctuary of the Havasupai Indians.

At twelve-thirty the white-handed Indian, a boy of about eighteen, leads up a skinny packhorse and loads on our sleeping bags, tarps, cooking gear, and the small amount of food we are taking for a three-day trip. He is handy at his diamond hitch, but uncommunicative; his hair grows down over his forehead and he wears big blunt spurs. The horses he brings up look to us like dwarfs, unable to carry our weight, but they do not sag when we climb on. My saddle is too small, and the stirrups won't lengthen to within six inches of where I want them; I console myself with the reflection that if I did put them down where they belong they would drag on the ground, the horse is so small.

For a quarter mile we circle the shoulder of a hill, and then, turning the corner, Mary looks back at me as if she can't believe what she has seen. Below us the trail drops in an endless series of switchbacks down an all but vertical cliff. And this is no cleared path, no neat ledge trail built by the Park Service. This trail is specially created for breaking necks. It is full of loose, rolling rocks, boulders as big as water buckets, steep pitches of bare stone, broken corners where the edge has fallen away.

Our guide, whose name turns out to be Hardy Jones, starts down casually, leading the packhorse, and we follow with our seats uneasy in the saddle, ready to leap to safety when the horse slips. We have ridden trail horses and mules before, but never on a trail like this. But it takes us less than a half hour to relax, and to realize that our horses have neither stumbled nor slipped nor hesitated. They know all the time where all their feet are. At bad places, with a thousand-foot drop under them, they calmly gather themselves and jump from foothold to foothold like goats.

As we descend, we learn too how these stunted horses got this way. Far up on the canyon walls, among house-sized boulders and broken rockslides, we see wild horses grazing as contentedly as if they were up to their knees in bluegrass in a level pasture. A half dozen of them are in absolutely impossible places, places where no horse could get. But there they are. And there are signs too that surefootedness is not innate: two thirds of the way down we pass a week-old colt dead by the side of the trail at the bottom of a fifty-foot drop. I ask Hardy what happened. "He fall down," Hardy says.

Ahead of us, in the bottom of a wide sandy wash, a wriggly canyon head begins to sink into the red rock. As soon as we enter this deepening ditch, Hardy turns the packhorse loose up ahead to set the pace. He himself dismounts and lies down in the shade with his hat over his eyes. After a half hour he catches and passes us, and after another fifteen minutes we pass him again, snoozing in the shade. I suspect him of all sorts of things, including nursing a bottle on the sly, but I finally conclude I am wronging him. He is simply sleepy. On occasion his yawns can be heard a half mile.

Once or twice he rides up close and starts a conversation. We discover that he is a good roper, and later in the month will ride to Flagstaff to compete in a rodeo. He has three good rope horses of his own, and he has finished the sixth grade in the Havasupai school. I ask him what he'll take for the pony he is riding, a sightly, tiny-footed, ladylike little mare, and he tells me, I am sure inaccurately, fifteen dollars. Then he asks me what I had to pay for the camera slung around my neck, and when I tell him, he looks incredulous and rides on ahead to take another sleep.

The canyon cuts deeper into rock the color of chocolate ice cream. At times the channel is scoured clean, and we ride over the bare cross-bedded stone. The *Grand Canyon Suite* inevitably suggests itself, and we are struck by the quality of the sound produced by hoofs on sandstone. It is in no sense a clashing or clicking sound, but is light, clear, musical, rather brittle, as if the rock were hollow.

The packhorse leads us deeper into the rock, going at a long careful stride down hewn rock stairs, snaking along a strip of ledge, squeezing under an over-hang. It is an interminable, hot, baking canyon, but there are aromatic smells from weeds and shrubs. None of the varieties of trees we meet are known to us. One is a small tree like a willow, with trumpet-shaped lavender flowers, another a variety of locust covered with fuzzy yellow catkins. Still another, a formidable one to brush against, is gray-leafed, with dark-blue berries and thorns three inches long. I pick a berry and ask Hardy what it is. "No eat," he says.

2

For three hours we see nothing living except lizards and the occasional wild horses grazing like impossible Side-hill Gazinks on the walls. Then around a turn comes a wild whoop, and a young horse bursts into view, galloping up the boul-dery creek bed past us. After him comes an Indian boy swinging a rope, and they vanish with a rush and a clatter up a slope that we have just picked our way down at a careful walk. In ten minutes the new Indian and Hardy come up behind us leading the colt, which has a foot-long cut across its chest as if from barbed wire, and which leaves bloody spots on the trail every time it puts its feet down.

Hardy is pleased at the neatness with which he roped the colt as it tried to burst past him. He breaks into a wild little humming chant, accented by grunts and "hah's," a jerky and exclamatory song like the chant of a Navajo squaw dance. As we ride he practices roping the hind feet of the horse ahead of him. After a while we are somewhat astonished to hear him singing with considerable feeling, "Oh, why did I give her that diamond?"

Now on a high rock we see a painted sign, "Supai." A handful of Indian kids whose horses are tied below sit on the top of the rock and wave and yell. We shift our sore haunches in the saddle and wonder how fourteen miles can be so long. At every turn the tight, enclosed canyon stirs with a breath of freshness, and we look ahead hopefully, but each time the walls close in around a new turn. A canyon comes in from the left, and a little brackish water with it, and there are cottonwoods of a cool and tender green, and willows head-high to a man on a stunted horse. There is a smell, too, sharp and tantalizing, like witch hazel, that comes with the cooler air as we make a right-hand turn between vertical walls.

Then suddenly, swift and quiet and almost stealthy, running a strange milky blue over pebbles like gray jade, Havasu Creek comes out of nowhere across the trail, a stream thirty feet wide and knee-deep. After more than four hours in the baking canyon, it is the most beautiful water we have ever seen; even without the drouthy preparation it would be beautiful. The horses, which have traveled twenty-eight miles today over the worst kind of going, wade into the stream and stand blowing and drinking, pushing the swift water with their noses. The roped colt tries to break away, and for a moment there is a marvelous picture at the ford, the white-toothed laughter of the Indian boys, the horses plunging, the sun coming like a spotlight across the rim and through the trees to light the momentary action in the gray stream between the banks of damp red earth.

That wonderful creek, colored with lime, the pebbles of its bed and even the weeds at its margins coated with gray travertine, is our introduction to Supai. After five minutes we come out above the village and look down upon the green oasis sunk among its cliffs. There are little houses scattered along a mile or so of bottom land, and at the lower end a schoolhouse under big cottonwoods. Men are irrigating fields of corn and squash as we pass, and fig trees are dark and rich at the trailside. At the edge of the village a bunch of men are gambling under a bower of cottonwood branches, and two kids, fooling away the afternoon, gallop their horses in a race down the trail ahead of us.

Both of us have from the beginning had the feeling that we shall probably be disappointed in Havasupai when we reach it. We have been deceived by the superlatives of travelers before, and we have seen how photographs can be made to lie. But this is sure enough the Shangri-la everyone has said it is, this is the valley of Kubla Khan, here is Alph the sacred river, and here are the gardens bright with sinuous rills where blossoms many an incense-bearing tree.

When we mount stiffly again and ride on after registering with Mrs. Guthrie, the wife of the Indian sub-agent, we pass little cabins of stone and logs, orchards of fig and cherry and peach, hurrying little runnels of bright water, a swinging panorama of red-chocolate walls with the tan rimrock sharp and high beyond them. Havasu Canyon is flat-floored, and descends by a series of terraces. We camp below the first of these, within fifty feet of where Havasu Creek pours over a fifty-foot ledge into a pool fringed with cress and ferns.

The terrace above our campsite is full of what I take at first to be the twisted roots of dead fig trees, but what turn out to be rootlike lime deposits left by the stream, which used to fall over the ledge here. Probably they were originally grasses and water plants on which the mineral deposit formed a sheath; now they writhe through the terrace, fantastically interwound, some of them six inches in diameter. In the center of each is a round hole, as if a worm had lived there. In these holes and in the rooty crevices is lizard heaven. Geckos and long-tailed Uta lizards flash and dart underfoot by hundreds, as harmless as butterflies.

The same kinds of deposits are being formed under the pouring water of the falls; the whole cliff drips with them. And all down the creek the water has formed semicircular terraces like those at Mammoth Hot Springs in Yellowstone. Each terrace forms a natural weir, and behind each weir the water backs up deep and blue, making clear swimming pools eight to ten feet deep and many yards across. No creek was ever so perfectly formed for the pleasure of tourists. We swim twice before we even eat.

When we crawl into our sleeping bags at dusk, the bats and swallows fill the air above us, flying higher than I have ever seen bats and swallows fly before. It is a moment before I realize that they are flying at the level of the inner canyon walls, catching insects at what seem from the valley floor to be substratospheric heights. For a while we wonder how bats fly so efficiently and dart and shift so sharply without any adequate rudder, but that speculation dwindles off into sleep. Above us the sky is clouded, and in the night, when my face is peppered by a spatter of rain, I awake to see the moon blurry above the rim. For a moment I think a real storm is coming on, until I realize that the noise I hear is Havasu Creek pouring over Navajo Falls and rushing on down through its curving terraces. It is for some reason a wonderful thought that here in paradise the water even after dark is blue—not a reflection of anything but really blue, blue in the cupped hands.

3

Below our camp a quarter of a mile, past a field half overgrown with apparently wild squash vines and the dark green datura, the Western Jimson weed, with its great white trumpet-flowers, Havasu Creek takes a second fall. Apart from its name, Bridal Veil, it is more than satisfactory, for it spreads wide along the ledge and falls in four or five streamers down a hundred-foot cliff clothed in exotic hanging plants and curtains of travertine. The cliff is green and gray and orange, the pool below pure cobalt, and below the pool the creek gathers itself in terraces bordered with green cress.

A little below the fall a teetery suspension footbridge hangs over a deep green pool, dammed by a terrace so smooth that the water pours over it in a shining sheet like milky blue glass. And down another half mile, after a succession of pools each of which leaves us more incredulous, the stream leaps in an arching curve over Mooney Falls, the highest of the three. At its foot are the same tall cottonwoods with dusty red bark, the same emerald basin, the same terraced pools flowing away, and below the pools is another suspension footbridge on which we sit to eat lunch and converse with a friendly tree toad.

It is a long way to the mouth of the canyon, where Havasu Creek falls into the Colorado in the lower end of Grand Canyon. We stop at the abandoned lead and copper mine below Mooney Falls, where we ponder the strength of the compulsion that would drive men to bring heavy machinery piecemeal down into this pocket on the backs of horses, set it up under incredible difficulties, construct an elaborate water system and a cluster of houses and sheds, bore into the solid cliffs for ore, and then tote the ore back out miles to some road where trucks could get it. The very thought gives us packhorse feet, and we make our way back to camp, yielding to temptation at every pool on the creek until we have a feeling that our skins are beginning to harden with a thin sheath of lime. After a day, we are beginning to realize how truly paradisiac the home of the Havasupai is.

There are in the West canyons as colorful and as beautiful as Havasu, with walls as steep and as high, with floors as verdantly fertile. There are canyons more spectacularly narrow and more spectacularly carved. But I know of none, except possibly Oak Creek Canyon south of Flagstaff, which has such bewitching water. In this country the mere presence of water, even water impregnated with red mud, is much. But water in such lavish shining streams, water so extravagantly colorful, water which forms such terraces and pools, water which all along its course nourishes plants that give off that mysterious wonderful smell like witch hazel, water which obliges by forming three falls, each more beautiful than the last, is more than one has a right to expect.

4

Yet even Shangri-la has its imperfections, the snake lives even in Eden. As we are working back from the canyon walls, where we have been inspecting a small cliff dwelling, we hear the barking of dogs. Below us is a field surrounded by fruit trees, and in the middle of the field, staked out in a line, we find four miserable starving mongrels. Each is tied by a length of chain to a post; at the top of each post is a bundle of branches loosely tied on to give a little shade. Around the neck of each dog is a collar of baling wire wrapped with rags, and near each a canful of muddied water is sunk in the sand. Yelps and whines grow frantic as we cross the field, and out of the bushes at the far end comes a staggering skeleton with a drooping tail. In the brush from which she emerged we find four squirming puppies.

The job of these dogs is obviously to serve as scarecrows, and they are obviously completely expendable. Clearly they have not been fed for days, and none of them can live beyond a day or two more.

The usual Indian callousness toward animals is not unknown to us, and we are willing in theory to accept that cultural difference without blaming the Indians. Perhaps this Indian thought it a good idea to get rid of some of his excess dogs, and at the same time protect his fruit. But our passing through the field has stirred the miserable animals into hopefulness. The tottering skeleton of a mother dog, dragging her dry teats, tries to follow us to camp; the others howl and whine and bark until we feel like running.

Our own food is meager, since we underestimated our appetites when we packed the grub bag, and there is nothing to be bought in the canyon. All we have left to serve us for our last two meals is a can of grapefruit juice, two oranges, a can of lamb stew, four slices of bacon, six slices of bread, and a handful of chocolate bars. The oranges and the grapefruit juice will be of no use to the dogs. Chocolate might make their starving stomachs sicker. The bread and bacon and lamb stew are slim pickings for ourselves.

After a half hour of trying not to hear the howling, I go back and clean out all the water cans, refilling them from the irrigation ditch. None of the dogs is interested in the nice clean water. They are all howling louder than ever when Mary and I start a fire and heat the lamb stew, butter half the bread, lay out the oranges and the chocolate bars for dessert. They howl so loud we can't eat; the stew is gravel in our mouths. We end by spreading two slices of bread with all our remaining butter and taking those and half the stew over to the field. What we bring is a pitiful mouthful apiece, gone so quickly that we wince. Hope has leaped so high in the starving mongrels now that Mary gets three chocolate bars and distributes them. Aware that we are absurd, that our humanitarianism is stupid and perhaps immoral, granting that the dogs have to starve to death day after tomorrow anyway, we carefully divide the meal according to size of dog, and give the skeleton mother a double dose of chocolate.

Then we go home and swim and crawl into our bags, but the dismal howling goes on after dark. It has dwindled off to an occasional sick whimpering by the time we get to sleep, and we have wondered seriously if we should not rather have knocked all nine dogs on the head and paid their owner a suitable fee for the loss of his scarecrows. James Russell Lowell to the contrary notwithstanding, it is a wretched thing either to give or to share when you haven't enough to do any good.

To heighten our disenchantment, we are both bitten during the night by the bloodsucking beetles known locally as Hualpai Tigers, which leave an oozing inflammation about twenty times as irritating as a flea or chigger bite. Next time we come down here we will come with a supply of roach powder.

Not an absolutely idyllic paradise, despite its seclusion and peace and its shining blue water. We see other things when we mount Hardy's horses the next morning and start on our way out. Looking with less eager and more critical eyes, we see girls and women and old men lying on couches in the sun outside the little stone and log cabins. Tuberculosis. We notice among the Supai what Dickens noticed among all Americans a hundred years ago—the habit of spitting all the time and everywhere, even into the creek—and we are glad we dipped our drinking water from a spring. We learn from Mrs. Guthrie that the tribe is less numerous than it used to be, and that it barely holds its own now at about two hundred. A year ago a dysentery epidemic carried off more than half the young children in the village, and measles has been deadly among them.

We learn too that some of the young men, especially those few who served in the armed forces, are restless in the static life of the canyon, and want to get out. We see signs of change in the tractor that the Guthries have had packed in, a piece at a time, and which the Indians can rent for a small fee. We hear speculation about the possibilities of an automobile road into Havasu, and of a guest lodge to be owned by the Indians and run by them and for them, with Indian Service assistance. We hear of the need of increasing the income of the tribe, and of the benefit that increased tourist travel might bring. Out at the fence we hear Hardy Jones, sitting and swinging his big spurs far under the belly of his little mare, singing "Oh, why did I give her that diamond?" which he has laboriously and inaccurately transcribed from the radio onto a piece of cardboard.

The problem of what is best for Havasu—the place and the people—is curiously complex and difficult. If one looks at it purely from the standpoint of conserving natural scenery, the conclusion is inevitable that an automobile road and a guest lodge would spoil a spot that is almost unbelievably beautiful, clutter it with too many people, bring the regulation and regimentation that are necessary when crowds come to any scenic area. Fifty people at one time in Havasu would be all the canyon could stand. The present two hundred visitors a year leave no real mark, but five times that many would. If the conservation of the canyon's charm is the principal end—and this is the view of the National Park Service, which does have a voice in the matter since the Havasu reservation lies within the Grand Canyon National Park—the canyon should be left primitive, a packhorse paradise.

5

What of the people, the two hundred Havasupai? Those who work with them and see the need for medical care and education and guidance know how difficult it is to bring the tribe even these minimal things under present conditions. Communication is by packhorse and telephone; the mail comes in twice a week, and supplies the same way, on the backs of horses. Though there is a school, Mrs. Guthrie is teaching everyone in it, both primary and advanced pupils, because it is impossible to get another teacher. It is equally impossible to find and keep a doctor and a nurse; when dysentery swept the canyon there was little anyone could do but bury the dead; when the Guthries' own son fell ill last winter he had to be taken out to a doctor by horse litter.

Though at the bare subsistence level the canyon can be nearly self-sufficient, there are considerable and growing needs induced by contact with civilization. There are clothes—because the Havasupai no longer wear the garments of beautifully dressed white deerskin that they used to wear. They wear boots and Levis and shirts and Stetson hats. They like sugar, candy, coffee, radios, dozens of things that take cash; and cash they can now obtain only from two sources: sale of horses or cattle to the outside, or charges at ten dollars a head for packing in tourists. The Guthries are inclined to feel that if the flow of tourists could be increased, and if accommodations could be created for them, the standard of living and health and education of the whole tiny tribe could be raised considerably.

There is no doubt about the truth of that opinion. The canyon could be made a commercial "good thing" with a little promotion, and if the enterprise were carefully watched, the Indians could get the whole benefit. But there is something to be said against this proposal, too. We are morally troubled as we talk about it, for how sure can we be that the loose and indefinable thing called "well-being" will necessarily be promoted by greater prosperity, better education, even better health, when these things may bring with them the dilution or destruction of the safe traditional cultural pattern? Is it better to be well fed, well housed, well educated, and spiritually (which is to say culturally) lost; or is it better to be secure in a pattern of life where decisions and actions are guided by many generations of tradition?

There is a threat that one feels in this paradise. The little tribe with its static life may be at the edge of stagnation, of fatalistic apathy, as some villages of the Hopi are reported to be; it barely holds its own, the dynamics of its life reduced to the simple repetition of a simple routine, its needs few and its speculations uncomplicated. It is easy for that kind of equilibrium to be broken, for that kind of society to be utterly confounded and destroyed by contact with the civilization of white America. It takes intelligence, and patience, and great strength of character, and a long period of time, for any people safely to cross a cultural boundary as these

Indians must. Perhaps doubling or trebling the number of tourists in Havasu Canyon each year would not materially increase the danger to the Havasupai. But build a road in, let the gates down on the curious and careless thousands, and the whole tribe would be swept away as the last big flood washed away the orchards of peach trees, introduced by John Doyle Lee when he was hiding from the Federal officers after the Mountain Meadows Massacre.

Yesterday I wanted to take a snapshot of an old Supai packer with bushy hair and prickly thin whiskers. His asking price was a dollar and a half. We finally settled for a half dollar, but even at that price that packer was getting dangerously close to the commercialized status of the Indians who with Sioux feathers in their Mojave or Paiute or Yuman hair wander around in populous tourist spots being picturesque for a fee. There is something to be said for the policy that urges keeping the barrier canyons around this tribe unbridged, for according to the ethnologist Leslie Spier, the Havasupai retain their native culture in purer form than any other American Indians. Other Indians, losing their hold on their native culture, have ceased to exist.

I doubt if there is a clear-cut answer to the problems the Havasupai face. Inevitably there will be more and more intrusion on their isolation, and inevitably they must proceed through the phase of falling between two cultures, of being neither Indian nor white American. If they are lucky, they can make that transition slowly enough so that eventually they can patch up a new order of cultural acceptances taking good things from both the warring cultures of their inheritance. I should say they might learn something from the white man about how to treat animals; they would do ill to lose their own native gentleness in dealing with children. They can borrow the white man's medicine and keep their own simple unspeculative friendliness with the earth. If they are lucky they can do this. If they are not lucky, their paradise might in fifty or a hundred years be like the retreat of old Yosemite, beaten dusty by the feet of tourists, and no trace of the Havasupai except squash vines gone wild in the red earth by a spring, or an occasional goat-wild horse on the talus slopes.

I should not like to be God in this paradise, and make the decisions that will decide its future. But I can hope, looking at Hardy Jones lolling in the saddle, singing, "Oh, why did I give her that diamond?" that on the difficult cultural trail he is traveling no one will crowd him too hard. The trail between his simple civilization and the inconceivably complex world beyond the rims is difficult even for those who can go at their own pace. Hardy has gone part way without apparent demoralization; he listens to his radio and will go to Flagstaff and perhaps win a roping prize. But the smoke-colored colt lying with his neck broken below Topacoba Hilltop is warning of what can happen to the too young and the too inexperienced on that path.

MOJAVE VALLEY TO BIG CANYON

Joseph C. Ives

In 1857, the United States War Department commissioned Lieutenant Joseph Christmas Ives to lead an expedition to assess the navigability of the Colorado River. Ives and his men journeyed five hundred miles upstream from the Gulf of California in a fifty-four-foot paddle wheeler named *Explorer,* which they were forced to abandon after it struck a rock. They continued on foot with the help of conscripted Mojave guides, and in late winter they reached western Grand Canyon, which they called "Big Canyon." For two weeks, Ives and his men explored Diamond and Havasu Creeks, homelands of the Hualapai and Havasupai tribes. After a series of nearly disastrous misadventures in the steep and bitterly cold canyons, they decided to turn back. In his 1861 report to the U.S. Congress, Ives reflects the strong prejudices of his day. He sarcastically calls the Hualapai "squalid, wretched-looking creatures," and he asserts that the Grand Canyon region is "altogether valueless." He concludes that his will be "the last . . . party of whites to visit this profitless locality."

• • •

Camp 65, Peacock's spring, March 31.—Leaving the Cerbat basin, the course lay towards a low point in the extension of Aquarius mountains—another chain almost parallel to the Black and Cerbat ranges. The gap much resembles the Railroad Pass. After entering it the trail took a sudden turn to the north, in which direction it continued. The sun was very hot, and the mules, not having had a plentiful drink of water for four days, showed marks of distress. Ten or twelve miles from camp, Mr. Peacock, who was riding in advance, discovered a large spring of clear, sweet water in a ravine near the road. There were no signs of the place having been used as a camp, and even Ireteba did not appear to have known previously of its existence. A Mexican subsequently found a running stream a mile or two further on, where the Indians passing this way had been in the habit of stopping.

Ireteba, at my request, again went in search of some Hualpais tractable enough to enlist for a few days in our service. After an absence of several hours he came back and reported that he had discovered two who were willing to go. In a little while, from the top of a neighboring hill, a discordant screaming was heard, proceeding from two Indians who were suspiciously surveying camp. It was some time before our Mojaves could persuade them to approach, and when they did they looked like men who had screwed up their courage to face a mortal peril. They were squalid, wretched-looking creatures, with splay feet, large joints, and diminutive figures, but had bright eyes and cunning faces, and resembled a little the Chemehuevis. Taking them into the tent occupied by Lieutenant Tipton and myself, with many misgivings as to how many varieties of animal life were being introduced there, I brought out some pipes and tobacco and told Ireteba to proceed with the negotiations. These were not soon arranged. The sententiousness belonging to Mr. Cooper's and other story-book Indians is not a gift of the tribes that one encounters in travelling. Our old guides and the two new candidates talked all at once, and with amazing volubility; they seemed to be recounting their personal histories from birth to the present date. The conclusion arrived at was that they knew nothing about the country—neither a good road nor the localities of grass and water; that they were out hunting and had lost their way, and had no idea of the direction even of their own villages. This very probable statement I correctly supposed to be a hint that they were not to be approached empty-handed; for when Ireteba had been authorized to make a distinct offer of beads and blankets, one of them recollected where he was, and also that there were watering places ahead to which he could guide us. It was thought advisable to again lie over for a day; and they went away, agreeing to be in camp on the day but one following.

A third Hualpais turned up this morning; he had features like a toad's, and the most villainous countenance I ever saw on a human being. Mr. Mollhausen suggested that we should take him and preserve him in alcohol as a zoological specimen; and at last he became alarmed at the steadfast gaze he was attracting, and withdrew to the edge of a rock overhanging the cook's fire, where he remained till dark, with his eyes fixed in an unbroken stare upon the victuals. The Hualpais are but little removed from the Diggers. They present a remarkable contrast to our tall and athletic Mojaves. The latter, as I discovered to-day for the first time, have suspected that the object of the expedition was to make war upon the others; and I had some trouble in convincing Ireteba that this was not the case. That we have come out to fight somebody he has fully made up his mind.

Deer and antelope are now frequently seen, but they are shy and hard to approach. A single antelope one of the Mexicans succeeded in killing; they are just in season, and the flesh was tender and delicately flavored.

Camp 67, Big cañon of the Colorado, April 3.—The two Hualpais preserved the credit of the Indian employés by being punctual to their engagement, and led off in company with the Mojaves as we ascended the ravine from Peacock's spring. It was a cool lovely morning, and a favorable day for travel. After proceeding a mile or two we issued from the hills and entered a region totally different from any that had been seen during the expedition. A broad tableland, unbroken by the volcanic hills that had overspread the country since leaving Fort Yuma, extended before us, rising in a gradual swell towards the north. The road became hard and smooth, and the plain was covered with excellent grass. Herds of antelope and deer were seen bounding over the slopes. Groves of cedar occurred, and with every mile became more frequent and of larger size. At the end of ten miles the ridge of the swell was attained, and a splendid panorama burst suddenly into view. In the foreground were low table-hills, intersected by numberless ravines; beyond these a lofty line of bluffs marked the edge of an immense canon; a wide gap was directly ahead, and through it were beheld, to the extreme limit of vision, vast plateaus, towering one above the other thousands of feet in the air, the long horizontal bands broken at intervals by wide and profound abysses, and extending a hundred miles to the north, till the deep azure blue faded into a light cerulean tint that blended with the dome of the heavens. The famous "Big cañon" was before us; and for a long time we paused in wondering delight, surveying this stupendous formation through which the Colorado and its tributaries break their way.

Our guides, becoming impatient of the detention, plunged into a narrow and precipitous ravine that opened at our feet, and we followed as well as we could, stumbling along a rough and rocky pathway. The Hualpais were now of great assistance, for the ravines crossed and forked in intricate confusion; even Ireteba, who had hitherto led the train, became at a loss how to proceed, and had to put the little Hualpais in front. The latter, being perfectly at home, conducted us rapidly down the declivity. The descent was great and the trail blind and circuitous. A few miles of difficult travelling brought us into a narrow valley flanked by steep and high slopes; a sparkling stream crossed its centre, and a gurgling in some tall grass near by announced the presence of a spring. The water was delicious. The grass in the neighborhood was sparse, but of good quality.

This morning we left the valley and followed the course of a creek down a ravine, in the bed of which the water at intervals sank and rose for two or three miles, when it altogether disappeared. The ravine soon attained the proportions of a cañon. The bottom was rocky and irregular, and there were some jump-offs over which it was hard to make the pack animals pass. The vegetation began to disappear, leaving only a few stunted cedars projecting from the sides of the rugged bluffs. The place grew wilder and grander. The sides of the tortuous cañon became loftier, and before long we were hemmed in by walls two thousand feet high. The scenery much resembled that in the Black cañon, excepting that the rapid descent, the increasing magnitude of the colossal piles that blocked the end of the vista, and the corresponding depth and gloom of the gaping chasms into which we were plunging, imparted an unearthly character to a way that might have resembled the portals of the infernal regions. Harsh screams issuing from aerial recesses in the cañon sides, and apparitions of goblin-like figures perched in the rifts and hollows of the impending cliffs, gave an odd reality to this impression. At short distances other avenues of equally magnificent proportions came in from one side or the other; and no trail being left on the rocky pathway, the idea suggested itself that were the guides to desert us our experience might further resemble that of the dwellers in the unblest abodes—in the difficulty of getting out.

Huts of the rudest construction, visible here and there in some sheltered niche or beneath a projecting rock, and the sight of a hideous old squaw, staggering under a bundle of fuel, showed that we had penetrated into the domestic retreats of the Hualpais nation. Our party being, in all probability, the first company of whites that had ever been seen by them, we had anticipated producing a great effect, and were a little chagrined when the old woman, and two or three others of both sexes that were met, went by without taking the slightest notice of us. If pack-trains had been in the habit of passing twenty times a day they could not have manifested a more complete indifference.

Seventeen miles of this strange travel had now been accomplished. The road was becoming more difficult, and we looked ahead distrustfully into the dark and apparently interminable windings, and wondered where we were to find a camping place. At last we struck a wide branch cañon coming in from the south, and saw with joyful surprise a beautiful and brilliantly clear stream of water gushing over a pebbly bed in the centre, and shooting from between the rocks in sparkling jets and miniature cascades. On either side was an oasis of verdure—young willows and a thick patch of grass. Camp was speedily formed, and men and mules have had a welcome rest after their fatiguing journey.

A hundred yards below camp the cañon takes a turn; but as it was becoming very dark, all further examinations were postponed till to-morrow. In the course of the evening Ireteba came into my tent, and I asked him how far we had still to travel before reaching the great river. To my surprise he informed me that the mouth of the creek is only a few yards below the turn, and that we are now camped just on the verge of the Big Cañon of the Colorado.

Camp 69, Cedar Forest, April 5.—A short walk down the bed of Diamond river, on the morning after we had reached it, verified the statement of Ireteba, and disclosed the famous Colorado cañon. The view from the ridge, beyond the creek to which the Hualpais had first conducted us, had shown that the plateaus further north and east were several thousand feet higher than that through which the Colorado cuts at this point, and the cañons proportionally deeper; but the scene was sufficiently grand to well repay for the labor of the descent. The cañon was similar in character to others that have been mentioned, but on a larger scale, and thus far unrivalled in grandeur. Mr. Mollhausen has taken a sketch, which gives a better idea of it than any description. The course of the river could be traced for only a few hundred yards, above or below, but what had been seen from the table-land showed that we were at the apex of a great southern bend. The walls, on either side, rose directly out of the water. The river was about fifty yards wide. The channel was studded with rocks, and the torrent rushed through like a mill-race.

The day was spent in an examination of the localities. Dr. Newberry has had opportunities for observation seldom afforded to the geologist. This plateau formation has been undisturbed by volcanic action, and the sides of the cañons exhibit all of the series that compose the table-lands of New Mexico, presenting, perhaps, the most splendid exposure of stratified rocks that there is in the world. . . .

Camp 73, Colorado Plateau, April 14.—Lieutenant Tipton, Mr. Egloffstein, Mr. Peacock, and myself, with a dozen men, formed the party to explore [Havasu] cañon. It was about five miles to the precipice. The descent of the latter was accomplished without serious trouble. In one or two places the path traversed smooth inclined ledges, where the insecure footing made the crossing dangerous. The bottom of the cañon, which from the summit looked smooth, was covered with hills, thirty or forty feet high. Along the centre we were surprised to find an inner cañon, a kind of under cellar, with low walls at the starting point, which were soon converted into lofty precipices, as the base of the ravine sank deeper and deeper into the earth. Along the bottom of this gorge we followed the trail, distinctly seen when the surface was not covered with rocks. Every few moments, low falls and ledges, which we had to jump or slide down, were met with, till there had accumulated a formidable number of obstacles to be encountered in returning. Like other cañons it was circuitous, and at each turn we were impatient to find something novel or interesting. We were deeper in the bowels of the earth than we had ever been before, and surrounded by walls and towers of such imposing dimensions that it would be useless to attempt describing them; but the effects of magnitude had begun to pall, and the walk from the foot of the precipice was monotonously dull; no sign of life could be discerned above or below. At the end of thirteen miles from the precipice an obstacle presented itself that there seemed to be no possibility of overcoming. A stone slab, reaching from one side of the canon to the other, terminated the plane which we were descending. Looking over the edge it appeared that the next level was forty feet below. This time there was no trail along the side bluffs, for these were smooth and perpendicular. A spring of water rose from the bed of the cañon not far above, and trickled over the ledge, forming a pretty cascade. It was supposed that the Indians must have come to this point merely to procure water, but this theory was not altogether satisfactory, and we sat down upon the rocks to discuss the matter.

Mr. Egloffstein lay down by the side of the creek, and projecting his head over the ledge to watch the cascade, discovered a solution of the mystery. Below the shelving rock, and hidden by it and the fall, stood a crazy looking ladder, made of rough sticks bound together with thongs of bark. It was almost perpendicular, and rested upon a bed of angular stones. The rounds had become rotten from the incessant flow of water. Mr. Egloffstein, anxious to have the first view of what was below, scrambled over the ledge and got his feet upon the upper round. Being a solid weight, he was too much for the insecure fabric, which commenced giving way. One side fortunately stood firm, and holding on to this with a tight grip, he made a precipitate descent. The other side and all the rounds broke loose and accompanied him to the bottom in a general crash, effectually cutting off the communication. Leaving us to devise means of getting him back he ran to the bend to explore. The bottom of the cañon had been reached. He found that he was at the edge of a stream, ten or fifteen yards wide, fringed with cottonwoods and willows. The walls of the cañon spread out for a short distance, leaving room for a narrow belt of bottom land, on which were fields of corn and a few scattered huts.

A place was found near the ledge where one could clamber a little way up the wall, and we thus got a view of the valley. The river was nearly as large as the Gila at low water, and, with the exception of that stream, the most important tributary of the Colorado between its mouth and our position. The cañon Mr. Egloffstein saw could not be followed far; there were cascades just below. He perceived, however, that he was very near to its mouth, though perhaps at a thousand feet greater altitude, and an Indian pointed out the exact spot where it united with the cañon of the Rio Colorado.

The Yampais [Havasupais] did not differ much from the Hualpais in general appearance. They were perhaps a trifle cleaner and more respectable. It is probable that, all told, they do not number more than two hundred persons. One of them accompanied Mr. Egloffstein to the foot of the ledge, and intimated a willingness to go with us to camp, but when he saw the broken ladder gave up his intention. The accident did not appear otherwise to concern him. There must have been some other trail leading to the retreat, for the use of the ladder had evidently been long abandoned.

Having looked at all that was to be seen, it now remained to get Mr. Egloffstein back. The slings upon the soldiers' muskets were taken off and knotted together, and a line thus made which reached to the bottom. Whether it would support his weight was a matter of experiment. The general impression was that it would not, but of the two evils—breaking his neck or remaining among the Yampais—he preferred the former, and fastened the strap around his shoulders. It was a hard straight lift. The ladder pole was left, and rendered great assistance both to us and the rope, and the ascent was safely accomplished. We invited the Indian to follow Mr. Egloffstein's example, but this he energetically declined. The examination being finished, it was time to return. On leaving camp we had expected to be back before night, and had brought along neither provisions nor overcoats. An hour or two earlier, finding that the day was rapidly slipping by, two of the party were directed to go back and tell those who had remained that we might be detained till the next day, and in that case to forward in the morning something to eat. We walked as fast as possible, in order to get out of the cañon before dark, but the ascent was laborious, and the trail, made in coming down over the rocks, difficult to follow. Numerous branch cañons, all looking alike, would have rendered it easy to become lost had the trail been once departed from. Night came before the foot of the precipice where the train had stopped was reached. It was impossible to distinguish the way in the dark, and we had to halt. A few minutes previously the tracks of the two men that had been sent ahead had been noticed diverging from the proper course, and it was concluded that they were wandering astray somewhere in the labyrinth. After nightfall, as is always the case in these regions, it became bleak and cold. Some of the party, attired for a walk under a hot sun, had not even their coats. The cañon was as dark as a dungeon. The surface of the ground being covered with rocks, a recumbent position was uncomfortable, and the rocks being interspersed with prickly pear and some other varieties of cactaceae it would have been unwise to walk about. The choice, therefore, lay between sitting down and standing still, which two recreations we essayed alternately for twelve hours that might have been, from the sensations of the party, twelve days. As soon as it was light enough to see the way we put our stiffened limbs in motion. Climbing the precipice was severe work. The summit once attained, it was but five miles to camp, but the violent exercise of the ascent, coming after a twenty-four hours' abstinence from food and rest, and a walk of more than thirty miles over a difficult road, proved so exhausting that, during the last stretch, two or three of the men broke down, and had to have coffee and food sent back to them before they could proceed. . . .

Our reconnoitering parties have now been out in all directions, and everywhere have been headed off by impassable obstacles. The positions of the main water-courses have been determined with considerable accuracy. The region last explored is, of course, altogether valueless. It can be approached only from the south, and after entering it there is nothing to do but to leave. Ours has been the first, and will doubtless be the last, party of whites to visit this profitless locality. It seems intended by nature that the Colorado river, along the greater portion of its lonely and majestic way, shall be forever unvisited and undisturbed. The handful of Indians that inhabit the sequestered retreats where we discovered them have probably remained in the same condition, and of the same number, for centuries. The country could not support a large population, and by some provision of nature they have ceased to multiply. The deer, the antelope, the birds, even the smaller reptiles, all of which frequent the adjacent territory, have deserted this uninhabitable district. Excepting when the melting snows send their annual torrents through the avenues to the Colorado, conveying with them sound and motion, these dismal abysses, and the arid table-lands that enclose them, are left, as they have been for ages, in unbroken solitude and silence. The lagoons by the side of which we are encamped furnish, as far as we have been able to discover, the only accessible watering place west of the mouth of Diamond river. During the summer it is probable they are dry, and that no water exists upon the whole of the Colorado plateau. We start for the south with some anxiety, not knowing how long it may be before water will be again met with.

MOJAVE CROSSING
TO ORAIBE PUEBLO

Francisco Garcés

Francisco Tomás Hermenegildo Garcés was a Franciscan priest who ran a small mission at San Xavier del Bac on the northern frontier of New Spain, near present-day Tucson. He joined Juan Bautista de Anza on his 1775 expedition to establish a route to the missions on the California coast, but soon branched off on his own. Traveling alone and unarmed for almost a year, Garcés walked beside his mule through much of Arizona and Southern California, usually following guides recruited from the various tribes that he met along the way. His goals were to explore unknown territory and identify tribes who were ready to convert to Christianity and become subjects of the king of Spain. In order to communicate his message, he carried a canvas painted on one side with "Mary Most Holy with the Divine Child in her arms" and on the other side with a "damned man." In June 1776, Garcés headed east from Mojave territory on the lower Colorado River, crossed the Hualapai mesas, visited Supai Village in Havasu Canyon, and eventually reached the Hopi villages at Black Mesa. Along the way, he became the second European to see Grand Canyon. Garcés was well received by most of the people he met, but the Hopi were uninterested in his preaching. They tolerated his presence as he camped on a street corner in Oraibi for a few days, but soon drove him off. He retraced his route to the lower Colorado and eventually returned to his mission, where he prepared the report from which this selection is taken.

· · ·

June 7, 107th day
 I travelled four leagues east and reached the territory of the Jaguallapais [Hualapais], who had a place ready for feasting us. . . . They behaved very well

toward me, in keeping with the warmth that I had shown toward them. I gave them to understand that I wanted to go to Moqui [the Hopi mesas]. The strongest of objections were raised by the Jamajabs [Mojaves], because they feared that the Hopi Indians might kill me; but my insistence finally prevailed.

At this place there is a little stream-bed with running water, good pasturage, good hunting, and an abundance of chia. I spoke to them of God and saw that they had some knowledge of Him. All of them kissed my crucifix and had their little children kiss it too. They wear garments of deerskin and some blankets from Moqui with Spanish-style sashes. They have awls and other tools given them by the Hopi Indians. I did not see any cultivated fields, and I think they live on mescal and game. I stayed one day. . . .

June 10, 109th day

After five leagues east I came to the Arroyo de San Bernabé, which in some places has running water and in others not. In the afternoon, after another league along this same watercourse in the same direction, I halted at an abandoned ranchería. My companions set fire to a hovel, raising clouds of smoke to see if there were any Indians near. None appeared, so we went on eastward. Soon one of my companions saw at the foot of a tree two children who, when asked where their father was, said he would soon come; and he did, about ten o'clock the next morning, with his wife, greeting us with pleasure. The man, seeing my mule, asked for it, to bring in a buck that he had left dead. It is remarkable how these Indians share whatever they get from hunting; though the amount be small they share it with everyone. On this occasion, before loading the deer on he cut it up and gave half to the captain who accompanied me. The days I stopped there, they both gave me of their portions.

This ranchería belongs to the Yavipais, who differ only in name from the Jaguallapais. The Indian sent a messenger to his relatives, telling them I was here. . . . On the second day the relatives began to put in an appearance, in troops of six or eight. The chief or head of each troop made a speech upon arrival, to which the Jaguallapai captain who was with me replied. Each captain on ending his speech turned to his men, asking them if what he had said was good, to which they all answered yes. Finally, the Jaguallapai captain said: "This Father has a good heart; he is on close terms with our friends the Jalcheduns [Apaches]; he has made peace for us with the Jamajabs. Now he wants to go to Moqui, and he asks your permission." All acquiesced in my desire, knowing that I was a Spaniard and that the Hopi Indians are on friendly terms with the Spaniards of New Mexico. Then three Indians, two men and a woman, came saying they were from near Moqui and offering to go there with me. They did go part of the way. Their bearing was superior, and their dress so good that they looked quite civilized. . . .

June 16, 111th day

After travelling four leagues northeast and north, with thickets of juniper and pines on either hand, and in the afternoon five leagues to the north, we stopped at a mountainous ridge where the earth was red, and the Indians told me that the Colorado River was nearby. We saw deep gorges of the same color. Where we halted there was very little water. The two Indian men and the woman gave me for food some of the mescal they had with them.

This day the married man chanted the Alabado in the same tone as is used at the missions. I was astonished and, giving him a string of beads, asked who had taught it to him. He gave me to understand that the Yutas [Utes], his neighbours, knew it because they used to hear it from the Tiguas. He went through it another time or two.

June 17, 112th day

I went two and a half leagues northeast along a very rugged mountain range and arrived at the ranchería where lived the unmarried Indian who accompanied me. He spoke to his captain, who rejoiced at my coming and sent a messenger with news of it to the rancherías toward the north, from which men and women came bringing me gifts of mescal, which abounds in that land. All of them were very festive, danced their fill, and rejoiced over the news that the Castillas (their word for the Spaniards) were tying up the southern Yavipais and taking them far off.

They drew on the ground a sort of map, pointing out all the surrounding nations and the ways to them. They were pleased and astonished when on the same map I outlined my journey. Thus we understood each other, and thus I gained information about all these nations.

The married Indian who came with me, and his wife, set out for their dwelling-place. The way there, they told me, was level and had plenty of water. I could have gone on to Moqui, but they urged me to go to their land, and desirous as I was of seeing more Indians and learning more routes, besides being most grateful for the favors of these companions, I could not refuse.

I spoke to the people of God and of Heaven, and they showed their acquiescence in all that I said. They kissed the holy crucifix and raised it heavenward, and thus it was passed from hand to hand, even to the smallest children. In this and in other rancherías there was not one maimed, sightless, infirm, or exhausted person who failed to entreat me to lay my hands on him and say some prayers for him. I would recite a little of the Gospel, or the Magnificat; and so I continued to do throughout the land of the Yavipais. . . .

June 19, 113th day

I travelled a league east, accompanied by the captain and three others from his ranchería, also one of the important Indians of those along the Jabesua River

[Cataract Creek, home of the Havasupai], who had a beard but only a scanty one. I came to a ranchería and near it a waterhole with abundant supply which I called the Pozo de la Rosa because it was overtopped by rosebushes. Throughout this land there are many and large pines. I went upslope northward and after two leagues stopped at a ranchería where the Indians begged me not to go further.

June 20, 114th day

I went on five leagues east, two northeast, and three north, the last four over most difficult terrain, through gorges which though immensely deep had abundant herbage and not a few trees, and thus came to a ranchería on the Jabesua River which I called San Antonio. To get to it I went along a narrow way . . . some three handbreadths wide with a very high cliff on one side and on the other a hideous abyss. What came next was worse. I had to get down from my mule and the Indians from their horses in order to descend a wooden ladder. All the earth here is red. There are many mescal plants. There are some cows and a few horses, most of them with a brand which I did not recognize; of only one did I have a suspicion that it might be from San Ignacio Mission. I asked these Indians, as I had asked others, where they got these horses and cows; they answered, from Moqui, where there are stolen livestock and many horses.

I arrived at night. The Jabesua Indians came so decked with pieces of red cloth that I thought they might be of the Apaches who harass these regions, the more since the women came also and among them were some who were whiter than one generally sees in the other nations. I was not afraid, since I saw how joyous they were at my coming and that they were accepting willingly the peace proposed by me with the Spaniards and the Jamajabs. I informed them that the Spaniards would soon come to live on the Colorado River with the Yumas, Jalcheduns, Cocomaricopas, Gileño Pimas, and Noraguas. They urged me so persistently that I had to stop there five days. During this time they treated me to deer-meat and beef, maize, beans, greens, and mescal, with all of which they were well provided.

It pleased me much to see that at daybreak the husband would go out with his wife and older children to work their fields, taking along the tools they needed such as digging-sticks, hatchets, and grub hoes; all these they get from Moqui. They are decently clothed and are fond of remnants of red cloth which they call Spanish because it comes from New Mexico. I think perhaps the women here are so light in color (I saw one who might be taken for a Spaniard) because the place where they live is so deep down that the sun scarcely gilds it before ten o'clock in the forenoon. In all my travels I have seen no better natural stronghold. It contains about thirty-four families and I believe it to be the largest of all the Yavipai rancherías. The Jabesua River flows through here. It rises in the tangled gorges that are in every direction, and runs northwest and north, flowing near here into the Colorado River. It is a medium-sized river but very rapid. The Jabesuas, by means of good dams, draw much water from it to cultivate crops.

June 25, 115th day

Accompanied by five Indians I went two leagues south and east with much difficulty, partly on foot, partly on horseback (they had taken our animals out by another path), and halted on the way up the heights at a watering-place with scant supply. In the afternoon I got to the top of that most painful ascent (its precipices are horrifying), and after a further three leagues southeast and north over land with much herbage, junipers, pines, and so forth, I arrived at a Jabesua ranchería where they had come to pick juniper berries. The principal man among the Indians said that next day he would go with me.

June 26, 116th day

Four more leagues southeast and south, and I stopped in sight of the succession of very deep gorges among which flows the Colorado River. From here I saw that in a very large mountain range extending from southeast to northwest and blue with distance a deep passage was cut, steep-sided like a man-made trough, through which the Colorado River enters these lands; I called it the Puerto de Bucareli. Although to my sight it seemed quite near, it was very hard to reach on account of the canyons in between. It lay to the east-northeast from where I looked. I saw toward the north some puffs of smoke which I was told were made by the Payuchas [Paiutes], who dwell on the other side of the river. Here, three families were waiting to go in company with us, since the way is very hazardous because of hostilities with the Tejua Yavipais and the Napacs [Navajo]. These Napacs live in a mountain range of the same name which, starting from that of the Puerto de Bucareli and running west, is in some places very high; it was still covered with snow. I think the Rio de la Asuncion rises there. This day they showed me some tracks of the Tejua Yavipais which went off to the north since in that direction lies their path for going to trade with their friends the Chemeguavas [Chemehuevi]. After travelling four leagues southeast in the afternoon, we spent the night in a pine forest. . . .

June 28, 118th day

After travelling three and a half leagues southeast, south, and east, I came to the Jaquesila River [the Little Colorado], which I called the Rio de San Pedro. It had an abundant flow, but the water was so turbid and red that it could not be drunk. In the pools along its banks there was good water. This river runs west-northwest; its bed, until it joins the Colorado (not far above the Puerto de Bucareli), is a very deep trough in the living rock, about a stone's throw in width, which even an unmounted traveller cannot possibly cross before reaching this place where I was, at which point with much trouble I was able to get down to it. The gorge continues upstream east-northeast, although not so deep. After crossing the river, I travelled eight leagues north in the afternoon through another canyon like the river channel. I had to branch off to reach a ranchería of about thirty Yavipais, who received me most warmly because there was among them the Indian who sang the Alabado as I have related above.

The captain of this ranchería, a noticeably long-bearded man, was the brother of the Jabesua Indian who accompanied me. Two Indians from Moqui had come to trade with these Yavipais. I found them dressed almost like Spaniards; they were wearing leather jackets. One of them kissed my hand. When I gave him a little tobacco and some shells he returned them to me. I called to the other, but he would not come near, nor kiss my crucifix, which the Yavipais offered to him. These Hopi Indians went away early the next morning, but I did not leave until the first of July.

July 1, 119th day

I went one and a half leagues east-southeast and came to a river that seemed to me to be the San Pedro Jaquesila. Near it was a pueblo in ruins. I was told that the pueblo had belonged to the Hopi Indians, and that the signs of crop-raising yet to be seen were their work since notwithstanding the distance from their homes they still come here to cultivate their fields. The river was low, with yellow water. After I crossed the river and some hills, I reached some very wide treeless plains. I travelled over them six leagues in the same direction and came to some of the Hopis' horse corrals, which were gorges or ravines not easy to enter or to leave, with not much water. From here the only mountain ranges that can be seen are to the south and southwest; they lead to the Apache country.

July 2, 120th day

I travelled three leagues east-southeast and three more east and south, and came to the pueblo called Muca by the Yavipais, which is Oraibe, the first settlement in Moqui. Meeting a young man, I offered him tobacco but he refused it. Two leagues further on, when I approached, as if to shake hands with them, two Indians who were well mounted and well clad, they drew away making signs to me to go back. The Yavipais with me spoke in my favor, but met with rebuffs and turned to me to ask what I wished to do. I gave the Hopis to understand that if they would not receive me I would go on to the Gualpes or to the Spaniards; and then, without waiting further, I continued forward since the pueblo was near. Of the eight Yavipais who were my companions only an old man and a boy caught up with me, and with them I entered the pueblo. The path up to the mesa is very narrow. Beside it was a sheep corral where they were guarding three flocks. Theirs are bigger than the Sonora sheep, and the black ones have the best color.

I ascended the slope and went across the mesa, passing some heaps of sand, to a spring that is in front of the pueblo. Although the soil is poor and there is no pasturage on the mesa, I saw many peach trees in the ravines, and at the edge of the spring I saw some beds of onions, beans, and other garden truck which they have cultivated only with much labor.

I came to the pueblo. At the entrance there are two or three tumbledown houses, and in the others neither door nor window is to be seen from this side. I entered through a rather wide street running from east to west as far as the pueblo exit, I think the only one. There come in at the sides of this street others of the same width, which in different blocks open into two small squares. The ground is not even, but it is firm, and the north-to-south streets are level because the slope of the place is toward the east.

The houses are built in storeys, some with more, some with fewer. Their arrangement is as follows. From the street level a wall rises to a height of about one and one-half varas, at which level is the courtyard, reached by a movable wooden ladder. The ladder has no more rungs than are needed for climbing to the courtyard, but its side rails reach to the flat roof. On the level of the courtyard there are two, three, or four rooms with wooden doors, bolts, and keys. If they keep chickens, the coop is here. The courtyard wall has a stairway leading to the upper storeys, which have each a big room in the middle and other rooms on both sides. There is also in the same wall a set of steps leading up to the roof, which commonly connects with the neighboring houses. The noteworthy thing is that all the living quarters of the houses turn back to, so that no one can see what another is doing indoors unless he climbs up to the roof. The shape is not square, nor is it exactly rounded.

As soon as I had entered and dismounted in the sight of a large number of women and children who were on the roofs, I approached, with the intention of climbing up, a house that was known to the old man; he had been speaking with its mistress, who was on the roof. She told him to come up but to warn me that I was not to come, nor my things either. I went to a secluded place I found by the street and unsaddled. The Yavipai took my mule to a corral for livestock.

All day long there were men, women, and children taking a look at me, but none would come close even though I offered them white seashells, at which their faces would light up because they like them so much. The old Yavipai said to me: "Stay here by yourself. These people don't like you and they are bad." With the corncobs thrown in the street I built a fire and made a little gruel. The rest of the Yavipais arrived and I heard them talking a great deal in the houses, undoubtedly pleading my cause. In the afternoon I saw coming into the pueblo the men returning from work, with their hatchets, digging-sticks, and grub hoes.

At nightfall an old man came to me. I gave him a present and held the crucifix for him to kiss. On receiving the gift he said in Spanish, "Díos te lo pague [May God reward you]"; and he went away. Another came, a young man, whom I treated similarly, and he began to say to me in Spanish: "Father, these are savages who do not wish to be baptized, nor do they believe that you are a priest; but I do, because I am baptized, and I am from Zuñi, where all the people are good and are content with their priest. We know that those who are baptized go to Heaven. Our priest came here, too, and when he returned he told us that these people were bad for they did not wish to be baptized. But the priest is satisfied with us of Zuñi. He came a short while ago from Mexico City and the old one went to Santa Fe. There is also a priest in Acoma and Laguna. You can go with us to him tomorrow, for there are three of us. The way is good, with water; it lies toward the sunrise. Before noon we shall arrive at the first pueblo, where there is plenty of fodder and the animals will feed well. Leaving on the next day and with all that day and the night for travel, you will reach the mission; if not, then on the following day. Don't be afraid of the Nabajai Apaches, for they have come down in peace and say that the Spaniards are brave and that a bearded man"—they mean me—"has come saying there is to be war no longer and the mission priest is writing to Santa Fe." I did not answer the Indian on this point; I only told him that I was glad we had met. I asked for the captain of the pueblo, and he said: "The captain doesn't want to come here. He has hid himself; where, who knows?" I urged him to tell the people that I was a priest, a minister to the Spaniards of Sonora and to other Indians like them. I asked him to say that they should permit at least the children to come near me, that I might give them presents and tell them about God. The Indian got up and spoke in a low voice to those who were near. Afterward, he asked me if I wished to sleep in the house where he was lodged, but I refused the offer since it had not been made by the master of the house.

At night, as the people went up to their roofs, where they sleep, there was much noise of singing and of flutes; but after a while there was silence. Then a high-pitched voice was heard giving a loud and very long oration or sermon. When it ended, the clamor started up again. After another interval a preacher with a harsh voice came out and while he preached there was dead silence. This night the men walked about the streets for two or three hours before dawn, quite as if it were a Spanish town.

After I had lain down, my companions the Yavipais came. I told them I had decided to go to Zuñi, but they said no, that I should return to the Jabesua country; that the Hopis did not want me. Although I offered them white shells with which to buy maize, they did not accept them because the Hopis would not supply it; and furthermore, the two youngest cast back at me the white shells I had given them on the road, from which I concluded that the Hopis had filled them with misgivings about my presents.

July 3, 121st day

At dawn the three Indians from Zuñi came to me. I told them I no longer wished to go to their pueblo because the Yavipais would not go with me and I would not be able to come back through Moqui, doubtful of the Hopis as I was, if I should come without the Yavipais. I had already been advised that the Yutas were friends of the Spaniards, as also of the Yavipais, but the way to them was long, requiring an escort and supplies, neither of which did I have. . . .

A little later my old Yavipai Indian came with one of the important men of the pueblo to urge me to go see the other pueblos of Moqui where they would give me something to eat, since here they would not do so. I saddled my mule and, accompanied by the two Yavipais and by many boys and girls as onlookers, went down the slope from the pueblo on the east side, where they pointed out the way to the other pueblos. I demurred, for want of a guide, but the old Yavipai said to me that both I and my mule were hungry and that he would wait here for me five days, as he had not finished selling the mescal and other things he had brought.

I resigned myself to going on alone and entered a vast sandy plain to the south. On both sides of my path I saw many fields of maize and beans, and many Indians working them. I went up another mesa and came upon two little shepherds guarding sheep and a woman with her hatchet getting kindling-wood. They ran off at my approach, which made me sensible of the antipathy of all these people. Reflecting that "Better the known evil of the present than the uncertain good of the future," and, in fine, that my friends the Yavipais were in Oraibe, I decided to go back there. After retracing the three leagues I had covered, I entered Oraibe at nightfall, astonished that so many were on the roofs watching me as I passed by on my mule seeking the secluded place where I had spent the preceding night, which I found after several turns.

In this pueblo the people are of two kinds and two languages: the first can be distinguished by the color and stature of both men and women; the second, by the difference in the mode of singing. Some are lighter and clearer in color, and well set up; others are small, dark, and ugly. When they go out from the pueblo they look like Spaniards in their dress, with leather jackets, tight sleeves, trousers, and boots or shoes. Their weapons are arrows and spears. In the pueblo they go about in shoes, and in sleeves of a spotted cloth and a dark-grey blanket such as they themselves make. The women wear a long, sleeveless smock and a grey or white blanket like a square mantilla. The smock is tied round the waist with a sash that is commonly of many colors. They neither daub nor paint themselves, nor did I see beads or earrings. The old women wear their hair in two braids and the younger ones in a whorl over each ear or all tied at one side. They take very good care of their hair.

Although they showed me no favor, I got the impression that among the Hopis there were many good people and that only their rulers were prejudiced. There may have been other reasons for the way I was received, apart from their not wishing to be baptized or to have Spaniards in their lands; for example, hearing that I came from the Jamajabs and the Yumas, friends of their enemies, they may have thought me a spy of the Tejua Yavipais and Chemeguavas. . . .

Within the pueblo I saw no water, but on the eastern slope I saw a copious spring with steps of worked stone leading to it and a curbing of the same material. In my secluded corner I slept that night. One of the Yavipais took my mule to the same corral as on the previous day.

July 4, 122nd day

As soon as day began to break I heard singing and dancing along the streets. The dance passed the place where I was and I saw some Indians with feather ornaments on their heads, and other finery, making a din with small sticks on a shallow wooden basin, in company with flutes. Many followed them and stopped here and there to dance. When the sun was up a great throng moved toward me and made me fear for my life. In the lead came four of the principal men, the tallest of whom demanded of me, with a smile: "Why have you come here? Don't stay. Go back to your own land." I made signs to them to be seated, but they did not wish to do so. I stood up, crucifix in hand, and partly in Yuma, partly in Yavipai, partly in Spanish, and with signs, which are the best language, I made known to them the path of my journey, the nations I had seen, and those that had passed the crucifix from hand to hand and had been good to me. I said, moreover, that I cherished the Hopis, and that I came to tell them that God is in Heaven and that the Crucified was God, Jesus Christ, who was good. To this an old man, contorting his features, said in Spanish, "No, no." At that I said, "Fetch my mule." When it was brought and my things were loaded on I mounted and, with a smile on my face, praising their pueblo and their dress, I left, surrounded by all the crowd until I was beyond the houses.

THE HOPI MESAS AND
THE COLORADO RIVER

Pedro de Castañeda

The first Europeans to see Grand Canyon and the Colorado River were members of a Spanish expeditionary army that explored, in 1540, what is now the American Southwest. Under the command of General Francisco Vásquez de Coronado, more than fifteen hundred soldiers and slaves marched across the deserts, searching for the seven golden cities of Cíbola mentioned in hazy reports from the northern frontier of what was then New Spain. When he reached the Zuni pueblos near the headwaters of the Little Colorado River, Coronado demanded food and shelter for his men. The inhabitants refused, so Coronado ordered his men to attack and occupy the pueblo of Cíbola. While recovering from wounds he sustained during the battle, Coronado sent a detachment led by García López de Cárdenas to the Hopi mesas, thinking they might be the fabled golden cities. The Hopi villages matched the fanciful reports in all respects except one: there was no gold to be found. According to the history of the expedition written by one of its members, Pedro de Castañeda, in 1540, Hopi guides then led Cárdenas and his men to the South Rim near the present location of Desert View Watchtower. Bewildered by thirst and by the unearthly scale of the place, Cárdenas felt sure that the river was just six feet wide. He sent three men down for drinking water. They returned exhausted several hours later and reported that even Grand Canyon's most insignificant rocks "were bigger than the great tower of Seville."

· · ·

Cibola being at peace, the General Francisco Vazquez found out from the people of the province about the provinces that lay around it, and got them to tell their friends and neighbors that Christians had come into the country, whose only desire was to be their friends, and to find out about good lands to live in, and for them to come to see the strangers and talk with them. They did this, since they know how to communicate with one another in these regions, and they informed him about a province with seven villages of the same sort as theirs, although somewhat different. They had nothing to do with these people. This province is called Tusayan. It is twenty-five leagues from Cibola. The villages are high and the people are warlike.

The general had sent Don Pedro de Tovar to these villages with seventeen horsemen and three or four foot soldiers. Juan de Padilla, a Franciscan friar, who had been a fighting man in his youth, went with them. When they reached the region, they entered the country so quietly that nobody observed them, because there were no settlements or farms between one village and another and the people do not leave the villages except to go to their farms, especially at this time, when they had heard that Cibola had been captured by very fierce people, who travelled on animals which ate people. This information was generally believed by those who had never seen horses, although it was so strange as to cause much wonder. Our men arrived after nightfall and were able to conceal themselves under the edge of the village, where they heard the natives talking in their houses. But in the morning they were discovered and drew up in regular order, while the natives came out to meet them, with bows, and shields, and wooden clubs, drawn up in lines without any confusion. The interpreter was given a chance to speak to them and give them due warning, for they were very intelligent people, but nevertheless they drew lines and insisted that our men should not go across these lines toward their village.

While they were talking, some men acted as if they would cross the lines, and one of the natives lost control of himself and struck a horse a blow on the cheek of the bridle with his club. Friar Juan, fretted by the time that was being wasted in talking with them, said to the captain: "To tell the truth, I do not know why we came here." When the men heard this, they gave the Santiago [a war cry] so suddenly that they ran down many Indians and the others fled to the town in confusion. Some indeed did not have a chance to do this, so quickly did the people in the village come out with presents, asking for peace. The captain ordered his force to collect, and, as the natives did not do any more harm, he and those who were with him found a place to establish their headquarters near the village. They had dismounted here when the natives came peacefully, saying that they had come to give in the submission of the whole province and that they wanted him to be friends with them and to accept the presents which they gave him. This was some cotton cloth, although not much, because they do not make it in that district. They also gave him some dressed skins and corn meal, and pine nuts and corn and birds of the country. Afterward they presented some turquoises, but not many. The people of the whole district came together that day and submitted themselves, and they allowed him to enter their villages freely to visit, buy, sell, and barter with them.

It is governed like Cibola, by an assembly of the oldest men. They have their governors and generals. This was where they obtained the information about a large river, and that several days down the river there were some people with very large bodies.

As Don Pedro de Tovar was not commissioned to go farther, he returned from there and gave this information to the general, who dispatched Don Garcia Lopez de Cardenas with about twelve companions to go to see this river. He was well received when he reached Tusayan and was entertained by the natives, who gave him guides for his journey. They started from here loaded with provisions, for they had to go through a desert country before reaching the inhabited region, which the Indians said was more than twenty days' journey. After they had gone twenty days they came to the banks of the river. It seemed to be more than 3 or 4 leagues in an air line across to the other bank of the stream which flowed between them.

This country was elevated and full of low twisted pines, very cold, and lying open toward the north, so that, this being the warm season, no one could live there on account of the cold. They spent three days on this bank looking for a passage down to the river, which looked from above as if the water was 6 feet across, although the Indians said it was half a league wide. It was impossible to descend, for after these three days Captain Melgosa and one Juan Galeras and another companion, who were the three lightest and most agile men, made an attempt to go down at the least difficult place, and went down until those who were above were unable to keep sight of them. They returned about 4 o'clock in the afternoon, not having succeeded in reaching the bottom on account of the great difficulties which they found, because what seemed to be easy from above was not so, but instead very hard and difficult. They said that they had been down about a third of the way and that the river seemed very large from the place which they reached, and that from what they saw they thought the Indians had given the width correctly. Those who stayed above had estimated that some huge rocks on the sides of the cliffs seemed to be about as tall as a man, but those who went down swore that when they reached these rocks they were bigger than the great tower of Seville. They did not go farther up the river, because they could not get water.

Before this they had had to go a league or two inland every day late in the evening in order to find water, and the guides said that if they should go four days farther it would not be possible to go on, because there was no water within three or four days, for when they travel across this region themselves they take with them women loaded with water in gourds, and bury the gourds of water along the way, to use when they return, and besides this, they travel in one day over what it takes us two days to accomplish.

THE STORY OF TIYO

G.M. Mullett

George Mullett was a popular illustrator and story writer for the turn-of-the-century children's magazine *St. Nicholas*. She also worked for twenty years as a scientific illustrator for the pioneering anthropologist Jesse Walter Fewkes at the Smithsonian Institution. Fewkes conducted excavations at many ancestral Puebloan sites, including Casa Grande and Mesa Verde, and he advocated government preservation of Native American sacred sites, which were being destroyed by looters and vandals. He also studied the continuing traditions of the Zuni and Hopi, recording many of their rituals, songs, and stories. Fewkes published a version of the story of Tiyo, an important Hopi cultural hero, in an account of the snake ceremonies at the village of Walpi in 1891. Because the direct transcript required readers to be familiar with many traditional characters and concepts, Mullett later adapted the story for a general readership. It tells the tale of a young man who floats down the Colorado River and, with the help of the goddess Spider Woman, learns the ceremonies that will ensure the arrival of life-giving rains every year. Mullett's version, with its poetic language and vivid storytelling, reflects her conviction that publishing Hopi stories would not only preserve them for future generations but also help to counteract the strong prejudices of her time. She left the manuscript of Spider Woman stories to her daughter when she died; it was published forty years later, in 1979, and has been a perennial favorite ever since.

· · ·

Back, far back, in the mists of time when the world was very young, at Tokonabi lived the Hopi lad Tiyo, of the Puma clan. First-born of his father, the Kikmonwi or village chieftain, he entered the world big with awe for the wonders of creation and a vast thirst for knowledge of their meanings. The eyes of his parents would meet in startled pride to see their wee lad watching the moving stream of sand sifting through the side of his small copper-colored fist and trying to see for himself that Life which his father had told him lay in the earth and caused the corn to sprout; or again, they would find him, ear close to some vessel of his mother's modeling, tapping on it to hear the Spirit of the Bowl make answer.

He would leave his romping to watch her make her brilliant pigments in small earthen vessels of her own molding and very early learned to select and chew a yucca stick into a proper paintbrush. When, with skillful fingers, she wove or painted design upon basket or bowl, there was he to watch her and his quick eyes were ever spying out a new "Why?"

"Why do you leave the black bands around the border unfinished, my mother? Why is a gap left?"

"So you saw that did you, little man? Surely you have the sharp eyes of Mourning Dove. Know then and remember that there is the Gate of Life for the Spirit of the Bowl to enter and to leave."

"But sometimes there is no opening," Tiyo would persist.

"Yes, and when it is that way it comes about that it is a burial bowl, so fashioned to hold good food for one who has left to join the Ancestors. A hole must then be knocked in its center so that its Spirit be released to go with the departed one's Breath Body to the Underworld."

The wisdom imparted by his parents passed like trickling water through the ears of his brother and two sisters, but Tiyo was ever held spellbound by the lore of his ancestors and stored and pondered it in his heart. When winter came and the hard, frozen ground held fast prisoner all the evil spirits who might work that one ill who was trying to pry into magic lore, how eagerly did he hang upon the tales whispered by the bolder of the old men. Sitting around glowing pinyon fires to carve the sacred dolls or gaily colored kachina masks, the old men told thrilling tales of those marvelous beings who peopled the Underworld. And when, filled with a tremendous yearning to know more of these mysteries, he would run to his mother with his scraps of knowledge, her eyes would light proudly even while she bantered with him.

"This is man knowledge—how should I know?" she would answer. "Have thou a care, little wise man, lest you be served the same dumpling as Brother Coyote."

"Tell me, my mother," Tiyo would demand, tugging at her arm and quick to scent a story.

"You know how it comes about that Brother Coyote is always prying into everything? My, but he is a meddlesome one, that one! On a day he was walking across the mesa looking here and there for some mischief when he came upon Tumblebug with his head close to the ground. At first Brother Coyote thought Tumblebug was playing dead, as he so often does, but finally he felt that he must find out. He touched Tumblebug gently with his paw. "Brother Bug, what are you doing with your ear thus close to the ground?"

"Yes," answered the Bug slowly. "I am listening to the gods talking down there in the Below."

"Ah," returned the Coyote, "and pray, Brother Tumblebug, what do the gods say?"

"'They say,'" said the Bug, glad to have a chance to teach meddlesome Coyote a lesson, "they say very solemnly that Brother Coyote would do well to run along home and attend to his own business."

And then when he had joined in lustily at her laughter at his own expense he would beg for other stories or songs about Brother Coyote, who, being such a busybody and altogether loose character, was always having thrilling adventures.

Now, because Tiyo was first born and because their thoughts were knit so closely together, the Kikmonwi bared his heart to his son. All his fears for his people, because of the thin clouds, small springs and scant rains, were shared with the youth, and his hope to make a great tribe of this small number became Tiyo's also. So when the boy became a youth, well muscled, clean-limbed and straight, he withdrew himself more and more from the games of his comrades, in which he easily surpassed them all, and gave himself more and more to the counsels of his father or to thoughtful brooding on the cliff's sheer edge.

Seated on the canyon's rim, like an atom hung in the immensity between the Above and Below, he would gaze for hours upon the wonders spread before him. His eager eyes tried to plunge beneath the surface of things that appeared, and the Eagle, Kwahu, himself, mounted no higher than did the questing thought of Tiyo as it strained to fly forth and learn the Why, the Where and the End of All. As he sat there, he watched Tawa march his shining course across the sky's blue arch; he gazed with rapture as the Sun God changed the canyon's walls from orange to pink, from pink to red; marvelled at the magic of him as he caused huge buttes to fade away and vanish and then, pulling long shadows behind him, splash the rocky walls with mighty pictures in a gorgeous riot of color. Or, on other days when lowering clouds hid Tawa from view, he watched the Great Plumed Serpent, Palulkon, strike and bite the earth, the while his blood would race and thrill as he listened to its angry bellowings thundering and reverberating through gorge and chasm.

But more potently than any of these wonders did the Far-Far-Below River draw his seeking eyes, coming as it seemed from the Unknown and travelling into the Unknown again. Like a great silver serpent it writhed its way, pulling behind it all the waters of his earth and vanishing with them into the Underworld. With such a wealth of water streaming into the Underworld, why could not Tawa on his nightly journey through the same region bring back enough for a bountiful rain for his people who so sorely needed it? But, alas! the rains that now came were so scant that the corn parched and Masauwuh, the Death God, continually skulked about their borders.

At last Tiyo, flaming with a high resolve, made up his mind to follow the Far-Far-Below River, brave every terror of the Underworld, fathom its mysteries, and win from the gods themselves the right to live and flourish.

Eagerly he sought his father: "Inaa, my father," he said, "I have been wondering where the Far-Far-Below River travels."

"So that is what you have been thinking about," said his father. "We do not know very much about that thing."

"I am convinced, after much long thinking, Inaa, that the Far-Far-Below River, which daily draws all the waters of the earth behind it flows down some great opening into the Underworld, for after all these years the gorge has never filled up, neither does any of the water flow back again."

"Maybe this is so, my son," said the Kikmonwi gravely, "but it may be that it travels so great a distance that the lives of many old men would be too short to follow it."

"Be that so or not, I must go and solve this mystery, Inaa, for I can find no peace in my mind until I do so," insisted Tiyo firmly.

Then his father took out his ancient stone pipe and smoked and smoked, while he searched his wisdom for the best way to help his son in this perilous undertaking upon which he was determined.

At last he spoke: "It is impossible for you to follow the river on foot, hence we must look for a hollow cottonwood tree, and I will show you how to make a winacibuh, in which you may float safely upon the waters of the Far-Far-Below River."

Eagerly did Tiyo search until he found such a tree, and the girth of it was such that it took the outstretched arms of the old Kikmonwi and his son's to span it. This they felled and cut from it a section as long as the body of the youth. Then, with stone ax and living embers, they gouged and burned out all of the inside, leaving only a thin shell like a huge drum. Small branches and twigs were then fitted into one of the open ends so as to close it completely, and the interstices were pitched thoroughly with pinyon gum.

At last all was done and his father looked upon Tiyo sadly. "After four sleeps, Itii (my son), you may start upon your journey. Your mother and sisters will make you kwipdosi from husked corn, boiled and dried and ground, while I with prayer and fasting will make you such pahos as I know you will need to win favor from those you will encounter on your journey."

When the morning of the fifth day had come Tiyo was chafing and straining to be on his way, so his father brought to him the prayer sticks and explained to him their meaning and their uses. Carefully he placed them on a fresh white cotton mantle—"This is Wupo Paho for Spider Woman; this for Hicanavaiya;

this for Woman of the Hard Substances; this for Tawa, himself, may it please him; while the last is for the Muiyinwuh, the Germ God." Beside these magic tokens he laid a small quantity of fluffy white down from the eagle's thigh. "This is kwapuha, my son. The greatest magic lies in these trembling breath feathers, and Spider Woman will show you how to use it. I beg you that you walk carefully, for if you step amiss and offend one of these great ones it will go ill with you. Wrap all of these things in this mantle and see that you guard them with greatest care."

Then his mother, as is the way with womenfolk, came forward with streaming eyes. Gently she handed him a tcakapta, and inside this food basin she had with cunning painted the sign of Spider Woman, while on the outer surface was the symbol of Tawa. Cunning magic! To this gift she and each of Tiyo's sisters added shallow circular trays of coiled grass wrapped about with yucca shreds and heaped generously with the kwipdosi they had made him.

Now all was ready, and Tiyo crept into his timber-box. After handing the youth a stout pole of honwi wood with which to guide his craft, the Kikmonwi reluctantly but with greatest care closed the open end of the winacibuh, gave it a mighty heave and away it floated, bobbing up and down on the rushing waters of the Far-Far-Below River.

Through a small circular opening that had been left for the purpose, Tiyo thrust forth his pole, pushing away from the rocks that lay in the way of his craft. On he floated over smooth waters, sped madly through swift, rushing torrents, plunged down cataracts, and for many hours spun through wild whirlpools where black rocks thrust forth their heads like angry bears. At times when the spray dashed through the small opening Tiyo caught it in his basin to quench his thirst or to mix with his kwipdosi for gruel, but when the roaring waters came about his timber-box he closed the opening with a plug.

Tossed and buffeted by whirlpool and rapid, Tiyo continued on. The journey was fearsome enough to daunt the staunchest heart, but through it all Tiyo remained undaunted and eager for his task.

TIYO MEETS SPIDER WOMAN

A sudden violent jolt, then that motionlessness that meant the winacibuh had come to a rest. Tiyo's heart leapt with such violence that his ears sang like small drums, and he swiftly tore himself an opening in the timber-box. When he peered through the opening he saw that he had come up against a sandy shore. No live thing could he see, but to his alert ears seemed to come a sibilant "hsss, hsss." Taking his paho mantle in one hand he sprang out expectantly upon the stretch of sand. The hissing became louder, and he saw that it came from a small hole near his feet. Then the "hsss" sounded distinctly four times, so he bent a listening ear close above it, and a voice issued from the depths.

"Um pituh, you have arrived," came in true Hopi greeting. "My heart is glad. I have been long expecting you, Tiyo. Come into the house of Kokyanwuhti."

Kokyanwuhti! How the heart of Tiyo thrilled at the name—Kokyanwuhti, the great Spider Woman.

"Alas, how can I come to you," cried the perplexed Tiyo, "I have looked on every side and see only this tiny hole through which your voice comes, and it will scarce admit the point of my great toe."

"Come," was the abrupt command. So Tiyo, without further question, placed his foot upon the hole; then, as if stirred to life, the tiny particles of sand began to whirl about and in a marvellous way the opening widened until it allowed the admission of his body as he was drawn gently downwards. When his feet touched solid rock he pressed impetuously forward in a dim passageway until he found himself in a great stone kiva. Then before his eager eyes appeared the Mighty One, she of whom since infancy he had heard with bated breath—Spider Woman.

Now, though Spider Woman is as old as time, she is likewise as young as eternity, for she is Earth Mother, so Tiyo, feeling the endless youth of her, hailed her "Kokyamana," Spider Maid, and in the way of woman she was pleased with the stripling's flattering tribute. Encouraged by her smile, he eagerly unrolled his mantle and reverently handed her the Wupo Paho and the trembling breath feathers of eagle down.

"Ah," cried she with pleasure as she scanned the prayer stick with care, "this was made by One Who Knows. I thank you. I can be seen or I can become as air; I go everywhere and I know all things; I know from whence you come and whither you are bound; I know your heart is good; I know the things you want. I have prepared food for you—partake of it," and she set before him two cornmeal dumplings that magically increased as he ate them, so that, though they were very small when he started, he ate and was filled to the chin.

For four days the youth stayed in the kiva of Spider Woman, listening to her words of wisdom, while she compounded the magic medicine that pacifies the snake and all angry animals. On the fifth day she gave it to him with these words, "Only the fearless can use this nahu; you keep your heart brave. There are Angry Ones who guard the kiva entrances to which you will go. You put this on the tip of your tongue and spurt it on such angry ones. You will see! They will become gentle as the rabbit. I will make myself small and sit behind your left ear so as to tell you what to do. See that your ears are keen and that you obey, or I shall leave you. Now take this down of Kwahu on your hand and step upon the sipapu over there."

Unquestioningly Tiyo obeyed his mentor, and as soon as he had done so the orifice opened just as before and he sank into the Underworld. When he came to a stop he stood waiting with his hand, upon which lay the eagle's down, outstretched before him. A miracle! Slowly the feathers stirred as if alive, rose gently and floated toward the northwest. With his eyes fixed upon it, Tiyo followed eagerly until he came to where the projecting ends of a ladder gave evidence of a kiva below. But alas! this entrance was guarded by a most fearsome monster. It was no less a one than the great Snake, Gatoya, himself. His gray body was only so long as the youth's arm, but its girth was that of a man's body. Two large eyes gleamed from a multi-colored head and, from a venomous mouth that could breathe death to a long distance, projected two great teeth capable of piercing the thickest buckskin. Here was his way barred by the Guardian of All Angry Snakes.

Tiyo did not blanch, and, because fear had not entered his heart to becloud his mind, he remembered the words of Spider Woman and put the nahu upon the tip of his tongue. As the hideous reptile reared to strike viciously with his poisonous fangs, Tiyo spurted the charm upon it just in time, and it drooped its ugly head meekly and allowed the youth to pass. He exulted over the danger passed, and more he would gladly meet if he could only gain for his people the gift of more abundant rain. But, as he passed on, there sprang before his startled eyes two angry bears, growling and reaching toward him with violent claws. The nahu, however, was ready on his tongue so that when he spurted it at them they bowed their shaggy heads submissively, allowing him to descend the ladder unmolested.

What a strange sight now met his eyes! He entered a great gray stone kiva, the walls, the roof and floors of which were hung and covered with snakeskins. Stranger still were figures—half man, half reptile—that squatted around a sand ponya on the floor. None spoke or seemed to notice him. And there was the stillness of death in the gloom.

Then came the welcome voice of Spider Woman whispering softly in his ear, "These are the Ancestors, show one of your paho." When Tiyo displayed a paho, an old chieftain merely bent his head and silently motioned to a sipapu which led still lower.

As he descended through this, a very different sight gladdened both his eyes and heart.

Everything before him was light and cheerful and many men sat around a brilliantly colored sand ponya chanting their songs to a low humming rhythm of many gourd rattles. Their garments and feather plumes were brightly colored, and from all came glad cries of welcome.

"You are now in Tchutcub kiva, the chamber of the Snake-Antelopes. Yonder chieftain is Hicanavaiya, Ancient of Six," whispered Spider Woman, who was now in the form of a tiny spider resting behind Tiyo's ear. "There stand the two beautiful daughters of the chief."

Standing on each side of the altar two maidens of wondrous grace and fairness of form caught Tiyo's attention. Both faces held his admiring eyes, but one held his gaze the longest, for she seemed as beautiful as the earth in its springtime unfoldment. It was with difficulty that he forced his eyes away from her face and turned to deliver the first Blue Paho to Hicanavaiya.

The chieftain looked at it very carefully before placing it by the sand ponya. "Now this is good," he said. "I can see that it was made by One Who Knows. I have been expecting you, and I thank you for coming. I cause the rain clouds to come and go. I cause the ripening winds to blow. 'Tis I who direct the coming and going of all mountain animals. Before you return to your home you will desire many things. Ask freely of me and you will receive, because your heart is good."

Tiyo would have been glad to tarry here in the home of the lovely maiden, but Spider Woman bade him resume his journey. Difficult though it was to leave, he did not hesitate in his obedience. Reluctantly he tore his eyes from the maiden and passed onward up the hatchway. At this point the eagle down floated toward the west, and he knew that he must follow in that direction though it seemed to lead only to a vast stretch of water. All the waters of the world must be here, like the Endless Waters of First Tale. Undoubtedly this must be the place to which the Far-Far-Below River journeyed. Far out he could see the long tips of a ladder projecting above the shimmering waters. There seemed no way to proceed, so he had stopped at the very brink.

The voice of Spider Woman came softly: "Behold the House of Huzruiwuhti before you. It is on dry land that floats upon the surface of this great water. Take some kwapuha (eagle down), spurt some of the nahu (medicine) upon it, and cast it before you on the water."

When Tiyo did this, the water drew back on this hand and on that, so that a dry path appeared which enabled him to travel dry-shod to the distant ladder ends. He was just about to place his foot on the ladder when two angry puma appeared, glaring, snarling and baring their teeth. It had gone ill with him had he not leapt lithely back as he blew upon them the magic nahu. In a most amazing manner they became humble and subdued. Hanging their heads meekly, they said, "Never before have we permitted any human being to pass us alive. But we can see your breath is pure and your heart is brave." As they lay down, one on each side of the entrance, he stepped fearlessly between them and descended the ladder.

Like no other ladder he had ever seen was this one down which he made his way into the kiva of the Woman of the Hard Substances. Skillfully was its frame-work overlaid with an ornate decoration of iridescent white shells from the Land of the Far Waters. The kiva walls were likewise resplendent with shell and tur-quoise. In jarring contrast to all this beauty was the huddled figure of an ancient crone wrapped in a shabby mantle of dingy gray. Scant snow locks of extreme age framed her face—lined as deeply as the age-old, storm-beaten rock face of Pisisbaiya (Colorado River)—from which her dim eyes peered at the intruders.

TIYO TRAVELS THROUGH THE UNDERWORLD

"You are thinking that you see an old woman, my Tiyo," whispered Spider Woman, "but judge not by the eye. There sits she who each day runs the whole course of her life, Huzruiwuhti. In her lord's absence she is as you now see her, withered and old, but every night upon his return she lays aside her drab mantle and becomes an enchanting maiden. At dawn she is clothed with radiant splendor, for here she lives with her always-bridegroom, Tawa.

Besides being beautiful, she is kind, and her heart is tender and generous."

So Tiyo paid the crone the reverence due the aged, and gently put into her hand the second Blue Paho. Holding it close to her dim eyes, she gave it the most intense scrutiny. At length a slow smile flickered over her shrivelled visage and she murmured: "Yes, this was made by One Who Knows. I thank you. Sit down and eat, and you may ask any of my possessions that your heart desires."

Then she placed before him a bowl of purest turquoise and began mixing in it an enchanted food of corn pollen, saying as she performed the rite, "This will be ready for you and the Father when he comes, that you may both eat of it and start away without delay."

There came a low injunction from Spider Woman, "Hold in readiness for Tawa." The words had scarcely entered Tiyo's ear when the air seemed to grow warmer, and there came the sound of a mighty rushing in the air above. Suddenly, with a crash as that of a terrific lightning bolt, something landed on the roof above.

Tawa, the Sun! As he descended, his shining beauty poised upon the glittering ladder was almost too great for mortal eye to bear. The white buckskin of his garment shone like unsullied snow, and on the sleeves and leggings hung a deep fringe of jingling white shells. While the youth gazed with wide-eyed awe, Tawa hung up the shining shield he carried on his arm, and as it glanced against the stone wall it sang out ching-a-ling and rained down a shower of golden sparks.

The garment of Tawa was thick, being fashioned for the intense cold of the Above, and it was hung about with great pockets. From these Tawa drew forth great numbers of pahos that he had collected from shrines he had visited on his daily journey and laid them before Huzruiwuhti. She was no longer the gray crone but stood slender and straight—a lovely maiden before her lord. Then she began to sort them, laying some on her left hand, others on her right. The latter she gathered to her with a warm smile, "These are from ones having good hearts. I will send them all they ask." Then her face became stern and she pushed the pahos on the left away from her. "But these are from liars and deceitful men. My eyes are offended at their sight."

From his right wrist Tawa took some scalps, and they were from those who had been slain on the right side of his path during the day; then from his left wrist he removed others, and they were of those who had been slain on the left side of his path. Over these the maid rocked her body, weeping and moaning bitterly over the gory locks. "I grieve when you are brought to me; it stabs me with pain as I touch you. My heart is sad and I tremble as I look upon your frightfulness. Oh, my people, my people, why can you not live in peace? Will you never cease to rend my heart with your quarrelling," and she arose with sad face to hang the scalps against the beautiful turquoise walls.

Then it was that Tawa turned to Tiyo. "Who are you?" he asked.

"Yes," answered Tiyo, "I have come from way over there by the cliffs at Tokonabi. I have brought you something. My father made it and told me to give it to you," and he handed Tawa the third Blue Paho. "We haven't enough rain over there. The Far-Far-Below River takes it all away, or else the Rainbow comes out and eats up the water when it tries to rain. How about this? Is that great water outside this kiva that which the river drags away from the earth, and may not some of it be spared for my people? Our corn sickens and dies, our people hunger and Masauwuh is always prowling near us."

"So that is what you have been thinking about. I have been seeing you there on the cliffs watching the Far-Far-Below River." As he talked, Tawa was turning the paho over in his hands, examining it closely, but at last a gratified look overspread his features and he nodded graciously. "It is well, my relative, my son. This was made by One Who Knows. Let us smoke together."

He filled the pipe with sweet native tobacco, and the two smoked together long and silently. When this ceremony was finished they partook of the magic pollen food that Huzruiwuhti had prepared for them. "Now we will make a journey through the Below across to the place where I start again tomorrow. Put your hand upon my girdle and see to it that your hold is firm."

Tiyo's strong young fingers had no sooner taken hold than with lightning swiftness they shot through the sipapu and started down to the house of the Germ God, Muiyinwuh, in the lowest depths of the Underworld. Down, down, down, they plunged their blazing way. As they neared their destination the air grew humid, and so vibrantly did it pulse with life that the heart of Tiyo beat with strange longings that put forth like green corn shoots in the spring. At the same time, with strangest magic did a vision of the Snake Maiden appear before his eyes.

"Here are we at the house of Muiyinwuh," said Tawa, leading him through a host of busy little men who swarmed to and fro like bees, working with eager haste. "Now you can see how it is done in this place. The life of all things starts here."

"So, you have come," said Muiyinwuh as he approached.

"Yes, I have brought you this Cakwa Paho. My father made it over there in Tokonabi," said Tiyo, placing the last blue paho in the god's hand.

"Yes, this was made by One Who Knows," declared Muiyinwuh nodding his head above it sagely. "Because of this I will always listen to the wishes of your people when they make it this way. At my word the life of all things starts—the seed of all green things that grow upon the face of the earth, the life of every animal and of all men. These creatures you see, they are always working at this task. They will always be working thus."

With wonder Tiyo looked upon these things, and he noted that the largest, finest workers were the most earnest and industrious, while the poor, wizened creatures were shiftless and indifferent. All about him life seemed to be pulsing like some gigantic heart, and Tiyo felt coursing through his being a mighty desire to accomplish great things and the ability to do so. Again Muiyinwuh gave the youth the most earnest assurances of his good will toward him and all of his people.

Tawa now motioned toward his red horsehair girdle, and Tiyo grasped it firmly as he had before. So, with a wave of farewell to Muiyinwuh, they started forth for the place where the sun arises. No stop was made until they came to Tawaki, Sun House of the East, and though it had seemed that no place could equal in beauty that of the Sun's western kiva, here beauty so resplendent met Tiyo's eyes that he could not decide which was the greater. Instead of blue, every shade of red and pink glowed, and they ate their food from a polished stone bowl that looked like the upturned rosy sky at dawn.

There was no woman in this kiva; Tawa and his brother Taiowa occupied it alternately. For four days Tawa carried the burnished shield across the heavens, returning each night to the kiva of Huzruiwuhti; thence through the Underworld, reaching the Above just in time to march across its blue arch. Then, while he rested in his beautiful rose kiva, Taiowa, whom he had created to relieve him, carried the shield for four days' time.

As they rested there, Tawa gave Tiyo wise counsel, bidding him be grateful that his desire to know the great mysteries had been granted and impressing upon him the importance of cherishing, not only the things he had already learned, but those yet to be revealed. As he talked, he showed him how to make the Great Sun Paho.

"When you have learned this magic your eyes will be opened, and for all time you will know all people; you will be able to look into their hearts; you will be able to read their thoughts," he promised. And, of a truth, when Tiyo had learned to make this paho he could hear his family mourning for him and calling upon him to return. His heart so yearned over their sorrow that had it not been that he had not yet won from the gods the promise of more abundant rains and that the face of the Snake Maid beckoned him, he would have returned at once to comfort them.

Tawa smiled, seeing into the heart of the youth. "Do not falter, my son. I counsel you that of all the gifts you will receive the one you will most prize will be the Rain Cloud, which you will receive at the hands of the chief of the Snake-Antelope kiva." Then Tawa gave him the skin of Gray Fox to hang upon the hatchway of the kiva, and when he had hung it upon the hatchway of the kiva it brought upon the White Dawn. The next day Tawa handed him the skin of Sikyataiyo, Yellow Fox, to hang over the gray skin and, behold, the Yellow Dawn appeared. This was most potent magic.

All had now been done, and Tawa was ready to leave Tawaki; but this time he took the youth upon his shoulder and, carrying him across the sky's blue dome, showed him all the world with its wonders outspread far below like a marvellously woven blanket. When, at sunset, they came to the House in the West, Huzruiwuhti brought forth gifts of all that was in the house—shell, turquoise and coral—saying, "Now you will leave me: Take these gifts!"

Gratefully Tiyo murmured "Kwakwai, kwakwai," as he wrapped them in his white cotton mantle. He turned to say farewell, and lo! he beheld the miracle of transformation with his own eyes. As Tawa approached the old woman, the decrepit female figure seemed to dissolve, as does gray mist before the morning sun, and, radiantly emerging, stood a beautiful maiden who awaited her lord with outspread arms.

At the top of the ladder Tiyo found himself again gazing at the shimmering waters that surrounded the kiva, but after a moment's pause he remembered what he must do. So, upon a remaining bit of eagle's down, he spurted the nahu and cast it upon the waters. As before, they rolled back to the right hand and to the left and so stayed, leaving him a dry path upon which to proceed. The golden glow of evening flooded everything. Far away he could see the projecting ends of the ladder that led down into the Snake-Antelope kiva, and hanging upon them was the red-fringed warrior's bow that betokened secret ceremonials below.

TIYO APPEARS BEFORE SNAKE MANA

Four sleeps have passed since you were last here, my Tiyo," said Spider Woman, "and what wonders you have seen and heard in that time. Now you are to go down here and receive the greatest blessing of all."

So this time, without challenge, Tiyo descended into the kiva of the Snake-Antelope priests. More wonderful to him than all the brilliance of Tawa's brazen shield was the light that leapt into the eyes of the Snake Mana when he appeared before her.

For four days Tiyo sat beside the sand ponya of this priesthood as one of them. He learned how to make this ponya with solemn ritual. It was rectangular in shape and outlined by a band of fine white sand; within this border were bands of red, green and yellow sand, separated each from the other by fine lines of black. The four sides represented the Four World Quarters, and the colors were those of the corn. Inside these bands was a field of white sand upon which were four sets of semicircles in the same colors, which represented rain clouds, while the parallel black lines running at right angles to them were rain. From between the set of white rain clouds lay four zigzag bands in the same four colors, outlined in black, and these were the snake symbols for lightning. Each snake had a horn on his triangular head, and each one wore a necklace. Set all about this altar were many magic ornaments and fetishes, and only those who had been tried and found both wise and good were permitted to sit beside it and learn its secrets.

While Tiyo sat here he listened to the wisdom of Hicanavaiya; he sang his songs, he intoned his prayers, and as he did so he learned to make pahos that would bring the rain and were known to these priests alone. "Here we have an abundance of rain and corn," Hicanavaiya told him, "while in your mesa land there is little of either, so thus shall you use your nahu. Fasten these prayers in your breast; these songs shall you sing and these prayers shall you make. Then, when you have painted your body in black and white bands as I have shown you, with the symbols of the snake, the clouds will come."

Then he gave Tiyo a part of everything that was in the two kivas, the bright one gay with feathers and the gloomy one hung with snakeskins. From the Snake-Antelope kiva he gave him all the colors of the sand so that he could make an altar of his own at Tokonabi. And because the youth had become learned in all this magic lore, the heart of the old chief was warm toward him as toward his own son, and he bound about his slim loins the woven white kilt of the Snake-Antelopes. When this had been done he caused the heart of the youth to leap like the mountain goat, for he waved his hand toward his two daughters saying:

"Here are the two mana who know the charm that prevents death from the bite of the rattlesnake. Take them with you also. The one toward whom your heart is soft is Tcuamana; take her for your wife. That other one you are to give to your younger brother, and she will become the mother of the Flute clan." When Tiyo turned to take this most precious gift, behold! he saw that both maids were enveloped about with fleecy clouds, like a mantle, which made them even more beautiful.

Now, with solemn mien, Hicanavaiya took a feathered object from beside the ponya. It was the sacred tiponi, the Snake chieftain's most precious emblem of office. Placing it most reverently in Tiyo's arms, he charged him solemnly to cherish it always with most jealous care.

"Truly, this is your mother, for it is made from the corn that nourishes the Good People." Then from the ponya he took another tiponi. "This is for your younger brother. See that he treasures it."

When Tiyo had put these with his other treasures in the white mantle, the chief gave to him these last words of wisdom: "See that you remember all you have heard and seen, and all that I have done, do you the same. Take my heart and my bowels and all my thoughts; then shall you become the father of a great clan and shall be called by my name."

So Tiyo bade him farewell, and as he stepped forth lithe, straight and good to look upon in the strength of his young manhood, the two daughters of Hicanavaiya followed behind him. The tiny magic spider still whispered into his left ear directions back to her kiva, from which his journey through the underworld had so lately started.

For four days he stayed there, hunting rabbits for her, while Spider Woman with cunning fingers wove him a hoapuh, a deep basket pannier with rounded ends, made of interlaced wicker strands, for him to carry on his back. When she had completed it, even to the fastening of a cotton cord upon it, she bade him farewell. "My Tiyo, thou hast learned all the secrets of the Four World Quarters and the Above and Below. Shut in thy heart all this wisdom, revealing it only to those whose hearts you have tried and found perfect."

Then she bade Tiyo get into the pannier, with a maiden on each side of him, and she disappeared up the hatchway. The three waited breathless, not knowing which way to turn next; then they beheld, slowly unwinding through the sipapu, a silvery filament. With fascinated eyes they watched the silvery spider line uncoil, swaying and shimmering—nearer and nearer, until at last it began like a live thing to wind itself around the cotton cord of the hoapuh.

The hoapuh stirred. It moved gently but irresistibly as an unseen force lifted it through the hatchway. Up, up and up, until it reached the white, fleecy clouds of the vast Above. Like some gigantic bird it sailed with them, following the silver thread of the Far-Far-Below River, until at last it hung over the rocky cliffs of Tokonabi. Then Spider Woman spun out the gossamer thread, and gently the hoapuh lowered to the ground. But as they neared the ground they could see the people fleeing in terror to their houses, or to any rock that might afford a shelter. Shrill cries of "Kwataka, Kwataka" floated to them, and Tiyo, knowing their thoughts, saw that his people had taken the hoapuh for some huge bird hovering aloft. Nay, they thought it was the dread Man-Eagle himself come to harass them. So, laughing mightily, he called out in a big voice for them to come forth and welcome him home.

TIYO RETURNS HOME

At Tiyo's shout of reassurance the people of Tokonabi crept fearfully forth from their hastily sought shelters, and when they saw that it was really their own Tiyo who had returned to them after so strange a fashion, they crowded about him, eager to make him welcome and listen breathlessly to his thrilling account of his travels through the Underworld.

Then Tiyo led the Snake Maidens to the house of his mother where they were to remain four days, unseen by anyone, grinding corn into fine meal, according to the marriage custom. Tiyo and his younger brother now called together all the male relatives to help them prepare wedding gifts for the brides. They wove two blue, cotton tunic robes, two white blankets bordered with red and black and having elaborate tassels at the corners, and long-fringed girdles to bind about the tunics. They also made moccasins, each pair having leggings that took half a deerskin in the making. For this outfit they made reed mats in which to keep them.

On the fifth day after their return Tiyo mounted to a housetop, as does the Speaker Chief, and proclaimed loudly:

"Hear, oh my people, men of Tokonabi! Back from my travels have come two strange mana, daughters of Hicanavaiya, the Ancient of Six. One of them I shall take to wife, the other is espoused to my brother, and from henceforth they will abide with us and be one with us. In sixteen days' time we will make their feast as it is meet we should do when a strange people comes among us.

"While at the House of the Rising Sun my eyes were opened, and it was given to me henceforth to know the mysteries and to know the hearts of all men. So now, ye men of Tokonabi, make ye ready, make ye ready, for it is my purpose to try you, and those among you whose hearts I find perfect shall be my priests and my brothers. These I shall teach new pahos, as I have been taught them, and you shall learn the prayers and sing the songs that Hicanavaiya gave me to carry in my breast. My heart that knows not fear shall be yours, my bowels and all my thoughts. In my kiva you shall be initiated into all those secret rites that will make the Rain Cloud do our bidding, and you will be priests of the Snake-Antelopes."

So all the men of Tokonabi set about making their hearts perfect and searching their thoughts that they might go before Tiyo for their test of worthiness.

Then the heads of both brides and grooms were washed in yucca suds by the mother of Tiyo, according to Hopi marriage custom. Upon the bride of Tiyo was placed a white blanket girt about with one of the long-fringed girdles. Her hair was brushed until its midnight hue took on the lustre of starlight; it was looped low over her ears and bound at the back. Over her rounded red-bronze shoulders a second white mantle was draped and upon this were tied feathers, one upon each shoulder and two in back over her shoulder blades. A white feather from the altar of her fathers was bound against her hair, and two large shell earrings hung from her ears.

Truly, Tiyo thought he had never seen anything more fair than this mana, when his mother gave her to him, and he led her proudly to her house that would henceforth be known as the Snake-Antelope House. And with the other brother went the other maid in her wedding finery to the Flute kiva.

Four times did Tawa and his brother Taiowa alternate in carrying the sun shield across the skies, and when the sixteenth day had passed the great feast for the Tcuamana commenced. Upon the fifth day of the feast low clouds trailed over Tokonabi, and from a rainbow descended a vast host of Snake people from the Underworld to do honor to their kinswoman. But, after they had been taken to the kiva for the feasting, they would eat nothing but corn pollen, and suddenly disappeared. For the next three days Tokonabi was overhung with the same lowering clouds, and upon each evening fresh hosts of Snake people from the Underworld descended from the rainbow, and, after partaking of nothing more than corn pollen, disappeared as the first visitors had.

On the morning of the ninth day a strange thing happened. When the Tokonabi men went forth into their valleys they found that their unearthly visitants had been transformed into venomous reptiles, and they knew not what to do. Therefore, they reproached Tiyo for the evil magic he had brought among them. Then the Tcuamana spoke to them, "We understand this; let the Younger Brothers go out and bring all these our people in. Then must you wash their heads and let them dance with you."

This seemed a most dangerous thing to do, but Tiyo reminded them that the Tcuamana knew the nahu that prevents death from rattlesnake bite. So they went forth unafraid and gathered up the reptiles as they had been bid. Then, when they had washed the heads of the snakes in huge stone jars, the men of Tokonabi danced with the snakes they had gathered in from the valleys.

They danced thus till sunset when Tiyo made a house of snake meal and they carefully laid the snakes within. All the people came to it that they might cast prayer meal upon them. When this had been done the Younger Brothers, for thus were the new Snake priests called, gently raised the snakes and carried them back to the valleys. Then, lo! the strange visitants all disappeared, carrying with them the prayers and petitions of the people of Tokonabi. Strangest of all, they had hardly left when the black clouds gathered, the great fiery serpent of the skies appeared biting and bellowing and the rains descended in abundance.

So now Tiyo had accomplished all his heart had longed to do. His mind was rich in magic lore. The Rain Cloud would now do his bidding so that the corn would grow and his people thrive. His heart sang at the sight of the Tcuamana who so ably cooked his food or busied her fingers in basket weaving or in modelling the yellow clay into vessels and decorating them with cunning designs in red and black. Truly it had gone well with him because he had kept his thought high and his heart unafraid.

TUDJUPA CREATES THE PEOPLE

Hualapai

The Hualapai, or "the People of the Tall Pines," like their close relatives and neighbors, the Havasupai, trace their ancestry to the Yuman-speaking peoples of the lower Colorado River Valley, who lived along what is now the Arizona-California border. This version of their traditional origin story, as told by the Hualapai elder Kuni, was first published in 1935 by anthropologist Gordon MacGregor. Kuni describes how the god Tudjupa created human beings at Wikame, or Spirit Mountain, near present-day Needles, California. Tudjupa divided the people into several tribes; then he gave each tribe a home and the knowledge of local plants and animals that would allow them to live well on the land. Like many traditional native stories, this one has evolved over time; Kuni's version explains the origin of the Euro-Americans who have so completely transformed the Southwest in the last 150 years. Today, the Hualapai have adapted to that change. They welcome tens of thousands of visitors every year at Grand Canyon West, with its famous Skywalk, and they run daily white-water rafting trips in the lower Grand Canyon.

· · ·

Once all the tribes of Indians were one, long long ago. At this time there were two gods, Hamatavila, the older, and Tudjupa, the younger.

In the west there is a mountain, Wikame, which stands all alone. It has little peaks at the top and deep gullies around the bottom. Wikame was made when the water dried up through a hole in the ground and left all the mounds of mud called *mataha'iatum*. From under Wikame the two gods appeared and climbed to the top and sat there. The younger one said to the older, "Do you know all things?" But the older one answered, "I am too old. I know nothing. You are young, you must take up and rule the world." Tudjupa said, "Since you don't know anything, I shall rule."

He took a piece of cane, *ata*, reed, and broke it into pieces. The longest strip he called the Mohave, and the next longest he called the Hualapai; the third he cut shorter and called it the Havasupai (people of the blue water). With the fourth piece he made the Mukwa (Hopi), with the fifth the Paiute or Chemehuevi, and with the sixth the Nyavpe (people of the rising sun, Yavapai). These pieces he made into a bundle and carried them east and laid them down. When they came alive, he called the time day. All these people came back and lived around Wikame.

There were frogs close by the river, and Tudjupa said, "Don't step on this frog, *hinya*, here." But Hamatavila did step on the frog and squashed out its excrement and viscera. This caused him to become ill in his bowels, from which he lost his excrement and viscera and died.

Tudjupa said to the people, "We shall take the body and burn it for four days." A fence was built around the pyre and he told them that after the fourth day of burning the body would come to life. Coyote, who was in the crowd, said, "Whoever heard of dead people coming to life? He will be gone forever." And so it happened, for Hamatavila never came back to life. Coyote told Tudjupa to cut his hair off. "Singe it short, also burn all Hamatavila's property."

Tudjupa said, "Since the body has not come to life on the fourth day, we shall bury it, and four days later a plant will grow on it." Coyote interrupted, "Whoever heard of such a tale, that something will grow on a grave?" But Tudjupa did not listen to him, and on the fourth day after he had said this, he sent Coyote to the grave. Here he found corn, pumpkins, watermelons, and beans growing. Coyote said, "Cousin, *nitca*, father's younger brother, now that we have this food, let us harvest it and eat." Tudjupa agreed, for he had planned all this, the people and the food that they should eat, and the water they should drink. All the people came to eat, and when they had finished, they planted crops from the food they saved. They sowed and harvested for years.

But quarrels broke out which grew more bitter as the days went by. These quarrels grew so intense that Tudjupa decided it was time the people were separated into tribes as he had planned in the beginning. . . .

Then Tudjupa left the Mohave at Wikame and took all the other peoples down to the west bank of the river. They picked up camp at Fort Mohave and started off and camped at Wikutula. . . .

Here he told the Paiute to leave and go to St. George and St. Thomas, and to be like the Mohave and be their friends.

From there they crossed the river to Saveula. Tudjupa had fed them at Wikutula, but at Saveula he taught them to prepare their food, all of which he had planned.

"Build a fire where you happen to be. First get wood, *okadja,* sandbar willow, juniper, then start your fires." These were already grown. He went to the juniper and took off the bark, and then the leaf of the yucca which he split and then bound round the juniper bark, making a slow match or torch. This he called *ohagwida,* and the drill *okada,* and the hearth *hamatavil.* He made a small hole in the hearth and placed the drill in it and rubbed the drill between his fingers. The loose end of the tinder stick he left close to the hole. When the sparks had lit this, he blew it into a flame and dropped little twigs on it to make a fire. Then he put three stones around the fire, and on these he placed pots which had been brought from the Mohave.

At Wikame pumpkins had been cut in slices and left to hang in the sun to dry. These had been brought along. They were put in the cooking pots. Water, which had been brought in jars from the Mohave, was poured in and the strips of pumpkin softened and boiled. This was cooled and eaten with their fingers.

Ears of corn they had brought were eaten green, and those in the shucks were thrown in the flames and roasted until the shucks were burnt. When this was done and the kernels looked yellow, the corn was eaten on the cob, or the kernels were picked off by the thumbnail into the hand and then tossed in the mouth. Corn was also cooked into mush, the kernels being ground on a metate. The stone was placed with the broad end away from the woman, the corn piled at the near end, and ground with the mano, the woman catching some from the pile as the stone was pulled in, and then grinding. The meal was poured into boiling water and stirred with the *sitava,* a bowed branch flattened on one side or split and the ends tied together with yucca fiber to set them closely together. They also had white beans with black eyes, which they boiled whole in cooking pots.

It took two days to teach them how to make fire and cook their meals.

They went their way again, to the White Hills, until they came to the spring Ahakwite and camped overnight.

Then they went to Hatu, Clay Springs, and camped.

The next camp was in Spencer Canyon.

Then they came to Meriwhitica. Tudjupa planned to leave the Hualapai here, but he did not tell them so at this time.

He turned to a pair of white people who had come from Wikame with the Indians. "You can do whatever you would like to do. Go your way." He gave them a horse, a cow, pigs, chickens. "I give you this for a start." Then the white man went to a spring, Halu, then to another, Minminyaha, and along the cliffs of the Colorado to Cataract Canyon, down this where the tracks of the animals still show, and up the wash to the east, where he disappeared. When he passed through the Indian country he saw the mines, and with the knowledge he gained in the east the white man later returned to work them.

Then Tudjupa turned to the Hualapai and said, "Now your turn has come. I shall leave you here and you can wander as you like over the mountains and valleys. There are springs here. Now you have seen all the trees and shrubs. Notice too the juniper, for you will need it for firewood and for shelters. It will bear blue berries for your food. Notice too the piñon tree and the cones it bears which will grow from winter till the fall when they will be ripe. You will have to climb the tree and break off a branch and pick the cones off. Dig a small hole and put juniper sticks across in a grate, and pile the cones on this grate, and build a fire underneath. Take a long stick and stir the cones. Take one out and crack it on the top with a stone and taste it. If the nuts are done, throw earth on the rest. Then spread the cones on a flat rock and beat them to separate the scales. When the nuts are out, gather them in a basket and with burning charcoal toss them on a basket tray to cook them."

"The yucca, *imenat,* will bear fruit, *menat,* in September. It will blossom in spring. The fruit will be soft when fully ripe. Take the ones that are partly ripe and not yet soft. Build a fire and put the fruit in. The top will be black and the rest yellow when it is cooked through. When it is soft, skin the fruit, open it, remove the seeds, and let it dry on a flat rock. Then roll this up for winter food. To eat it, cut a piece off to chew or boil it into a stew."

"Mescal, *viyal,* will be another plant to eat. This is for the women to prepare. Take a stick so big (two feet long, one to two inches thick), sharpen one end like a chisel, and hammer it with a stone against the butt of the stem and cut this out. With a knife cut the leaves off and carry the mescal butt, *qeluk,* home in your basket. Do this from early in the morning for four days. Dig a hole as deep as your waist. Shovel it out with your mescal cutting stick, *tapa,* and carry the dirt out in your basket. Cover the hole with crossed juniper sticks. Lay large stones over the wood. Put a large stone at the corner as a sort of door through which the wood is lit with cedar bark. When the wooden roof is burnt, the hot stones will fall into the hole. Then push these against the walls and put the mescal in to roast. Throw dampened juniper bark over this and pile dirt on and allow it to cook two days. Spread the cooked butts on rocks and mash them. The juice comes out and makes a wet mash. Make a mat of sticks and spread the mescal mash on it to dry. Then it is rolled up to store away."

He pointed out the tuna cactus, *alaya* (prickly pear), to them. "This will bear fruit which I planned for you to pick off." But Coyote said, "Whoever heard of fruit without thorns?" So he shaved up juniper bark and threw the splinters over the cactus, and it has always borne spines since. "The tuna cactus blossoms in spring, and the fruit grows green in May. It is gathered in August when it has turned reddish purple. The meat is eaten raw, after the spines are beaten off with a bunch of *kuwaiya* brush. To store the tuna, cut it up without paring and crush the seed and juice into a pot. Spread the meat of the fruit on a bark blanket. Drink the juice after the seeds are strained out. The dried meat grind into coarse flour and store in buckskin bags to be hung in caves until winter." . . .

"All these fruits I have made ready for you to eat. I shall tell now about the animals.

"The ground will be covered with thorns. You may be starving. Hunting will whet your appetite. First, to protect your feet, you must make sandals, *manyo*, of yucca and cover them with piñon gum."

"The rat, *amalga*, is small but smart. He will make a house for himself of twigs and brush under a cactus or bush. His flesh will be food for you. When you go to hunt rats do not go alone, but with a boy or girl, or a dog, to watch the many holes of the rat's house. All the holes must be blocked so that he cannot run away, so that you will not have to pull up all the tunnels."

"Take a cane, stick it in the nest to chase out the rat or use a hook to rip up the nest. The rat will be hard to catch. When he has been cornered in a hole, push in a pointed stick wet on the end and twist it around. This will catch in the fur, and you can pull the rat out."

"The rat's fur is valuable. Skin him carefully and save the skins until you have enough for a blanket. Carry a bow and arrow to shoot him if he escapes you."

"There may be many people in a place. If you kill one rat or twenty, you must divide equally with all the people that live there."

"Trapping will relieve you from spending too much time hunting. Make a trap of a flat rock and three short sticks. Set as many traps as possible; go to each of these early in the morning. You may catch mice or rats or rabbits. Cook and eat them. You may catch a snake or a lizard. Eat them too if you are starving or else throw them away."

"Divide your game with all the camp."

"To hunt the cottontail rabbit, *hilo, halo,* you must take a bow and arrow. Remember, you are hunting. You must not walk straight through the desert, but you must wander through the brush and search in all places where a rabbit might be. Shoot and kill him with your arrow; never let him get away. Then look close by, for there may be another one."

"If you don't have a bow and arrow, take a club. You can catch a rabbit by chasing if you run fast enough. If four or five men are hunting together, one of them may not kill any. Then give him a rabbit to help him out. Allot one apiece. Boil them for a feast."

"Remember the fur. Cut and twist it into long ropes to weave into a blanket. When winter comes you will need it for a covering."

"Hunting the jackrabbit, *ikule*, is about the same as catching the cottontail. Go alone, taking a bow and arrow, or in a party to hunt him. They are cooked the same way. If you care for rabbit meat very much and cannot kill them with the bow and arrow, make a net from the *qilo,* twisting the fibers into cord and weaving the cord into mesh just large enough to catch a rabbit. The net should be sixty feet long. Find the paths of the jackrabbits and stretch the net across. You must take a party of men to drive the rabbits into the net. Perhaps you may catch three or four rabbits for each man. The fur will be like the cottontail's. Make blankets of it."

"The wildcat will be easy to catch because he will stop in the trees where you can shoot him."

"The fox and the coyote you shall have to chase. This will be hard. But in the winter you can catch them with less difficulty, for you can track them in the snow. Keep all the furs, for you will need them when it is cold to make into gloves, blankets, and quivers. These animals will be good meat for you if you wish to eat them. The coyote will be shy and hard to catch, but when he is careless you may get him."

"The badger you can use, especially to make a blanket to keep you from the cold."

"I shall make the deer, *aqwaqa,* the wildest and fastest animal. I have made the smaller animals to eat, but if you feel like killing the deer, you will have meat that will last you longer. There will be both male and female deer. They will be shy and hard to see because they will have sharp hearing and sensitive scent. If you get in the wind he will smell you and run. Only by trailing the tracks from a long way off will you be able to kill him. Going after the deer, you must know the sex. In summer when it is hot it may be necessary for you to chase him a long way, until you tire him and he runs into the shade. You may kill him in this way, but it will take at least a day, maybe longer. You may have him in sight for a long time but far away. In the evening you may get close and see him and kill him then."

"Not all of you will be good runners. A bad runner might have to chase two or three days. Never come back until you have killed your deer. You may find many tracks, but you must be able to distinguish your game from the other tracks."

"When you kill a deer, take good care of the hide, dress it well to make it soft, and keep it. If you need clothing you will have the buckskin to make shirts and moccasins and leggings for your women and children and yourself, and also to make sacks. Then when you move from place to place you have something in which to put your property. Pack it and go."

"The range of deer is wide. Their trails go over mountains and open plains and generally in the roughest places, which will make them hard to find, and the deer hard to kill. Go to the nearest trail and build a rock wall along it. Have a party to set fire to the brush or to shout and scare the deer. When they run by the wall, the men hidden behind it can shoot them."

"Some will be good and some bad hunters. All the hunters will have a hard time, but the good ones will catch their deer. When the good hunter has plenty of skins for clothes and meat to eat, he must go and help the poor hunter, for he may not be lucky enough to kill a deer."

"When the deer is dead, take the horns and cut off the head. Pack the skin of this with damp dirt so it will dry slowly and not get rough. The next time you go hunting wear the deer head and imitate a deer. Go into the brush, stalk him, and shoot him."

"Relatives must help the man who has not been lucky enough to kill a deer, by giving him meat and hides. You may not keep all your deer, you must divide. Dry the meat. Use both the buck and doe skins for clothing. Sometimes one may get a doe or fawn when he cannot kill a buck."

"I make everything for you people, large and small animals. There are more big animals to be made."

"When I make the antelope, *imul, umul, muul,* he will be wise and hard to kill. He will not be like the deer in the mountains but he will roam the open plains. When you go hunting you will find the antelope in a herd. They will run in a circle. If you are a good hunter and know their habits you will try to get where you can shoot close by. If you are a fast shooter you may get two or more. If you kill a buck, take the horns and skin the whole antelope as you would a deer, but leave on the head. Stuff the skin with moist soil and leave it to dry. Dress the skin and paint the markings with white mineral paint to make them look like antelope legs and tail. If you want to kill two or three more antelope, take this hide on the hunt. Do not wear it at the start, but when you find the herd on the plain. Go out as early as you can when the antelope are grazing. Don't run into them but play around, walk, lie down like an antelope, and work closer that way. The reason I tell you to imitate an antelope is to get food for the family. If you imitate and stalk them, you will never starve. The antelope is for clothing as well as for meat."

"The mountain sheep, *imu, umu,* will be found in the rocky places and mountains, not on the plains. Most them will be on the cliffs and benches of the canyons along the Colorado. When you hunt, look for the sheep tracks in the soft dirt of a bench and find which way the sheep went. Let the party circle around ahead of the sheep and one man stay behind to drive them into the party. Some may hide behind a pile of dirt on the bench and shoot the sheep when they are driven across the bench. Make your clothes from sheepskin and eat the meat. Take the horns too, heat them in ashes to make them soft, and make them into two spoons to eat with."

"Every animal is for some purpose. Be careful when you hunt."

"For a bow, take a strong, straight mulberry, *puima,* and smooth it down on one side so you can bend it. Take a strong sinew cord and string the bow."

"The arrow is made of reed or cane, *ata.* This will be found near the water. It will be green first, but when it is ripe, it will turn yellow. Now this is ready. Take a number. Take a small stone, heat it, and work out the joints and curves of the reed in the grooves of the rock. You want feathers on your arrow. Watch a nest of eagles or hawks until the young are big enough to be fed. Catch one and feed him until the feathers are full grown. Take the good feathers and split them in two. The arrow needs three of these. Get a sinew and wrap it around so the feather will stick. Take some hard wood that won't break or split, set it into the shaft, split the end of the foreshaft, *maval,* and set in the arrowhead. The arrowhead is made of white stone and worked to a sharp edge. Set the tang of the head in the split of the foreshaft and bind it. Now it is an arrow and ready to use."

"Arrows cannot be carried in the hand. You must have a carrier for them. If you kill a fox or wild cat, make a long sack of the skin so you can carry a number of arrows in your quiver."

"When you feel like smoking, you will find wild tobacco, *uva;* pull this out by the roots, dry it in the sun, much of it. And you will need a pouch. Make this out of squirrel skin. Rub the tobacco between your hands. Smoke it."

"What are you going to make the pipe, *mehlu,* with? Take clay, mold it into a pipe, hollow it with a stick. Bake it slowly in ashes. Take the bowels of a young rabbit when it is sucking and mix the grass in the bowels with tobacco to smoke."

"All this is for you: clothes, food, hunting, games. Now do all that I have told you that I may see if you have learned everything right. Gather food, and cook."

Then they did all these things, and everything came out perfectly. . . .

"Here is the land where you will live. Go to the places where you find water. Mark off your land and live by the water. Name these places. In summer live by berries and wild food plants. In winter go live in caves on your own land. In these you will have stored your food that you gathered in summer. The land that you own must have a name. There will be a piece for a family. They own the food and game on this piece. They can move within its boundaries to the caves, the berry patches, and the hunting ground."

"To get trees for your house set fire to them at the roots and burn them down. Work off the limbs with a rock. With these limbs make your house. Cover the house with bark. Burn the dead wood; have plenty of this ready for the cold day. In summer you will need a shade. Lay branches and brush against the limb of a tree from both sides. Leave two sticks forked for the opening. Never tear down your winter houses. Keep a fire inside."

"If the head of the family dies, his boy must live on in the same place and take care of the land. Do not be afraid to do this."

"You do not know how they will die. Some will go in old age, others in youth. They will die thus. A man will go to sleep and dream. He will dream of sickness and death. He will think of this misfortune when he wakes. He will think sickness and die later. If you dream of sickness, but also how you will get well, and when and why, and don't forget this dream, you may get well."

"When you are sick you must have a doctor. He will know of night and evils.

He will read your mind. But what will help him? The creator of people will help him. A gourd is for you to rattle over the sick. If the doctor cures you, you must satisfy him. Pay him a buckskin or whatever you have on hand. The doctor will sing. What can help him if he keeps on singing? The spirits will help him. If he does not have a good understanding of spirits, he cannot cure you."

"If a man fails to be cured and dies, all his property, clothes, skins, must be burned. Also for a woman, her property, pots, and baskets must be burned up. If a relative feels bad, he can choke himself, hang himself on a tree, shoot himself with a bow and arrow. If a doctor fails to cure a sick man, any of the relatives may kill the doctor. My advice is, even if you lose your only child, accept it. You know you are a man or woman. Keep out evil spirits. Be good, behave. Thus take care of yourself and you will live to an old age."

"As you go on then through the generations, try and grow up to be men and women of good people. Hand down this advice.

"This land will be your country to settle and get your living in."

Then Tudjupa gave the Mukwa (Hopi) a flock of sheep and a flock of goats and told them to start out from Meriwhitica and go make their living. On their way they stopped in the Havasupai country. It was not wide enough, so they moved on beyond Grand Canyon and settled down.

"When you have come to this place take good care of your flocks. You have these for your meat. Plant the corn I give you even though you have dry land. Sing to the spirits and this will bring rain. Sheep and goats will give wool for spinning thread; weave this into blankets for use in your houses. Make on the plains your adobe house for the summer. But in the winter build your houses in the caves. If it is hot in summer you can do your weaving in your cave homes."

"Some people will be your friends. Trade blankets for buckskins with them. Make your moccasins and clothes from these buckskins. Realize this: your children will be cold, so you will need this for their clothing."

"Your wife will make baskets like other women. Your main food will be peaches. Plant the peach trees on the plains. Do your gardening with corn, watermelons, pumpkins, and beans. In the winter go trade with the Hualapai for mescal and any other wild foods they gather in the valleys or in the mountains for their winter storage. Keep peace with the other peoples and be friends always, for they are your own people and will always be. I want you to keep these rules and let your children's children carry them on. When you die or any member of your family dies, burn any of your belongings you like."

After he had settled the Hopi, his plan was to have the Hualapai, Havasupai, and Yavapai all one tribe. "This is my plan, to have you all one tribe, and I have given you directions what to do."

But the mean people started a quarrel right away, so he separated these and called them Nyavpe (Yavapai).

He told these, "You know all the matters that I have been telling you. Take what you have learned and go to your country. You will find there all the things that I have given these people here. Once you were Hualapai but now you are a different tribe, the Yavapai. Yet you will have the same food and rules as the Hualapai." Ever since, the Yavapai have been the enemies of the Hualapai. . . .

There were so many Hualapai people that a small number of these followed after the Hopi. They came to the Hopi Camp at Cataract Creek and, liking the place, they stayed and became the Havasupai. They were named after their river. The Hopi had left peach seeds at this place, and in this way the Supai got their peach trees. When they left the Hualapai, they took four seeds with them, corn, melon, bean, and squash. The Yavapai had taken these four seeds also. Tudjupa told the Havasupai, "You understand the Hualapai language. You may use this, but there will be differences, for you will call things after your own way." The Havasupai do all things as the Hualapai do. "The Hualapai will be your friends. They will come to where you live and meet and make trade there with the Hopi and the Navaho. . . . "

Tudjupa had told the Indians in the beginning that the whites would return, and the only way to drive them out was shoot them. At Wikame Tudjupa had made a white man and a white woman, who left the Indians at Meriwhitica and went far to the east where they learned a great many things. Afterwards they returned when there were many, many of them.

After their return there were disputes about the land, then great numbers poured into the country. The whites had guns but the Hualapai had only bows and arrows. More Indians were killed than whites, but they fought to the end. From the time my great-grandfather was alive white men have been coming into the country, and wars continued until the soldiers stopped them and the miners came in.

THEY TOLD STORIES

Ramson Lomatewama

Ramson Lomatewama is a painter, sculptor, glass artist, and poet whose several books include *Silent Winds: Poetry of One Hopi* (1983), *Ascending the Reed* (1987), and *Drifting through Ancestor Dreams* (1994). Born in California and raised in Flagstaff, Lomatewama moved to the reservation after college to immerse himself in Hopi culture. He worked as a teacher at the Hotevilla-Bacavi Community School, grew corn using traditional dry farming practices, and carved kachina dolls using centuries-old techniques that rely on entirely handmade materials and pigments. At the same time, he began writing poetry, using it as another means of reinhabiting tradition. His frank, meditative poems about corn, rain, nightfall, and the seasons capture the texture of daily life in the Hopi homeland, which he describes as "a place where people live by faith and sweat." In this poem, he reflects on the meanings of the petroglyphs and pictographs created by his ancestors, seeing in them another kind of writing, another kind of story that can help him understand the past that made him who he is.

. . .

They told stories
with rough hands
and drops of sweat,
sharing with us
fragments of their journeys
pecked into sandstone walls.

I follow their footsteps
as my fingers gently follow
every curve,
every worn line—
feeling another time,
finding warmth in ancient spirals
and lightning of those
who left long ago.

I stand alone
and feel their faces,
frozen in the centuries of seasons.
I gaze deep into their mottled eyes
remembering words handed down,
tracing with my fingers each and every antelope;
following migration patterns chipped into memories;
looking for songs in snakes and water waves;
letting upraised arms of ancestor spirits
hold my numbed hands.

I follow their journey in stone
from our third world,
reaching hand over hand,
ascending the reed;
coming into canyons,
reaching higher and higher
like sprouted corn
stretching upward to light.
I feel their words
and hear echoes of past lives.

I brace myself, breathing hard and steady.
I stay to drink every drop of their grit-filled stories,
taking in every moment,
every image of who I am,
before winter's jagged wind
drives me from this place.

FURTHER READING

Anderson, Michael F. *Living at the Edge: Explorers, Exploiters, and Settlers of the Grand Canyon Region.* Grand Canyon, Ariz.: Grand Canyon Association, 1998.

Berger, Todd. *It Happened at Grand Canyon.* Guilford, Conn.: TwoDot, 2007.

Beus, Stanley S., and Michael Morales. *Grand Canyon Geology.* New York: Oxford University Press, 1990.

Boyer, Diane E., and Robert H. Webb. *Damming Grand Canyon. The 1923 USGS Colorado River Expedition.* Logan: Utah State University Press, 2007.

Brooks, Juanita. *Jacob Hamblin, Mormon Apostle to the Indians.* Salt Lake City: Westwater, 1980.

———. *John Doyle Lee: Zealot, Pioneer Builder, Scapegoat.* Glendale, Calif.. A.II. Clark Co., 1961.

Butchart, Harvey. *Grand Canyon Treks: 12,000 Miles through the Grand Canyon.* Bishop, Calif.: Spotted Dog Press, 1998.

Butler, Elias. *Grand Obsession: Harvey Butchart and the Exploration of Grand Canyon.* Flagstaff, Ariz.: Puma Press, 2007.

Clark, Georgie White, and Duane Newcomb. *Georgie Clark: Thirty Years of River Running.* San Francisco: Chronicle Books, 1977.

Corle, Edwin. *Listen, Bright Angel.* New York: Duell, Sloan and Pearce, 1946.

Courlander, Harold. *The Fourth World of the Hopis.* New York: Crown, 1971.

Crampton, C. Gregory. *Sharlot Hall on the Arizona Strip: The Diary of a Journey through Northern Arizona.* Flagstaff, Ariz.: Northland Press, 1975.

Dellenbaugh, Frederick. *A Canyon Voyage: The Narrative of the Second Powell Expedition.* New York: G. P. Putnam's Sons, 1908.

Holmstrom, Buzz, and Brad Dimock. *Every Rapid Speaks Plainly: The Salmon, Green, and Colorado River Journals of Buzz Holmstrom.* Flagstaff, Ariz.: Fretwater Press, 2003.

————. *Sunk without a Sound: The Tragic Colorado River Honeymoon of Glen and Bessie Hyde*. Flagstaff, Ariz.: Fretwater Press, 2001.

————. *The Very Hard Way: Bert Loper and the Colorado River*. Flagstaff, Ariz.: Fretwater Press, 2007.

Dolnick, Edward. *Down the Great Unknown: John Wesley Powell's 1869 Journey of Discovery and Tragedy through the Grand Canyon*. New York: HarperCollins, 2002.

Dutton, Clarence. *Tertiary History of the Grand Canyon District*. Washington, D.C.: United States Government Printing Office, 1882.

Euler, Robert C., and Frank Tikalsky. *The Grand Canyon: Intimate Views*. Tucson: University of Arizona Press, 1992.

Farquhar, Francis P. *The Books of the Colorado River and the Grand Canyon: A Selective Bibliography*. Los Angeles: G. Dawson, 1953.

Ford, Mike S. *The Books of the Grand Canyon, the Colorado River, the Green River, and the Colorado Plateau: A Selective Bibliography, 1953–2003*. Flagstaff, Ariz.: Fretwater Press, 2003.

Fradkin, Philip. *A River No More: The Colorado River and the West*. Berkeley: University of California Press, 1996.

Ghiglieri, Michael. *First through Grand Canyon: The Secret Journals and Letters of the 1869 Crew Who Explored the Green and Colorado Rivers*. Flagstaff, Ariz.: Puma Press, 2003.

Goldwater, Barry. *Delightful Journey: Down the Green and Colorado Rivers*. Tempe: Arizona Historical Foundation, 1970.

Grattan, Virginia L. *Mary Colter: Builder upon the Red Earth*. Grand Canyon, Ariz.: Grand Canyon Natural History Association, 1980.

Henry, Marguerite. *Brighty of the Grand Canyon*. New York: Rand McNally, 1953.

Hinton, Leanne, and Lucille Watahomigie. *Spirit Mountain: An Anthology of Yuman Story and Song*. Tucson: Sun Tracks and the University of Arizona Press, 1984.

Hirst, Stephen. *I Am the Grand Canyon: The Story of the Havasupai People*. Grand Canyon, Ariz.: Grand Canyon Association, 2006.

Hughes, J. Donald. *In the House of Stone and Light: A Human History of Grand Canyon*. Grand Canyon, Ariz.: Grand Canyon Natural History Association, 1978.

Huisinga, Kristin, Lori Mackarick, and Kate Watters. *River and Desert Plants of the Grand Canyon*. Missoula, Mont.: Mountain Press, 2006.

James, George Wharton. *The Grand Canyon of Arizona: How to See It*. Boston: Little, Brown and Company, 1910.

Kinsey, Joni. *The Majesty of the Grand Canyon: 150 Years in Art*. Cobb, Calif.: First Glance Books, 1998.

Kolb, Ellsworth. *Through the Grand Canyon from Wyoming to Mexico*. New York: Macmillan, 1914.

Lamb, Susan. *The Best of Grand Canyon Nature Notes, 1926–1935*. Grand Canyon, Ariz.: Grand Canyon Natural History Association, 1994.

Lavender, David. *River Runners of the Grand Canyon*. Grand Canyon, Ariz.: Grand Canyon Natural History Association, 1985.

Leavengood, Betty. *Grand Canyon Women: Lives Shaped by Landscape*. 2nd ed. Grand Canyon, Ariz.: Grand Canyon Association, 2004.

Locke, Raymond Friday. *The Book of the Navajo*. Los Angeles: Mankind, 1979.

Martin, Russell. *A Story That Stands Like a Dam: Glen Canyon and the Struggle for the Soul of the West*. Salt Lake City: University of Utah Press, 1999.

McCroskey, Mona Lange. *Summer Sojourn to the Grand Canyon: The 1898 Diary of Zella Dysart*. Prescott, Ariz.: HollyBear Press, 1996.

McNamee, Gregory. *Grand Canyon Place Names*. 2nd ed. Boulder, Colo.: Johnson Books, 2004.

Morehouse, Barbara J. *A Place Called Grand Canyon: Contested Geographies*. Tucson: University of Arizona Press, 1996.

Neumann, Mark. *On the Rim: Looking for the Grand Canyon*. Minneapolis: University of Minnesota Press, 1999.

Poling-Kempes, Lesley. *The Harvey Girls: Women Who Opened the West*. New York: Paragon House, 1989.

Pyne, Stephen J. *Dutton's Point: A Natural History of the Grand Canyon*. Grand Canyon, Ariz.: Grand Canyon Natural History Association, 1983.

———. *Fire on the Rim. A Firefighter's Season at the Grand Canyon*. New York: Weidenfeld and Nicolson, 1989.

———. *How the Canyon Became Grand*. New York: Viking, 1998.

Reilly, P. T. *Lee's Ferry: from Mormon Crossing to National Park*. Logan: Utah State University Press, 1999.

Reisner, Marc. *Cadillac Desert: The American West and Its Disappearing Water*. New York: Viking, 1986.

Ryan, Kathleen Jo. *Writing Down the River: Into the Heart of the Grand Canyon*. Flagstaff, Ariz.: Northland Press, 1998.

Sadler, Christa. *There's This River . . . Grand Canyon Boatman Stories*. 2nd ed. Flagstaff, Ariz.: Red Lake Books, 1994.

Smith, Dwight L. *The Photographer and the River, 1889–1890: The Colorado Cañon Diary of Franklin A. Nims*. Santa Fe, N.M.: Stagecoach Press, 1967.

Stanton, Robert Brewster. *Through the Grand Canyon of the Colorado*. New York: C. Scribner's Sons, 1890.

Stegner, Page. *Grand Canyon: The Great Abyss*. San Francisco: HarperCollins West, 1995.

Stegner, Wallace. *Beyond the Hundredth Meridian*. Boston: Houghton, Mifflin, 1953.

Stone, Julius. *Canyon Country: The Romance of a Drop of Water and a Grain of Sand*. New York: G. P. Putnam's Sons, 1932.

Suran, William. *The Brave Ones: The Journals and Letters of the 1911–1912 Expedition down the Green and Colorado Rivers by Ellsworth L. Kolb and Emery C. Kolb*. Flagstaff, Ariz.: Fretwater Press, 2003.

Teal, Louise. *Breaking into the Current: Boatwomen of the Grand Canyon*. Tucson: University of Arizona Press, 1994.

Trimble, Stephen. *Lasting Light: 125 Years of Grand Canyon Photography*. Flagstaff, Ariz.: Northland Press, 2006.

Van Dyke, John. *The Grand Canyon of the Colorado*. New York: Charles Scribner's Sons, 1920.

Warner, Ted. *The Domínguez-Escalante Journal: Their Expedition through Colorado, Utah, Arizona, and New Mexico in 1776.* Provo, Utah: Brigham Young University Press, 1976.

Waters, Frank. *The Book of the Hopi.* New York: Viking, 1963.

———. *The Colorado.* New York: Rinehart, 1946.

Webb, Roy. *High, Wide, and Handsome: The River Journals of Norman D. Nevills.* Logan: Utah State University Press, 2005.

———. *Riverman: The Story of Bus Hatch.* 3rd ed. Flagstaff, Ariz.: Fretwater Press, 1989.

Welch, Vince, Cort Conley, and Brad Dimock. *The Doing of the Thing: The Brief Brilliant Whitewater Career of Buzz Holmstrom.* Flagstaff, Ariz.: Fretwater Press, 1998.

Woods, G. K. *Personal Impressions of the Grand Cañon of the Colorado River.* San Francisco: Whitaker and Ray, 1899.

Zolbrod, Paul G. *Diné Bahane': The Navajo Creation Story.* Albuquerque: University of New Mexico Press, 1984.

CREDITS

Page 7: Detail of *Rounded Inward Curves and Projecting Cusps of the Walls,* by H.H. Nichols, reproduced by permission of the David Rumsey Map Collection, www.david rumsey.com.

Page 91: Detail of *Grand Canyon Scroll Map,* by Les Jones, reproduced by permission of Les Jones and Marriott Library, University of Utah.

Page 173: Detail of *Provincia de Moqui,* by Silvestre Vélez de Escalante, reproduced by permission of The Newberry Library, Chicago. Ayer ms. map 229.

"Grand Canyon" reprinted from Amil Quayle, *Grand Canyon and Other Selected Poems* (Lincoln, NE: Black Star Press, 2009), by permission of Amil Quayle.

"Fear of God" excerpted from *The Secret Knowledge of Water,* by Craig Childs, published by Sasquatch Books (Seattle), 2000.

"Bright Angel Trail," from *Downcanyon,* by Ann Zwinger (Tucson: University of Arizona Press, 1995), copyright © The Arizona Board of Regents 1995. Reprinted by permission of the University of Arizona Press and Ann Zwinger.

"Havasu" reprinted from *Desert Solitaire: A Season in the Wilderness,* by Edward Abbey (New York: McGraw-Hill, 1968), by permission of Don Congdon Associates, Inc. © 1968 by Edward Abbey, renewed 1996 by Clarke Abbey.

"The Man Who Walked through Time," from THE MAN WHO WALKED THROUGH TIME, by Colin Fletcher, copyright © 1967 by Colin Fletcher. Used by permission of Alfred A. Knopf, a division of Random House, Inc.

"Where Solitude Is Easy to Find," pages 3–17 from *Grand Canyon,* by Joseph Wood Krutch, copyright © 1957, 1958 by Joseph Wood Krutch. Reprinted by permission of HarperCollins Publishers, William Morrow.

"A Cougar Hunt on the Rim of the Grand Canyon" reprinted from *A Book Lover's Holidays in the Open,* by Theodore Roosevelt (New York: Charles Scribner's Sons, 1916).

TEXT
10/12.5 Minion Pro

DISPLAY
Minion Pro, Gotham, Condensed Akzidenz Grotesk

COMPOSITOR
BookMatters, Berkeley

PRINTER AND BINDER
Maple-Vail Book Manufacturing Group